In this work, Solomon Sule-Saa undertakes a fascinating project to validate, through the stories of the encounter between the Dagomba and Konkomba of northern Ghana with Christianity, especially the translated Scriptures, Lamin Sanneh's claim of Christian mission as a dynamic vernacular translation and anti-hegemony movement. In my view, Sule-Saa succeeds in this enterprise.

The author offers a brief and meaningful portrait of Sanneh, biographically and intellectually, and thus sets the stage for the application of his ideas in regard to the two people groups involved in this study. Using both primary and secondary sources, Sule-Saa presents the stories of the Dagomba and Konkomba, their origins and pre-Christian history, capturing, among other things, their social organisation, governance structures, rites of passage, festivals and religions. He also deals with the interactions of these two people groups with other people groups as well as the colonial authorities, Christian missionaries and churches.

In the end, in this well-structured piece of work that does not shy away from engaging with critical questions arising from gospel and culture engagement, we have a readable account of the positive and far reaching effect that Christianity, especially mother-tongue Scriptures in Dagbani and Likpakpaaln, have had on the Dagomba and Konkomba respectively. In recounting the story of the significant effect of the translated Scriptures on all aspects of the lives of the Dagomba and Konkomba, this book itself is missionary in outlook and thus must be read by all Christians, especially those involved in mission work at all levels as well as in the translation of the Bible.

Reverend Professor Benhardt Y. Quarshie, PhD
Rector, Akrofi-Christaller Institute of Theology, Mission and Culture, Akropong-Akuapem, Ghana

The eminent Gambian theologian, Professor Lamin Sanneh, has taught us that, instead of assessing the gains of the Christian enterprise solely through the lens of Western missionary activity and their colonial collaborators, we should look more closely at the twin factors of Bible translation and the role of local agency in the transmission of the Christian faith. In *Making a Difference: Bible Translation among the Dagomba and Konkomba of Northern Ghana*, Dr. Sumani Sule-Saa employs Professor Sanneh's *hermeneutic of mission as translation* as an intellectual grid to examine the effect of Bible translation on the lives of these two very important language groups. The book also assesses the nature of Christian mission to the Dagomba and Konkomba prior to the translation of the Bible into their respective mother tongues and draws attention to the seismic changes that have occurred in the wake of the apprehension of the gospel in terms that are indigenous to these local communities. *Making a Difference* offers mission historians and biblical scholars, particularly those in Africa and the two-thirds world, an opportunity to make a difference in their approach to the study of these disciplines. It is a must-read book!

Professor Philip Laryea, PhD
Dean of Accredited Studies, Akrofi-Christaller Institute of Theology, Mission and Culture, Akropong-Akuapem, Ghana

This work is a most comprehensive and captivating exposition of the historical and religio-cultural heritage of the Dagomba and Konkomba peoples, made alive through the translation of the Holy Scriptures. It is one of the most lucid affirmations of Lamin Sanneh's principle of Christian mission as the revitalisation of the indigenous consciousness, made possible, in a real sense, through a journey of self-discovery by the author. The study offers Sule Saa opportunity to both analyse and interpret the exciting encounter between the gospel and two specific indigenous cultures. Through a most thorough and systematic narrative of the history of the two ethnic neighbours, the author succeeds in revealing great, rich and hidden treasures that continue to produce transformation in succeeding generations of the Dagomba and Konkomba. A great work of research worthy of commendation for the great impression it is sure to make on readers generally and the academy in particular.

Professor David N. A. Kpobi, PhD
Director of Graduate Studies, Trinity Theological Seminary, Legon, Ghana

Solomon Sumani Sule-Saa has given us a work that deals with the interface between indigenous languages on the one hand, and the importance of translating the message, on the other. The ability of the author to study northern Ghanaian cultures and translation provides a refreshingly new study that is a shift away from previous studies based on southern experiences. We have in this volume an important study that also engages such leading minds in the field as Lamin Sanneh, whose groundbreaking work on mission and translation has shaped discourses in this field for many years.

Reverend Professor J. Kwabena Asamoah-Gyadu, PhD
President, Trinity Theological Seminary, Legon, Ghana

This book tells the story of Christian mission and Bible translation among the Dagomba and Konkomba peoples of northern Ghana. The author has assembled material from credible sources and communicated his findings in reader-friendly format. The book is indeed a classic contribution to attempts at highlighting the many priceless untold stories about heroes and heroines through whom the Bible has been made available to communities in their own mother tongues. It is a must read for all who wish to appreciate the wonders of "Pentecost" on the Ghanaian terrain.

Very Reverend Professor John D. K. Ekem, ThD
Vice President, Methodist University College, Ghana
Translation Consultant, The Bible Society of Ghana
Kwesi Dickson-Gilbert Ansre Distinguished Professor of Biblical Exegesis & Mother Tongue Hermeneutics, Trinity Theological Seminary, Legon, Ghana

In this work Dr. Sule-Saa addresses Professor Sanneh's views of Christian mission as translation in a receptor language and culture. Sanneh contrasts this with Islam, which he asserts is cultural diffusion, and focuses on cultural uniformity. This is because of the Muslim claim that the Qur'an is not translatable. Further, Sanneh asserts that at Pentecost God revealed multilingual translation as the paradigm for Christian mission. Dr. Sule-Saa tests this theoretical position by studying the work done by Christian missionaries in two specific ethnic groups in northern Ghana, namely among the larger, more dominant Dagomba and the smaller acephalous group, the Konkomba. When missionaries first began their work, these groups viewed Christianity as an alien foreign religion; this was especially true for the Dagomba who are approximately 60% Muslim. [The German] Basil missionaries began the Dagomba Bible translation in the early 1900s, but because of WWI, the British colonialists forced them to leave Ghana. It was not until the 1960s that the translation and literacy project was continued under the auspices of SIL and GILLBT. When the Bible translation, published by the Bible Society of Ghana, was completed and available for the Dagomba, it was read on Radio Savannah. This made the scriptures available to all the Dagomba: Muslim, Christian, and non-Christian alike. God was speaking their language and they listened faithfully. Missionaries and the Konkomba team also translated the Bible into their language. When they received their translation, they developed a new sense of pride in their language and culture; it destigmatized them. The Bible in the local languages was redemptive and transformative in very positive ways. This contradicts the perspective of various anthropologists and others that mission work is a form of colonialism and cultural hegemony that destroys the local culture including their religion. This study found that the opposite happened. Christianity as translated through the Bible in the local language and in everyday life serves to affirm and contributed to retaining the local language and culture. This is a must-read story of God's work among the Dagomba and Konkomba through Bible translation. It also includes a similar result found among the Bimoba in northern Ghana. This study also serves to confirm Sanneh's hermeneutic of mission as translation.

Carol McKinney, PhD; *Anthropology Consultant with SIL*
Member of the Bible translation team of the Jju language, Nigeria
Senior faculty of Dallas International University, Dallas, Texas
Recent books by SIL International include Baranzan's People of the Middle Belt of Nigeria *(2019) and* Bajju Christian Conversion *(2019)*

Making a Difference
Bible Translation Among
the Dagomba and Konkomba of Northern Ghana

SIL International®
Publications in Ethnography

49

The Publications in Ethnography series focuses on cultural studies of minority peoples of various parts of the world. While most volumes are authored by members of SIL International® who have done ethnographic research in a minority language, suitable works by others also occasionally form part of the series.

Series Editor
Susan McQuay

Managing Editor
Eric Kindberg

Editorial Staff
Joyce W. Park, Volume Editor
Newton Frank, Copy Editor
Bonnie Brown, Copy Editor

Production Staff
Lois Gourley, Composition Director
Judy Benjamin, Compositor
Barbara Alber, Graphic Designer, Cover photograph and design

Making a Difference
Bible Translation Among the Dagomba and Konkomba of Northern Ghana

Solomon Sumani Sule-Saa
with Joyce W. Park

SIL International®
Dallas, Texas

©2021 by SIL International®
Library of Congress Control Number: 2020947471
ISBN: 978-1-55671-371-2
ISSN: 0-0895-9897

All rights reserved

No part of this publication may be reproduced, stored in a retrieval system, or transmitted in any form or by any means—electronic, mechanical, photocopy, recording, or otherwise—without the express permission of SIL International®. However, short passages, generally understood to be within the limits of fair use, may be quoted without permission.

Data and materials collected by researchers in an era before documentation of permission was standardized may be included in this publication. SIL makes diligent efforts to identify and acknowledge sources and to obtain appropriate permissions wherever possible, acting in good faith and on the best information available at the time of publication.

Copies of this and other publications of SIL International® may be obtained through distributors such as Amazon, Barnes & Noble, other worldwide distributors and, for select volumes, publications.sil.org:

SIL International® Publications
7500 W. Camp Wisdom Road
Dallas, TX 75236-5629 USA

General inquiry: publications_intl@sil.org
Pending order inquiry: sales@sil.org

Contents

Abbreviations xi

Maps xii

1 Introduction 1
   1.1 The intellectual framework of, and motivation for, the writing of this book 3
   1.2 How this study was conducted 4
   1.3 Overview of the book 4
   1.4 Review of relevant literature 6
   1.5 Sanneh's perspective on translation 8

2 Christianity as a Vernacular Translation Movement 11
   2.1 A brief academic biography of Lamin Sanneh 11
   2.2 Sanneh's journey of faith and thought 12
   2.3 A new reading of Christian mission history 13
   2.4 The significance of vernacular Scripture translation in mission 14
   2.5 New approach to Christian mission in Africa 15
   2.6 Sanneh, on the effects of mission as translation 18
      2.6.1 Translation and empowerment 18
      2.6.2 Translation and the enhancement of identity and confidence 18
      2.6.3 Bible translation preserves indigenous languages ... 19
      2.6.4 Challenging Western hegemony 20
      2.6.5 Sanneh, on World Christianity 23

3 The Dagomba of Northern Ghana 25
3.1 Introduction 25
3.2 Sources 25
    3.2.1 Non-written sources 25
    3.2.2 Written sources 27
3.3 History of the Dagomba 28
    3.3.1 The jihads 28
    3.3.2 Possible origins 29
    3.3.3 The colonial era 31
3.4 Administrative capitals 32
3.5 Demographic data 33
3.6 Dagomba relationships with other ethnic groups 33
    3.6.1 The Mamprusi 33
    3.6.2 The Mossi and Nanumba 34
    3.6.3 The Gonja 34
3.7 The impact of the Asante empire on the Dagomba and the Asante decline 35
3.8 Post-independence developments 36
    3.8.1 Recent history 37
    3.8.2 Urban Dagomba and rural Dagomba 38
3.9 Language 38
3.10 Social organisation 39
3.11 Rituals governing traditional life 40
    3.11.1 Marriage 40
    3.11.2 Beliefs around pregnancy 43
    3.11.3 Birth 43
    3.11.4 Circumcision 43
    3.11.5 Death and burial 44
    3.11.6 Festivals and celebrations 44
3.12 The Dagomba response to Western education and development 45
3.13 Dagomba Religion 47
    3.13.1 Effect of migration on religions 47
    3.13.2 Dagomba primal religion 48
3.14 History of Islam in Dagbon 51
3.15 Dagbon chieftaincy and religion 53
3.16 The Dagomba of Northern Ghana: Conclusion 54

4 The Konkomba of Northern Ghana 57
4.1 Introduction 57
4.2 Sources 58
4.3 History: Origins of the Konkomba 59
4.4 The Konkomba under colonial authority 61
4.5 The Konkomba after Ghanean independence as a republic 65
4.6 Recent history 65

Contents

    4.7 The Konkomba and their neighbours 66
    4.8 Language 67
    4.9 The Konkomba and related ethnic groups 68
        4.9.1 The Mamprusi kingdom 68
        4.9.2 The Nanumba 69
        4.9.3 The Gonja 70
    4.10 The stigmatisation of the Konkomba 70
    4.11 The Konkomba and ethnic pride 71
    4.12 Education and literacy 72
    4.13 Social organisation 72
    4.14 The traditional beliefs and worldview of the Konkomba 73
        4.14.1 *Uwumbor* 'supreme God' 73
        4.14.2 The *kenjaa* 'lesser gods' and 'nature spirits' of
                 the Konkomba 75
        4.14.3 *Bininkpieb* 'ancestors' of the Konkomba 75
        4.14.4 *Oubwa* 'diviners' 76
        4.14.5 *Njog* 'sorcerer's medicine' 76
        4.14.6 *Kesuo* 'witchcraft/sorcery' 76
    4.15 The Konkomba and Islam 77
    4.16 The Konkomba traditional festivals 78
    4.17 Traditional ritual and belief 79
        4.17.1 Marriage 79
        4.17.2 Circumcision 80
        4.17.3 Death and burial 80
    4.18 Conclusion 80

5 Christian Mission in Northern Ghana: The Dagomba Story 83
    5.1 Introduction 83
    5.2 Colonial authorities and Christian mission in the
         Northern Territories 84
         Relations between colonial authorities and Christian missions. 86
    5.3 Beginnings of Christian mission 88
        5.3.1 The pioneer missions amongst the Dagomba 89
        5.3.2 Role of southern Christians 93
        5.3.3 The challenges to the Christian mission enterprise 93
    5.4 Another phase of the Christian mission to the Dagomba 94
        5.4.1 The Assemblies of God mission to the Dagomba 94
        5.4.2 The Catholic church 98
        5.4.3 The Evangelical Presbyterian Church 101
        5.4.4 The Baptist church 102
        5.4.5 The second mission of the Presbyterian Church of
              Ghana to the Dagomba 104
        5.4.6 The Scripture Union 111
    5.5 Current challenges and opportunities in Christian mission
         to the Dagomba 112

        5.5.1 The challenge of Islam 112
        5.5.2 Initial perception of Christianity as alien 113
        5.5.3 Poverty 113
        5.5.4 Ethnic conflicts 113
        5.5.5 Church structures and the Christian mission to the
             northern peoples 114
  5.6 Good will towards Christianity 114
      Role of Christian NGOs 114
  5.7 Translation of Christianity among the Dagomba 114
  5.8 Early attempts at Dagbani Bible translation 115
        5.8.1 The Basel Mission 116
        5.8.2 The Assemblies of God Mission 116
  5.9 The translation and use of the Dagbani Old Testament 117
        5.9.1 The Bible Society of Ghana and Dagbani Bible translation .. 117
        5.9.2 Faith Comes By Hearing and Scripture engagement 118
        5.9.3 The role of GILLBT in the Dagbani Literacy Project 119
  5.10 Conclusion 120

6 **Christian Mission in Northern Ghana: The Konkomba Story .. 121**
  6.1 Introduction 121
  6.2 Colonial policy and the evangelisation of the Konkomba 122
        6.2.1 Assemblies of God mission to the Konkomba 122
        6.2.2 The Evangelical Presbyterian Church 123
        6.2.3 The Worldwide Evangelisation Crusade 124
  6.3 An evaluation of the missionary enterprise among the Konkomba .. 126
  6.4 Konkomba preference for Christianity 127
  6.5 Mission as a translation movement: The Konkomba Christian
      Scriptures 129
        6.5.1 Literacy among the Konkomba 131
        6.5.2 SIL International and GILLBT 131
  6.6 The role of the indigenous Konkomba in Bible translation 133
      The Konkomba traditional religion in the translation process 136
  6.7 Some aspects of the translation process 140
        6.7.1 Anthropological research 140
        6.7.2 Sociolinguistic survey 141
        6.7.3 Literacy 142
        6.7.4 Securing funding 142
        6.7.5 Personnel 142
        6.7.6 Involvement of the churches 143
  6.8 Conclusion 143

7 **Sanneh's Hermeneutic of Mission as Translation and
Anti-hegemony: Test Case of the Dagomba and the Konkomba... 145**
  7.1 Introduction 145
  7.2 The effect of mother-tongue Scriptures in light of Sanneh's paradigm 147

7.3	The Dagomba and Konkomba use of the Bible since publication.. 148
7.4	The effect of Bible translation on the Dagomba........................ 149
	7.4.1 Testimonies from Faith Comes By Hearing 149
	7.4.2 Dagbani Scriptures and social change............................ 155
7.5	The effect of the Likpakpaaln Scriptures on the Konkomba 158
7.6	The effect of Bible translation on the Bimoba people – a comparison.. 170
7.7	The mother-tongue Scriptures and conversion 173
7.8	The effect of the Scriptures on theological understanding....... 174
7.9	Socio-cultural effect... 175
7.10	Mother-tongue Scriptures and modern challenges.................. 176
7.11	Mother-tongue Scriptures and primal religious aspirations ... 177
7.12	Bible translation and renewal of Dagomba and Konkomba cultures 178
	7.12.1 The vernacular Scriptures and festivals 179
	7.12.2 The mother tongue and guidance 180
	7.12.3 Mother-tongue Scriptures as the moral frame of reference.. 180
	7.12.4 Mother-tongue Scriptures and subversion of hegemony.. 181
	7.12.5 The Dagbani and Likpakpaaln Scriptures and holistic development.. 182
	7.12.6 Bible translation as holistic mission............................. 185
7.13	Summary.. 189

8 A Revitalised Indigenous Consciousness: The Fruit of Translation .. 191
- 8.1 The troubled beginnings of Christian mission in northern Ghana... 192
- 8.2 Lamin Sanneh's new look at Christian mission........................ 193
- 8.3 Christian mission against cultural hegemony 193
- 8.4 A new approach to evangelisation: learning the languages of the people 194
- 8.5 Translation of culture along with translation of Scriptures 194
  - 8.5.1 The Dagomba response to vernacular Bible translation 194
  - 8.5.2 The Konkomba response to vernacular Bible translation... 195
- 8.6 Other effects of the translated Scriptures.................................. 197

Appendix: Dagomba and Konkomba Anthems Sung in Churches... 203
1. Two Dagomba anthems sung in churches................................ 203
2. A Konkomba anthem sung in churches.................................... 204

Archival Source References.. 205

Textual References 209

Index 219

Abbreviations

AG	Assemblies of God
EPC	Evangelical Presbyterian Church
FCBH	Faith Comes By Hearing
GILLBT	Ghana Institute of Linguistics, Literacy and Bible Translation
KOYA	Konkomba Youth Association
NGO	Non-governmental organisation
PCG	Presbyterian Church of Ghana
PRAAD	Public Records Administration and Archives Department
RILADEP	Rural Integrated Literacy and Development Programme
SIL	Summer Institute of Linguistics (currently, SIL International)
SU	Scripture Union
UNESCO	United Nations Education, Scientific and Cultural Organization
WEC	Worldwide Evangelisation Crusade
WVI	World Vision International

Map 1. Country of Ghana showing administrative regions

Source: The United Nations. https://www.un.org/Depts/Cartographic/map/profile/ghana.pdf. Accessed 4 December 2018. Used with permission.

Maps xiii

Map 2. Ethnic map of Ghana, highlighting Dagomba and Konkomba

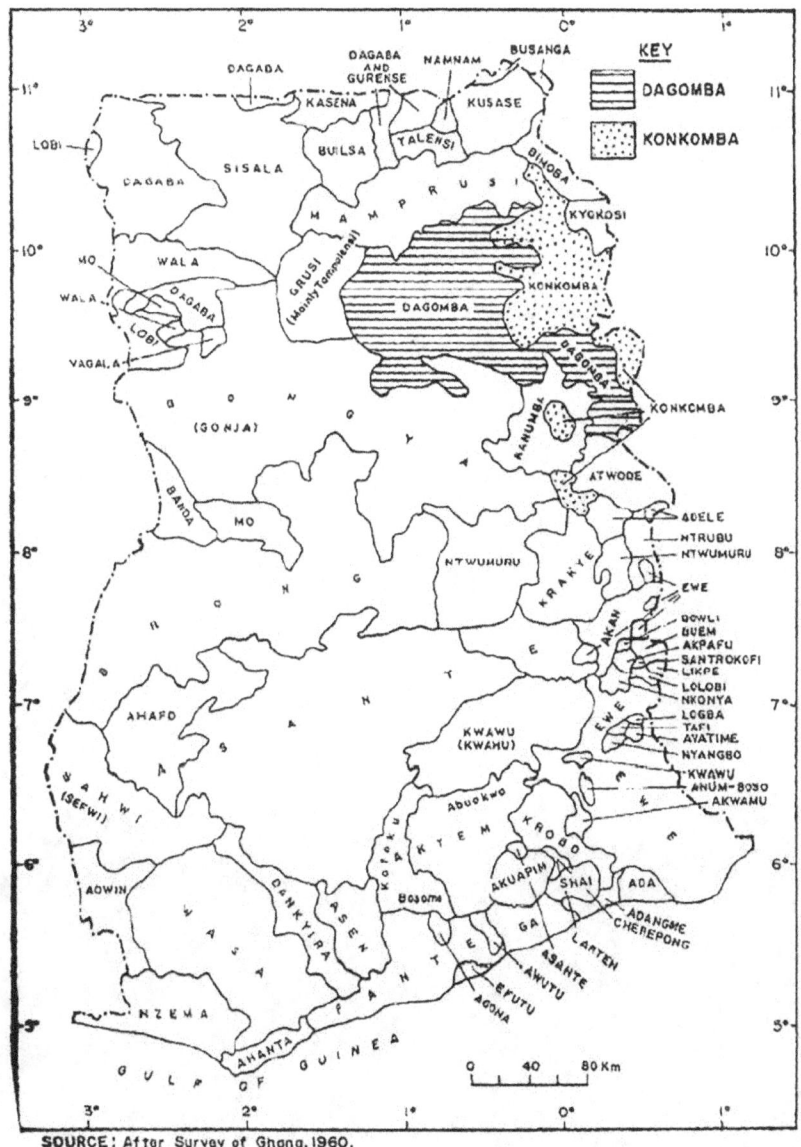

Source: Department of Geography, University of Ghana, Accra.
Used with permission.

1

Introduction

The encounter of the Dagomba and Konkomba peoples of northern Ghana with the Christian gospel[1] is a case study in culture change, church development and the spread and influence of religious and philosophical ideas. In succeeding chapters I focus on that encounter referencing Lamin Sanneh's theoretical framework of the translation of the gospel. According to John Mbiti, to place this gospel at the heart of African culture, missionaries had to translate it (1994:27). "Mission is impossible without communication, and Christianity purports to be Good News in any language" (Gittins 2002:81). The focus of this work, therefore, is on the effect of Bible translation into the native language of the Dagomba (Dagbani) and Konkomba people (Likpakpaaln[2]) and on the lives of those who speak these languages. This work also provides an opportunity to examine the nature of Christian mission[3] in the context of two very different societal structures[4]

---

[1] The "gospel," is used in this work to mean the revelation of God through Christ Jesus, which encompasses the written word about the person of Christ, the Christian message; the gospel is also referred to as "Good News." Gospel is capitalized when reference is made to the first four books of the New Testament: Matthew, Mark, Luke and John.

[2] There are several variations of the spelling of the Konkomba language; we use *Likpakpaaln* in this book.

[3] In this work, "Christian mission" is used in the sense of *missio Dei*, that is, an initiative of God. As Bosch says: "mission is not primarily an activity of the church, but an attribute of God. God is a missionary God" (1991:389–390).

[4] As described in PRAAD Accra. ADM 56/1/204, PRAAD (Public Records Administration and Archives Department), Accra, Ghana.

in the Northern Region of Ghana, the largest of eighteen administrative regions (see map 1),[5] namely, the so-called chiefly or centralised Dagomba, and their acephalous or non-centralised Konkomba neighbours (see map 2).

The Dagomba belong to the chiefly type and exercised hegemony (dominance) over the so-called non-chiefly Konkomba throughout their history of coexistence. The relationship of these two groups to each other has generally been characterised by hostility even though there have been inter-marriages between some segments of these two groups. The Dagomba people have a traditional, centralised political system. The Konkomba people, on the other hand, belong to a decentralised socio-political system, who once were subjects of the Dagomba king. Because of their structured and hierarchical society, the Dagombas were more easily influenced early on by Islam as a society in general, resulting in a religious predisposition toward the Islamic religion. The Konkomba are predominantly adherents of primal religion, commonly known as African traditional religion (Rattray 1932).[6]

In recent times the Dagomba, especially those who live in rural territory, and the Konkomba have become more open to Christianity. The Konkomba have had the full Bible translated for some time, while the Dagomba had only the New Testament and portions of the Old Testament available until 2007 when the complete Dagomba Bible was launched.

Although Christians constitute a minority segment of the populations of both people groups, one can observe a growing Christian presence and influence among them. Missionaries to the Dagomba and Konkomba embarked upon a holistic mission (Sim 2004) that laid the groundwork for acceptance of change.[7] The focus of this book, however, is limited to the effect mother-tongue Bible translation has had – with respect to domination and empowerment, and regarding a qualitative culture change. Is there a difference between the influence observable among the Dagomba, who do not have a long history with the complete Bible, and on the Konkomba who have had a longer duration of biblical contact?

Other questions we address include: How did these two people groups encounter the gospel? What was the medium of communication for the Christian message, and how was that message encoded by the missionaries and decoded by the Dagomba and Konkomba? By what means can we determine if Christianity has been indigenised into their respective worldviews and thought patterns, and how far has the Christian faith effected those worldviews, their ethos and the behaviour of the Dagomba and

---

[5] The map shows ten administrative regions that were current at the time of writing.
[6] Rattray's study coincided with the second phase of missionary work among the Dagomba and Konkomba. The perspective in his book, *The Tribes of the Ashanti Hinterland*, would have been useful to the missionaries of that time.
[7] Some would say mission work is purely evangelistic; others, just social action. John Stott, *Christian Mission in the Modern World*, suggests we understand Christian mission as a partnership of evangelism and social action (Stott 1975).

Konkomba? Finally, how can one assess the encounter of the Dagomba and the Konkomba today with Christianity?

1.1 The intellectual framework of, and motivation for, the writing of this book

In this work[8] I borrow Professor Lamin Sanneh's concept of Christian mission as a DYNAMIC VERNACULAR TRANSLATION MOVEMENT. I frame Bible translation as integral to effective Christian mission, specifically with respect to the Dagomba and Konkomba of northern Ghana, between 1912 and 2007. Sanneh's work is key to elucidating the data.

Bible translation plays a pivotal role in interpreting Christian mission comprehensively because Christian faith depends principally on the Bible. It is the preponderance of translating the Christian message, not just from one language to another but also across cultures, that Sanneh refers to as a translation movement. We have chosen to examine the religious trajectories of the Dagomba and Konkomba in the context of northern Ghana within Sanneh's paradigm of mission because of its uniquely creative potential to analyse and interpret the encounter of these two cultures with Christianity.

The motivation to write on this theme is both academic and personal, in that it arises in part from my desire to understand the nature of Christian mission. Most Western scholars using social science and Marxist methodologies conclude that Christian mission is cultural imperialism and religious bigotry (Sanneh 2003:20). I find refreshing Sanneh's departure from other approaches. He presents Christianity as a faith-seeking-translation on a cross-cultural journey; he thus makes the Christian faith liberating and true to its mission. Sanneh interprets Christian mission essentially as a vernacular and dynamic translation movement, and therefore "anti-structure" (1997a:291ff) or ANTI-HEGEMONY. An historical trajectory of the transformative effect of Bible translation on the Dagomba and Konkomba, gives us a specific case study from an African viewpoint that substantiates Sanneh's perspective of Christian mission.

Sanneh, a world leading scholar in African Christian mission history, had immense knowledge of African traditional religion, and experience in both Islam and Christianity. His historical perspective provided helpful insights into how the Dagomba and Konkomba encountered Christianity and adopted Christianity into their own cultural parameters making it their own, not a religion exclusive to Westerners, southern Ghanaians or "elite" literates.

The northern Ghanaian context provides an ideal environment for testing Sanneh's paradigm of mission because of the prevalence of African

---

[8] This work is based on my doctoral dissertation presented in 2007 to the Akrofi-Christaller Institute, Akropong-Akuapem, Ghana.

primal religion and Islam, in addition to Christianity, among the different ethnic groups (Boi-Nai and Kirby 1999:133ff). We can find ample evidence to contrast the attitude of Christians and Muslims towards the translation of Christian and Muslim Scriptures into the common vernacular of the local communities.

On a personal level, Sanneh's religious itinerary, that is, his conversion from Islam to Christianity that moulded his scholarship, was an experience that resonates with mine. His perspective assists me with the intellectual, analytical tools to understand Christian mission among the Dagomba and Konkomba, in addition to understanding my own religious journey. His perspective of the Islamic missionary approach as a counterpoint to Christian mission is especially helpful.

1.2 How this study was conducted

In this work, I consulted both primary and secondary materials. The primary sources include archival materials, reports and correspondence on Christian missionary work in northern Ghana. Also included in these resources are interviews with members of the Dagomba and Konkomba communities in both northern and southern Ghana, as well as an interview with Professor Lamin Sanneh. Among the groups interviewed were ten focus groups, mission scholars, traditional rulers or opinion leaders, church leaders, and Bible translators and their assistants. The oral interviews were recorded with an audio-recording device, transcribed and then analysed.

Sanneh's writings, especially those related to his perception of Christian mission, comprise the bulk of the secondary resource material for this book and provide the intellectual framework for the work. Other scholars' writings relevant to the study of mission history, especially in relation to Ghana, were also consulted.

1.3 Overview of the book

In chapter one we introduce the background and the framework, motivation and methodology for this work. After this introduction we look at some of the relevant literature on the subject.

In chapter two we introduce Lamin Sanneh and his paradigm of Christian mission. The chapter covers his educational background as well as his journey of faith and his contribution to scholarship. His concept of "mission as translation and anti-hegemony" forms the final part of the chapter.

Chapters three and four deal with the histories of the Dagomba and Konkomba peoples respectively, their origins and their relationships to other ethnic groups. This historical section discusses the political systems of these people groups and their effect on national politics. It also examines their

1.3 Overview of the book

traditional religion and worldview, as well as their encounters with Islam. In the final parts of the two chapters, attention is given to the Dagomba and Konkomba attitudes to education and development, and also to their challenges and aspirations.

These two chapters provide a basis for assessing the influence of mother-tongue Scriptures on the Dagomba and Konkomba people, their institutions and their interrelationships. It also gives us the opportunity to examine what cultural resources were drawn on for the translation of the Christian message.

In chapters five and six we consider Christian mission as a translation movement – a TRANSLATABLE FAITH – in light of the effect of the Dagomba and Konkomba Christian Scriptures. Chapter five, gives an overview of the Christian mission agencies that have made an effect on the Dagomba. We then discuss the coming of the mother-tongue (*Dagbani*) Scriptures to the Dagomba. A similar pattern is followed in chapter six with the Konkomba people and the translation of the Scriptures into *Likpakpaaln*.

In dealing with Christian missionary activity to the Dagomba and Konkomba prior to Bible translation into their mother tongues we limit discussion to missionary agencies or denominations that made a significant effect on the evangelisation of the Dagomba and Konkomba. These include the Presbyterian Church of Ghana (PCG), the Assemblies of God (AG)[9], the Catholic church, the Baptist church, the Evangelical Church of Ghana, the Scripture Union and other Christian groups. We consider the role of the Dagomba and Konkomba who practice traditional religious customs, and the preparations of the translators for their task of Bible translation. Other areas taken into consideration include the Dagomba and Konkomba traditional religions, and Islam, in the translation process. The chapters also look at how the Dagomba and Konkomba Scriptures have been received, and their role in socio-cultural development. We consider the influence of vernacular Christian Scriptures on those who practice traditional Dagomba and Konkomba religious customs and their influence on Muslims in northern Ghana.

Chapter seven deals with the test of Sanneh's hermeneutic of mission as translation and anti-hegemony, with special reference to the Dagomba and Konkomba. We explore the impression vernacular translation has had on the worldviews and modes of problem solving of the two people groups. In addition, we examine the effect of the mother-tongue Scriptures on attitudes, culture and churches. Finally, we discuss the anti-hegemonic role of vernacular translation in the relationship between the Dagomba and the Konkomba with focus on their self-esteem. Other themes covered in this chapter on the role of translation include empowerment of the people and the destigmatisation of indigenous cultures.

Chapter eight includes a summary of findings and the conclusion.

---

[9] Officially, the World Assemblies of God Fellowship.

1.4 Review of relevant literature

For the most part, early scholarly studies of the Dagomba and Konkomba cultures concentrated on socio-cultural issues but did not record Christian missionary activity. However, those studies offer insight into how these people groups with complex and highly developed cultures encountered and adopted Christianity.

British anthropologist R. S. Rattray was one of the earliest to produce an ethnography on the peoples of the then Northern Territories of Ghana.[10] His work, *The Tribes of the Ashanti Hinterland* (1932) is very informative, though it has little to say regarding Christian mission work. David Kimble (1963) in his study of the political history of Ghana provides the reader with invaluable insights by situating the peoples of northern Ghana in the political history of the country and describing factors that have influenced social change in Ghana following Western colonial contact. The issue of language use and a development of national consciousness also engaged his attention.

More recent literature also lacks reference to the contribution of Christian mission in the life of the peoples of northern Ghana. Abudulai Yakubu, an attorney of Dagomba heritage, published a book in 2005 on the Dagomba, entitled *The Abudulai-Andani Crisis of Dagomba: A Historical and Legal Perspective of the Yendi Skin Affairs*. While helping the uninformed understand the political polarisation of the Dagomba that is threatening to break up their kingdom, there is no reference to the role of Christian mission activity, athough he acknowledges that of Islam.

Peter Barker's *Peoples, Languages and Religion in Northern Ghana* (1986) is the earliest study to acknowledge the influence Christianity and Islam have had on the Dagomba and Konkomba peoples. Barker's survey of all the peoples of northern Ghana helps fill the gap in our knowledge of the contribution of religion in the development of these societies. He highlights the need to use vernacular language in religious encounters if the local people are to adopt a religion as their own.

This work explores how the local people choose the religion to which they ascribe; and whether the indigenous cultural worldview and Christianity are accepted side by side; or does Christianity syncretise indigenous concepts so that the two appear to be one and the same?

What role does the traditional religion of the Dagomba and Konkomba play in their encounter with the gospel? How did the missionaries convey the gospel to them? How did the Dagomba and Konkomba comprehend the missionary message? But, most important, by what means do Dagomba and Konkomba "domesticate" or embrace the gospel as their own and not that of the missionaries? How did they move from "their gospel" to "our gospel"?

---

[10] "The Northern Territories of the Gold Coast consisted of the present Northern and Upper Regions of the Republic of Ghana" (Thomas 1974:fn 2).

1.4 Review of relevant literature

Christian ministry to traditional people has been subjected to criticism in the Western media. Whereas some are balanced in their criticism others are overly critical. For instance, some Western journalists such as Julian Pettifer and Richard Bradley (1990), Geoffrey Moorhouse (1973) and anthropologists like the Comaroffs (1997) criticise missionary outreach to the extent that they fail to recognise the positive role of Christianity in African society. In their view, Christian ministry emerged as an intruder and destroyer of non-Western cultures.

The attitude of some missionaries no doubt left much to be desired. Restating Western missionary negative perception of African culture, V. Y. Mudimbe observes that the negative attitude of many Westerners informed their view that the African could only be a slave (1988:8). It is a fair observation that some missionaries never saw value in Africans and their culture. However, in exceptional cases missionaries did embrace Africans and their heritage. Willem Saayman (1990:312) acknowledges that some colonial missionaries made commendable contributions. He notes, however, that they also committed serious mistakes in relation to culture. In his view, many missionaries regarded African culture negatively and, in some cases, waged a military-style campaign of words against it. In his analytical article on Western Christian mission amongst southern African peoples, on the other hand, Anthony Balcomb (1998) has shown evidence that the recipients of Christian mission outreach embraced the gospel in light of their own cultural experience. The Christian message was received and acted upon on the basis of what the recipients already knew from their own religious background. Furthermore, Balcomb has demonstrated how the recipients also resisted any perceived domination from Western missionaries.

Ali Mazrui is an important Muslim African scholar-historian. Like Sanneh, he had a deep interest in Christianity in Africa and a profound inside knowledge of East African Islam. The former was a Muslim, whilst the latter was a Christian convert from a Muslim background. Mazrui sustained that the discussion of Christian mission in Africa is important, and that it should be an inter-African discussion.

In his seminal article on "Religion and Political Culture in Africa," Mazrui (1985:817) examined historically the theme of translation in both Islam and Christianity and describes how Islam took root in Africa in two processes. The first process, which typified the spread of Islam in the North African context, was political, including conquest, control and suzerainty; whilst the second, typical of the sub-Saharan African situation, was economic, involving trade and migration.

Mazrui observed a striking paradox between Christians and Muslims with respect to language use in worship. He pointed out that Islam has been less compromising than Christianity in that respect, as though the God of Islam understood only one language, Arabic. As Mazrui elaborated: "Most of the hymns in mosques in Africa are in the Arabic language, which are memorised and recited, not necessarily with a command of their meaning. It is in this sense that Islam in Africa is linguistically uncompromising, demanding due conformity with the language in which God communicated with humankind" (1985:23).

Mazrui described the contrasting attitudes of Christianity and Islam toward the translation of religious materials into the languages of the local people:

> ...Christianity has quite often communicated with Africans in the language of their own societies. The Bible was translated into indigenous African languages quite often decades before the Qu'ran was. Services in African churches are often conducted in indigenous African languages. Hymns, though sometimes originating in Europe, have been translated quite early and are often sung in indigenous African tongues. At least at the level of language, Christianity has made more concessions to Africa than Islam has done. (1985:23)

He was however quick to add that "in other respects Islam has appeared to be more accommodating to the wider culture of Africa, more ready to compromise with African ancestral customs and usages" (Mazrui 1985:23). This statement is debatable, considering the fact that jihadists, who claimed to uphold the pure form of Islam, were opposed to accommodations with African cultural practices. They held that such practices of compromise had adulterated pure Islam (Azumah 2001:313).

1.5 Sanneh's perspective on translation

Basing his arguments on empirical evidence from mission field experience, Sanneh arrived at a conclusion on Christian mission different from other scholars studying missions. In his view, "missionary interest helped to protect many ethnic societies from extinction, or at least helped to preserve a record of such societies before they disappeared altogether" (1990:313).

Sanneh's perspective of vernacular translation as anti-hegemony was not alien to the Byzantine missionaries. According to Emilianos Timiadis, Photius, the Patriarch of Constantinople (810–895) was one of the pioneers in this movement. Timiadis explains that Photius "defended pluralism and liberty in a time of a monolithic latinization" (Timiadis 1985:237–244). By fighting for the vernacular expression of the Scriptures, Photius was calling the church back to authentic Christian mission whereby the gospel was clothed in the mother tongue.

Sanneh's 1989 treatise on translation, *Translating the Message: The Missionary Impact on Culture,* made clear that it is the nature of Christianity to be adaptable to all cultures. Sanneh asserted, "Christianity is remarkable for the relative ease with which it enters living cultures." Christianity, he argues, "in becoming translatable, renders itself compatible with all cultures" (1989:50). This is possible because genuine Christian mission is translating Christ, who is the content of the mission. If Christianity can be described as a cross-cultural faith, it is because of its essential nature of being translatable.

In *Piety and Power: Muslims and Christians in West Africa* (1996:49ff.), Sanneh observed that after Pentecost, Christianity became a religious movement on the peripheries of Jewish communities as Christian communities sprang up in Gentile society. He noted further that Pentecost allowed the church to dispense altogether with the original Aramaic and Hebrew of Jesus' preaching. Sanneh's view was that, Jerusalem was dismissed as being exclusive to Christian orthodoxy. Consequently, Christianity embraced other languages and cultures that were considered alien to the Law and the Prophets.

In contrast to Christianity, Sanneh contended that the Islamic *hijrah*[11] confirmed and preserved the "Arabicness" of Islam, the indispensable universality of Mecca and Medina (Arabic centres) (1996:49ff.). Muslim fixed and limited centres stand as a counterpoint to the Christian view of multiple centres that are not fixed – except Rome for the Catholics.

Sanneh was not alone in his understanding of Christian mission as vernacular translation of Scripture. The Ghanaian theologian, Kwame Bediako, comes to the same conclusion in his *Christianity in Africa: The Renewal of a Non-Western Religion*. Bediako perceives the achievements of vernacular translation of the Christian gospel in Africa as stripping Christianity of its Western garb. Christianity can therefore be perceived as an indigenous African religion. He interprets mission as translating Christ from one cultural medium into another. In his view, therefore, Christianity has no abiding "city" or "culture" because it can be accommodated by every society. Christianity, he argues, can therefore be justifiably called an African religion because it is "fully coherent with the religious quests in African life" (1995:60).

Bediako argues further that God speaks to Africans in their mother tongue (i.e. vernacular). His argument is based on the fact that "the ability to hear in one's own language and to express in one's own language one's response to the message which one receives must lie at the heart of all authentic religious encounter" (Bediako 1995:49).

By implication, conversion of Africans to Christianity is not informed by cultural manipulation but rather by a genuine religious quest for fulfilment. Therefore, in spite of the historical circumstances surrounding the Western missionary enterprise in Africa, Christianity can be seen as an African religion.

---

[11] The journey of Muhammad and his followers from Mecca to Medina in the year 622; the beginning of the Muslim era itself.

In light of the above, a fresh approach to the contemporary study of mission in Africa is appropriate. Sanneh called for a shift from viewing mission from the perspective of Western missionaries and imperialist ideology, to viewing mission in the African socio-religious context. Examining the context on the ground and seeing mission from the indigenous African point of view, is bound to recast Christian mission in Africa in a new image as "translation and anti-hegemony" (1989:175).

Sanneh interpreted Christian mission as "translation" and that of Islam as "cultural diffusion." In the former, the message is transmitted from one cultural medium to another receptor culture. Thus, the message is encoded in the medium and idiom of the receptor culture in order to make translation complete. Unlike Islam, which prohibits the translation of the Qur'an and insists on cultural uniformity, Christianity is remarkable for its effort to approximate the speech of the common people (Vanhoozer, referencing Sanneh 2005). With respect to Islam, the message, in this case the Qur'an, is not translatable. Islamic mission requires the receptor culture to apprehend the entire Qur'anic message with its Arab culture. Translations of the Qur'an are not given equal status with the Classical Arabic Qur'an. Christian mission, however, is translatable because all cultures are considered equal, cleansed and elevated, and therefore imbued with transcendent status and able to become vehicles of divine communication. When viewed in this light, Christian mission is better understood as a vernacular translation movement than as a colonial relic.

This study of the Dagomba and Konkomba encounter of the Christian faith, especially the coming of their mother-tongue Scriptures, provides us with the concrete context to assess Sanneh's thesis.

2

Christianity as a Vernacular Translation Movement

As we saw in chapter one, there are different approaches by scholars to the study of Christian mission, based on social science methods. These social science methods have their merits as well as their limitations. It is a search for another relevant method that has motivated Sanneh to re-interpret Christian mission as a translation movement (1983:168–171). The Dagomba and Konkomba of northern Ghana serve as case studies to ascertain the soundness of Sanneh's thesis.

2.1 A brief academic biography of Lamin Sanneh

To understand Sanneh's paradigm of Christian mission, it is important to understand him as a person. Lamin Sanneh, a leading African scholar on Christian mission, combined deep religious commitment with academic rigor. Born in Georgetown, The Gambia, in 1942 to an ancient royal family of an elite Muslim ruling class, the *nyanchos*,[1] he is now a naturalised U.S. citizen and lives in the USA with his South African-born wife, Sandra, and two grown children. As a member of the *nyanchos*, Sanneh had his earliest education with other sons of traditional rulers in a Muslim government school in The Gambia. He secured a U.S. State Department scholarship to

---
[1] *Nyanchos* means 'royalty' in the Mandika language according to Lamin Sanneh. Also see Martha T. Fredriks, *We have Toiled all Night: Christianity in The Gambia 1456–2000* 2003:49.

pursue studies in theology and history in the United States. His area of interest at this level of study was the intellectual history of Europe, which culminated in a thesis on the Evangelical Movement. He pursued further studies that took him into the fields of Islamics and Missiology.

Following a Master of Arts degree from the University of Birmingham, England, in Classical Arabic and Islam, he pursued studies in the Near East School of Theology, Beirut, from 1968 to 1969. In 1974 he earned a PhD in Islamic History, with a thesis on "The Origin and Dispersion of the Jakhanke People of Senegambia," a unique pacifist Islamic movement. His broad area of studies has equipped him for a versatile academic career that would take him to four continents for studies and lecturing. He is the author of over a hundred articles on religious and historical subjects in leading academic journals and of several books, many of which are referenced in this work.

2.2 Sanneh's journey of faith and thought

When Sanneh wished to convert to Christianity at the age of eighteen he encountered apathy on the part of Western missionaries in his native country. He recounts how he approached a Methodist missionary in The Gambia asking to be baptised, signalling his conversion to Christianity from Islam. It was not until after a year's persistent attempts that he received the baptism he so desperately desired. The missionary was reluctant to accept, or did not see the need for, Sanneh's conversion. In his article, "Christian Mission and the Western Guilt Complex," Sanneh recalled these incidents of his journey to Christian faith. Without a compelling conviction that he needed this conversion, Sanneh would have given up, as he vividly recounts:

> I had this absurd idea that the gospel had marked me out for something, whether for reward, rebuke or ridicule I did not know; whatever it was, I felt inexorably driven toward it. On the night of my baptism I was overcome with emotion, finding it hard to believe that my wish was being [fulfilled]. (1995:393)

That incident and subsequent events brought Sanneh to the view that there exists a Western guilt complex in relation to Christian mission. Some Western Christians seem to have concluded that Christian mission has been destructive rather than redemptive. For Sanneh, these Westerners feel embarrassed or even guilty that people from the non-Western world have become Christians. To assuage this feeling of guilt associated with Western missions, Sanneh explained that his conversion was at his own volition and not by coercion from missionaries. He explains emphatically: "When I have told them [Westerners] that I was in no way pressured into joining the church, they have seemed gratefully unburdened of a sense of guilt" (1995:393).

It is possible to replicate and confirm Sanneh's experience in several accounts of Christian conversions in the non-Western world, even in the era of the modern missionary movement from the West. In light of Sanneh's experience, it is not surprising that he offers a more creative approach to the study of Christian mission, which departs from the usual stereotype as Western hegemony.

2.3 A new reading of Christian mission history

In the article, "Christian Missions and the Western Guilt Complex" referred to earlier, which first appeared in the *Christian Century*, April 8, 1987, Sanneh pointed out that some Western scholars continue to insist upon the claim "that missionaries instilled a sense of inferiority in natives" (1995:394). This perspective has perhaps had a negative effect upon Westerners, and they may carry needless "guilt about the mischief of the white race in the rest of the world, importing this guilt complex into Africa" in particular (1995:394). Consequently, many Westerners accept responsibility for atrocities that some Westerners have committed in their relationships with other races of the world. Perhaps if God and indigenous agency are brought more into the study of Christian mission as Sanneh advocated, the negative perception of mission could be replaced with a more objective assessment of it.

Sanneh observed, accurately, that this "Western guilt complex" is so pervasive that the Western church and Western scholarship tend to undermine the Christian faith and Christian mission. In further analysis of this attitude, Sanneh contended that the "Enlightenment" is also partly responsible for questioning the rationality of Christian beliefs such as the virgin birth and miracles in general. His assessment is that both "guilt complex" and the "Enlightenment" have negatively affected Westerners with the resultant paranoid feeling. Consequently, the Western church appears to have lost confidence and enthusiasm in Christian mission. Western Christians seem to shy away from and hesitate to be involved in the discussion of religious matters. Rather than being driven by missionary conviction, the post-modern Western church characterised by cultural relativism mentality seems to be driven by the liberal secular culture (Sanneh 1995:394). Thus, Western secularism seems to be setting the agenda now for the Western church as religious fervour seems to be waning. Could the leadership of the Western church be shifting to the non-Western world which now has the majority of Christians (Walls 2002:ch.3)?

Some nationalists in Africa have viewed Christian mission as being part of the colonial chain of oppression that needed to be broken. Hence mission has been seen as a camouflage for gain and power, and some had even predicted the demise of Christian mission in the non-Western world with the collapse of colonialism. This has been described in Sanneh's article "Mission and the Modern Imperative – Retrospect and Prospect: Charting a Course" (1990:301). Could the fact that this prediction was not realised tell us that something inherent in Christianity made Africans reject Western hegemony but embrace the Christian faith that the missionaries introduced?

As a religious historian, Sanneh has examined what actually happened in the encounter between Western missionaries and non-Western peoples, leading him to criticise the widely accepted Western view that Christian mission has been destructive. He observes in his analysis of the standard Western scholarship on Christian mission history that the critical view tends to focus on missionary motives and faults (1995:394) without considering their overall positive effect on indigenous people's life in its totality.

Sanneh demonstrated in two major analyses, *Translating the Message: the Religious Impact on Culture* and *Whose Religion is Christianity? The Gospel Beyond the West,* that Bible translation has been central in Western Christian mission activity and that Scripture translation has been redemptive and transformed recipient societies in positive ways. Perhaps Sanneh was making a legitimate argument here, but clearly Christian missionary work has not been redemptive in all cases. The outcome of missions has been determined to a large extent by the kind of missionaries, the missionary policy they employed, the prevailing political environment and local socio-cultural factors. Yet incontrovertible evidence demonstrates that when Christian missions embarked on vernacular Bible translation they also boosted the development of languages, the positive transformation of culture and the improved general life of communities. *Making a Difference: Bible Translation among the Dagomba and Konkomba of Northern Ghana* details case studies that point to positive effect among the Dagomba and Konkomba as the effect of vernacular Bible translation. Let us now turn our attention to related themes Sanneh examined in his scholarly works.

2.4 The significance of vernacular Scripture translation in mission

The translation of the Scriptures into vernacular languages has affected Christian mission in three significant ways. First, it has made religious language accessible to all people, thus breaking the monopoly of the traditional religious specialist (Sanneh 1993b:89). This development has had ripple effects, for it has empowered ordinary people to participate in the expansion of Christianity in Africa and elsewhere.

Second, according to Sanneh, achievement of Scripture translation also "desacralises" religious language by rendering it in ordinary daily discourse.

He demonstrates insights and deep thought on the wider implications of vernacular translation for society when he writes: "Culture was purged of the sin of deification. Tribal cultures, regardless of how profane or despised, were constituted into expressions of God's living purpose through the vernacular Scriptures" (1993b:90).

In *Translating the Message*, Sanneh described this purging of culture as "destigmatisation" (1989). From his perspective, no culture is too mean for God to use as a vehicle of divine self-disclosure. It is equally important to him to note that in Christianity there is no one special divine language in which to receive God's revelation. Neither are Christians enjoined to use a particular language as the only sacred language for liturgical worship.

A third achievement of vernacular translation is the fulfilment of the purpose of mission, namely, the Christian conversion of all peoples. The accomplishment of this task has helped to dispel the notion that Christianity is a Western religion. The achievement, therefore, has made a shift in Christian mission (Sanneh 2003:25), lifting it to a higher plane by making indigenous people the key agents of mission. Thus, the early elements of Western features in missionary churches, from Sanneh's perspective, were only temporary, awaiting mother-tongue Scriptures to transform and indigenise them.

For Sanneh, the vernacular Scriptures challenge any notion of exclusivity in Christianity; vernacular translation is another way of acknowledging the universality of Christianity and its plural nature (1993b:91). He contended that, on the day of Pentecost, multi-lingual translation of the gospel took place simultaneously; the languages of the world represented in Jerusalem on that day were exalted by the Holy Spirit to the same plane and became carriers of God's revelation to all the peoples of the world. In that one event, Sanneh argued, God revealed multilingual translation as the paradigm for Christian mission.

2.5 New approach to Christian mission in Africa

In reassessing early European missionary attempts in Africa, Sanneh enumerated the difficulties the missionaries had to contend with in the form of diseases, local resistance to the Christian message and the trade in slaves. These missionary problems were further compounded by the fact that other Europeans often accompanied the early missionaries with varied interests and motives. The earliest missionaries' initial ministry was not to the indigenous Africans but rather it was restricted to the forts and castles. This lead Sanneh to conclude that this era of missionary enterprise "produced Fortress Christianity...quarantined...and defended by cannon and gunboats" (1997b:558). However, if Christian mission was seen to be good for the African, then it had to be released from the comforts and protection of the castles and forts.

Later missionaries had to risk their lives as they carried their mission activities to the indigenous peoples in turbulent African society. Sanneh again observed that the Protestant Reformation and the later Roman Catholic Reformation pushed missionary outreach in a new direction of what he terms "modern missions." In Sanneh's perspective,

> When we speak of modern missions...we have in mind not merely a simple chronological change but a fundamental alteration of worldview from the religious territoriality characteristic of the Middle Ages to the social buoyancy conducive to the emergence of a new middle class and gender mobility, and a rising sense of risk-taking and personal responsibility, attributes that became central to the culture of the modern missionary enterprise. (1997b:558)

The era of modern missions came about when Europeans came to the realisation that they had to discard the idea of Europe as the exclusive realm of Christendom or "Christian territory." Consequently, Christian commitment was to be the main prerequisite rather than race, gender or age in this era. This new understanding was to revolutionalise the Western missionary enterprise.

The hallmarks in modern missions, according to Sanneh, were volunteerism and broad-based participation that transcended gender. This shift in focus from the powerful to ordinary Christians transformed Christian mission and attracted the masses in times of crisis. In this way, it functioned as a means of peaceful social change and mobility.

The concept in Africa of "religious territoriality," or Christendom led to the designations of geographical places as either Christian territories or mission fields. Initially, royalty and aristocrats were sponsors of early missionary expeditions. Thus, early attempts adopted the approach of appealing to political or economic authorities who declared that all in their territory were "Christians." With the inception of modern missions, however, conversion of individuals was on their own volition and this became the hallmark of the missionary bodies.

When modern missionaries came to Africa they encountered initial resistance from the people. Sanneh explained that this reluctance of Africans to be converted to the Christian faith had to do with the political implications of conversion. It meant changing allegiance from one's indigenous rulers to foreign ones. This explains why converts were referred to as "pacified" tributary natives who could be absorbed as colonial dependants or vassal subjects of Ferdinand and Isabella, king and queen of Spain." It is for this reason, Sanneh explained, that "evangelization was colonization" and vice versa (1997b:559). Evangelisation as colonisation might have helped to sow the seed of the gospel but little reaping was done because the price was too high for many Africans to pay. A more culturally sensitive approach needed to come to the fore if Africans were to be won to Christianity.

The new credible strategy, which looked to indigenous institutions but played down territorial conquest, can be seen as the watershed for modern missions. The ultimate goal of this mode was "to guarantee success and to create milder Christendom or missionary spheres of influence" (Sanneh 1997b:559). This called on the church to engage traditional religions and cultural values in dialogue, and took the path of persuasion rather than coercion, respecting human free will. It was the missionary translation project that facilitated this. Missionaries had to know the terrain well in order to evolve an effective mission approach that met the felt needs of the people.

Sanneh outlined a number of key elements in the approach by the modern missionary movement. First, missionary organisations had to embark upon geographical and scientific exploration to facilitate transportation. Second, they had to incorporate cultural and linguistic research and documentation into their work. Third, missionaries could not neglect the physical needs of their target audience. They played key roles in the development of the areas where they worked, undertaking projects in education, in medical services, and in suppressing the slave trade and encouraging in its place lawful trade and general economic development. In this way they took agriculture and education seriously. Hence his argument, that "modern missionary enterprise involves preaching and teaching and healing and building community" (1997b:560).

Although critical scholars continued to ignore clear evidence and summarily dismiss missionaries as colonial collaborators and therefore oppressors, there had been instances of "genuine missionary alignment" with local people. For example, when the colonial authorities bombarded Osu because they refused to pay the poll tax, the Basel missionary Zimmermann moved with the Ga people to settle at Abokobi, a suburb of Accra, Ghana, rather than stay with his fellow Europeans. It is also noteworthy that there is evidence of serious rift and conflict between missionaries and the colonial authorities, who were thought of as being their natural allies (Sanneh 1990:304). Further, it is "an incontestable fact" that most of the nationalist leaders were educated in mission schools (1990:305). Thus, an objective analysis of facts on the ground reveals that mission and colonialism had different agendas and were therefore not bedfellows as critics have sought to project. The missionaries were often pro-indigenous whilst the colonialists pursued their own materialistic interests. Sanneh concluded that mission in its most authentic form was distinguished by the development and promotion of the vernacular languages. He carries his argument further by pointing out that, whereas the colonial empire sought to spread universal values, mission committed itself to the development of vernacular cultures, and that this had far-reaching consequences throughout the indigenous world.

2.6 Sanneh, on the effects of mission as translation

2.6.1 Translation and empowerment

The Gnostics of the New Testament era believed that the divine message came in esoteric language accessible only to specialists or a selected few with special gifts. The Christian gospel, however, is meant for all categories of people and this is why Sanneh contended that the translatability of the gospel had led to its accessibility to all persons and cultures. Ordinary people and unrecognised cultures now have equal access to the divine. For instance, women who are or have been marginalised in most cultures now have access to the gospel, and consequently, have been empowered (1995:396).[2]

The vernacular translation embarked upon by the missionaries employed the speech of the common workaday world. Sanneh noted that the Christian approach to translatability strikes at the heart of gnostic tendencies, first by contending that the greatest and most profound religious truths are compatible with everyday language, and second, by targeting ordinary men and women as worthy bearers of the religious message (1995:396).

In Sanneh's scheme of things, translation "destigmatises culture," by which he meant it denies that culture is "profane." By implication, he was asserting that the sacred message may legitimately be entrusted to the forms of everyday life; thus, all aspects of culture can serve as vehicles of the gospel. He continued to argue that translation revitalises, revives and renews culture. In relativising culture, it shows that there is more than one normative expression of the gospel. If the gospel relativises culture, then Christian mission should result in a pluralism in which only God is the revitalizing centre (1995:396).

2.6.2 Translation and the enhancement of identity and confidence

If translation really effects culture, then it must be felt in the identity and confidence level of recipient cultures. Sanneh noted that when non-literate populations were equipped with a written Scripture for the first time, from the wonder and pride of possessing something new that is also strangely familiar, "they burst upon the scene with confidence in the 'whos and whys' of their existence" (1995:396). Euphoria normally accompanies the launching of Bible translations. Mother-tongue speakers are elated that they now have written literature in their language; the status of their language has been elevated to the level of other languages enabling them to enter into the wider intellectual community and also contribute to knowledge.

Vernacular translation empowers indigenous people by stimulating self-awareness among them and enables them to question the actions of missionaries. Sanneh cited an example from Kenya of the Luo Christian leader and

---

[2] This empowerment has to do with the elevation of minority languages and destigmatising cultures deemed inferior.

2.6 Sanneh, on the effects of mission as translation

founder of the Church of Christ in Africa, Matthew Ajuoga. Having had access to translation, Matthew criticised the missionaries since he saw that, "'Love,' as the Bible explained it, was absent from the missionaries' treatment of Africans" (1995:397). Mother-tongue Scripture translation helped indigenous people challenge Western cultural practices and to recover from colonialism.

What was the motivation for this attitude of the missionaries toward the local communities, languages and cultures? In Sanneh's opinion, missionaries saw God's word as superior to any other message; hence they attached considerable importance to their translation work. They consistently adopted "the language and culture as vehicle for the transmission of the gospel," and in his view, "they never questioned whether the language was fit to carry the gospel" (1995:398).

Explaining the missionaries' motive, Sanneh argued that "whatever judgment the missionaries brought with them, it was not about the fitness of the vernacular to be the hallowed channel for communicating with God" (1995:398). This was a theological paradox in which missionaries who entered the field to convert others were themselves also being converted, thus enabling them to participate in the indigenous worldview. As mentioned elsewhere, in the translation process, "it was missionaries who first made the move to "convert" to a new language, with all its suppositions and ramifications" (1995:397). Indeed, the missionaries who actually left indelible marks on their parishes were those who were converted by the cultures in which they worked. As they did this they incarnated the gospel and thus inevitably made it easier for the indigenous people to embrace it.

It is not only the missionaries who were converted by the translation of the gospel into local languages and cultures; the translation has engendered cross-cultural fellowship among diverse ethnic groups that hitherto were not on speaking terms. Bible translation has helped in no small way in challenging people to look beyond their cultural walls. Thus, it has enabled Christians from diverse ethnic backgrounds to congregate and by so doing has paved the way for "pluralism in language, social encounter and ethnic participation in the Christian movement" (1995:397). For example, most Christian denominations in Ghana have multi-ethnic membership with multi-lingual church services.

2.6.3 Bible translation preserves indigenous languages

Vernacular translation also helped to preserve languages that were threatened by a lingua franca. For example, European languages such as English, French and Portuguese might have supplanted indigenous African languages if the latter had not had their vernacular Scriptures. Through Bible translation, missionaries ensured indigenous languages preserved their culture because: "In their grammars, dictionaries, primers, readers and systematic compilations of proverbs, axioms, customs and other ethnographic materials, missionaries furnished the scientific documentation by means of which the modern study of cultures could begin" (1995:398).

That there is a close connection between the growth of Christianity and the widespread employment of the vernacular is Sanneh's contention. Christian growth has been slightest in areas where vernacular languages are weak – that is, where a lingua franca such as English, French, Portuguese, Arabic or Swahili has succeeded in suppressing mother tongues (1995:399). Sanneh accounted for this trend by explaining that the nature of Christian mission is that the Good News message is always seeking vernacular incarnation. It is as if Christian mission abhors cultural domination. There seems to be a built-in compulsion in the gospel demanding that every people group be given an opportunity to hear God's word on its own terms.

Using Islam as a counterpoint, Sanneh argued that though it, too, is a missionary religion, it does not translate its Scriptures. Accordingly, "Islam is strongest in societies where a lingua franca exists, and weakest in places of vernacular preponderance" (1987:333). For this reason, Islam has promoted Arabic in its mission. On this, Sanneh, himself a Christian convert from Islam, was categorical: "I know of no Muslim language institutes dedicated to the systematic study of the vernacular. Islam has succeeded brilliantly in its missionary enterprise, promoting at the same time a universal devotion to the sacred Arabic" (1987:334).

Whereas Christian mission proceeds with the sense of being incomplete without the unevangelised people groups' mother tongues, Islam sees itself as complete and demands that all people groups should embrace its Arabic form. Therefore, Christian mission by translation proceeds as a learner, whereas Islamic mission by cultural diffusion proceeds as teacher.

2.6.4 Challenging Western hegemony

Sanneh saw another contribution of translation as empowerment in the sense that translation sets a standard and emboldens Africans to challenge the West's claim of cultural superiority (1993a:17) and questions the legitimacy of foreign domination.

In his book, *Encountering the West: Christianity and the Global Cultural Process* (Sanneh 1993a:15ff.), Sanneh identified a logical inconsistency in most Western scholars who are opposed to Christian missions, in that while they claim that culture is independent of Christianity on the one hand, they see religion as something that is reducible to its cultural forms. To these Western scholars, indigenous societies were living in a state of cultural innocence prior to imperialist missions that subsequently contaminated them (1993a:15). Thus, in their view, Christian missions have had a negative, if not destructive, effect on indigenous culture.

2.6 Sanneh, on the effects of mission as translation

In this book, Sanneh provided us with the key to understanding his perspective on the issues he wrote about. He testified that the four strands he enumerated shaped his scholarship and perspectives:

> This book is...something of a personal intellectual testament, one individual who was educated on four continents and who carries within him some of the formative strands of several distinct cultural traditions: the African, the Islamic, the Christian and the modern West. Often these four strands are unalterably intertwined, and when one strand is drawn out to provide a perspective, the others resonate in sympathy, and their combined synthesis becomes the unspoken rationale for whatever merit there is in a multicultural vocation such as mine. (1993a:24)

Sanneh found the concept of cultural purity as championed by defenders of indigenous cultures as unsatisfactory and untrue in real life. He convincingly pointed out that multiple cultural boundaries may coexist harmoniously and fruitfully. In real life, cultural inclusiveness is indispensable because cultures continue to borrow from each other. For this reason, Sanneh contended that past excesses on the part of some missionaries against some indigenous cultures do not in themselves invalidate religion. In his thinking, "the answer to such excesses is to repossess the religious subject in its multicultural dimensions rather than abandoning it to commissars and zealots" (1993a:26).

In this multi-cultural context, we can begin to pay serious attention to Christianity as a religion with integrity and subsequently, its encounter with indigenous peoples and their cultures. Rather than Christianity being labelled the destroyer of indigenous cultures it can be shown that it "has successfully penetrated African societies largely because it has been assimilated into local idiom" (1993a:15). That Africans have embraced Christianity is not a case of Western cultural imperialism, but rather Christianity has found a home in African indigenous cultures.

Sanneh found a kind of misconceived dialectic among Western writers who tend to polarise the issue between a "Christianity that is opposed to culture and a Christianity that is culturally determined." He continued that, this perception was bound to lead to controversy evidenced in the boxing of African converts into a mould of Western cultural imperialism, and consequently, considering them as "cultural orphans and traitors" (1993a:16). To hold this view is to suggest that Africans were passive receivers of the Christian message. This view is not only faulty but is equally an insult to the African's intelligence and ability to adopt and process new information.

Moreover, this view also postulates that violence and alienation are the only forms of cultural contact Western missionaries have had with indigenous societies. Western scholars often perceive this contact in terms of domination and the submission of non-Western people to missionaries. Unsatisfied with this interpretation, Sanneh's resolve was to confront the view that African Christianity could not be shaken out of its Western cultural forms. For him, Africans received the Christian message in terms of their own religious and cultural resources and not as a result of cultural imperialism. Cultural imperialism is more of an ideological statement than a critical analysis of the interaction of cultures. The anthropologist Conrad Phillip Kottak argues in his *Mirror for Humanity* (1999:234–238) that when cultures meet they tend to selectively borrow from each other. Thus, no culture is passive in cross-cultural encounters.

Sanneh's methodology has been the pursuance of the historical roots of the "religion-versus-culture controversy" in Western intellectual thought. Furthermore, he also endeavours to show how mother-tongue projects of scriptural translation have encouraged local people to embrace Christianity along with their own cultures (Sanneh 1993a:16).

Sanneh was not unaware of some missionaries who "wanted to dismantle the older indigenous cultural dispensation and to subvert the native genius." Their attempts however only worked as long as the mother-tongue Scriptures were not available. For, as he noted, missionaries' employment of the mother tongue in their scriptural translation "was a tacit surrender to indigenous primacy and complicates the arguments of Western cultural superiority." Whereas some missionaries were ready to learn and work with cultural categories, others were ethnocentric. For instance, a French missionary in Africa, as late as 1960, is said to have claimed, "…for European culture a unique, normative status, saying it possessed the 'high degree of perfection which the entire world recognizes'" (Sanneh 1993a:17).

For many other missionaries, the Bible is the highest authority and for that reason they believed it should become the life standard for the people to whom they brought the message of Good News. They therefore set out to translate it into the mother tongue. This accounts for the commitment that attended these missionaries' efforts to develop a written system for indigenous languages and then translate the Bible into them. By translating the Scriptures into the mother tongue of local societies, missionaries were indirectly communicating to Africans that their languages were equal in worth to those of the missionaries.

While Western writers tend to criticise Christian missionary endeavours as being a tool of colonialism and Western hegemony, Sanneh declared that Christian mission in its authentic form is anti-hegemony. He identifies the anti-hegemonic function in translation. A successful translation "[w]ill minimize," and even "prevent, continued Western cultural and political domination and the subversion of other people." This anti-hegemonic tendency may partly explain why "colonial authorities were not always supportive of mother-tongue translation." We noted earlier how Sanneh was able to show that in many parts of French and Portuguese Africa, colonial authorities acted to disenfranchise the mother tongue (1993a:18) in that they did not encourage the use of indigenous languages. Christianity in Western hegemonic terms did not take root in Africa with the earliest attempts by European missionaries (Sanneh 1989). Sanneh argued that the African discovery of this liberating Christianity was as a result of the translation of the Bible into African languages (in Donovan 2001:151).[3] The first understanding is that the vernacular Scriptures are read as God speaking to the individual and community in the most intimate way possible. As people read and reflected on these Scriptures, they evaluated the Europeans' attitude in relation to God's perception of human worth and conduct. Thus, it was no longer what the European missionaries said that was final but what God said in the Scriptures. "What they learned convinced them that mission as European cultural hegemony was a catastrophic departure from the Bible" (1989:162ff.).

In his book, *Whose Religion is Christianity? The Gospel beyond the West*, Sanneh argued that Africans received the vernacular Scriptures and used them as the measuring rod both of their lifestyle and that of the European. In other words, they realised that they were on the same plane with Europeans before God and therefore were of equal worth in the sight of God. The translation of the Scriptures into the mother tongue of a people could therefore be seen as subversive [to the dominant power] because it opens access to power for the strong and the weak, the ruler and the ruled (2003:98).

The successful fight to end the slave trade, for example, was achieved not only through legislative process by European abolitionists; Africans themselves contributed in no small way to wipe out the menace (1999:239). Sanneh explained how this happened: "In reading the Bible in their mother tongue, Africans discovered stories about slavery and liberation, about captivity and restoration, about injustice and vindication and about God's promises to the long-suffering tribes of Isaac and Jacob and drew appropriate lessons of empowerment from that" (1999:151).

For Sanneh, therefore, vigorous promotion of vernacular translation of the Christian Scriptures has acted variously to preserve indigenous cultures and their values; it has had a liberating effect on the person and community where such "deep" translation has taken place. Therefore, in this way MISSION AS TRANSLATION has acted as anti-hegemony.

2.6.5 Sanneh, on World Christianity

Sanneh's examination of the history of Christian mission lead him to conclude that through setback and opportunity Christianity is now a

---

[3] Sanneh argued in his analysis of Vincent Donovan's *Christianity Rediscovered* that, "Christianity offered Africans the language of liberation and equality with which to oppose colonial repression." These mother-tongue Bibles coupled with literacy empower Africans to assert their identity and to fight for their freedom. Translation suggests that mother-tongue Scriptures function by awakening people to discover themselves and their potential.

world religion, far from being the ploy of a Western cultural imperialism (2003:22). The inherited apostolic faith has, through translation, become genuinely multicultural. It is no longer a monolithic church but is now characterised by the forms and habits of other languages and cultures, thus making it a lively cross-cultural and inter-religious religion. He recognised that this development is not uniformly evident everywhere. For him, the exciting features of this World Christianity are the creative production of new hymns, music, artistic and liturgical materials and fresh categories for doing theology. This has thus given impetus to mother-tongue Christianity, which in turn has promoted the preservation of valuable cultural values, ecumenical sharing and partnership (1997b:572).

Sanneh appreciates the crucial shift of disentangling Christianity from its Western missionary roots and giving recognition to local initiatives.

> The dawn of a new dispensation, a fresh, if sometimes uneven, point of departure for apostolic heritage, a galvanizing hope born of proven confidence that we can move beyond Day One of the missionary landing to enter the fields and spheres with our hearts and minds fixed on the right things. It represents a landslide change in the old order, an axial shift of mass and direction. (1997b:572)

And yet when we make this axial change and differentiate Christianity from colonialism, also indigenous assimilation from missionary transmission, then shall we indeed perceive Christian mission both as translation and anti-hegemony.

3

The Dagomba of Northern Ghana

3.1 Introduction

In the previous chapter, we dealt with the person of Lamin Sanneh and his theology of Christian mission as a translation movement which serves as our intellectual point of reference. This chapter explores the history and culture of the Dagomba of northern Ghana. To fully assess the encounter of the Dagomba with Christianity, it is imperative that we trace their origins, their identity and their religious history. This will enable us to assess the level of effect of the vernacular Scriptures. Primary and secondary sources on the Dagomba help us understand their history, language, social organisation, literacy and religion, as well as show how these have shaped their identity and prepared them within their context for Bible translation.

3.2 Sources

3.2.1 Non-written sources

The history of the Dagomba, like that of most traditional, non-literate societies, is shrouded in a mist of obscurity. The earliest historical information on the Dagomba is embedded in a collection of oral traditions which need to be analysed critically (Shinnie and Ozanne 1962:13). The Dagomba traditional drummers, the *lunsi* and fiddlers, the *gunji* (Oppong 1973:13), who recite their traditional narratives, are an invaluable source of the people's tradition (Vansina 1985:3-10).[1] Like the Dagomba, the other chiefly ethnic groups in northern Ghana such as the Mamprusi and Gonja have their *lunsi* and *gunji*. These are all male and depend on their association with the traditional authority, *naam* 'chieftaincy', for their livelihood. The oral sources used in this work include recorded interviews with the drummers and some of the traditional leadership of the Dagomba.

The office of the *lunsi* and the *gunji* rests with families that have a long association with the royal court as custodians of the dynastic history. Over the years these traditional functionaries have been the source of information about the origins, migrations, battles and the royal genealogy of the Dagomba and other related peoples (Oppong 1973:13ff.). Traditional festivals and royal funerals provide occasion for the recitation of the historical past of the people.

The recitation reproduced here provides some insight into the founding of the Mole-Dagbani kingdoms and the genealogy of their ruling dynasties:

> This is how the kingdoms of the Dagomba, Mamprusi, Nanumba and Moshi[2] began. Tiyaawumya begat Tohi-zee. And Tohi-zee also begat Kpuginambu. Kpaginambu begat three sons. Gbewaa and Namzisheli and Nyagili. Nyagili's descendants are the Nabdam, and Namzisheli's descendants are the Tallensi, who are in the Bolgatanga area now. Gbewaa begat Kufogu, Zirili, Tohigu and Shitobu and Nmantambo.
>
> Other children he gave birth to in addition are Subee, Bugiyeligu and Biemoni. Gbewaa gave birth to daughters who are Kachagu and Yentori. Kufogu and Zirili did not have dynasties. Tohigu's descendants are the Mamprusi, Shitobu's descendants are the Dagomba, and Nmantambo's descendants are the Nanumba. Gbewaa's daughter whose name is called Yentori has as her descendants the Moshi. King Gbewaa's other children left and became chiefs in Dagomba towns. All these happened about the year 1300 (more than 700 years ago). (Dagbani Almanac 2003)[3]

---

[1] Vansina notes that oral traditions, though valuable, are not without limitations and points out some of the limitations of oral sources. Because the narrators may only be saying a fraction of what they know, the history may be presented in a particular interest or to reflect a particular point of view.

[2] This is the same group referred to as Mossi elsewhere in this book. Individual scholars use various spellings of vernacular names.

[3] Abdulai Lunga 'drummer' and Yendi Yiwogunaayili *lunsi* 'drummers' and others. On Saturday, 20 January 2007, at Gumani in Tamale, another group of drummers I interviewed confirmed this narrative.

3.2 Sources

That the Dagomba, Mamprusi, Nanumba, and the other ethnic groups are considered to be descendants of Tohajie (alternate spelling Tohi-zee) has been corroborated by an interview with an elderly Dagomba, Pastor Moses Yahaya, and colonial reports on the Dagomba.[4] Furthermore, the works of historians such as A. W. Davies and A. A. Iliasu writing on the "Kambonse" of Mamprusi and Dagomba confirm the consanguinity of the Mole-Dagbani peoples.[5] These peoples are believed to have helped the king of Melle (Mali) and intermarried with his people. According to Davies, they picked up some Mandingo words and dances during their migration to modern Ghana from the Lake Chad region.[6]

The Dagomba cherish their history and tend to portray themselves as powerful people, who once wielded considerable power and influence over other ethnic groups in northern Ghana. Although the sources of their history tend to express a strong bias in their favour in their dealings with other ethnic groups, valuable information can be gleaned from them (Vansina 1989:54–61). This tendency is not peculiar to Dagomba, for history is often presented from the point of view of the strong.

To sum up, the *lunsi* and the *gunji* view Dagomba myths and legends in a positive light and faithfully recite them. Muslim scribes and colonial authorities apparently showed sympathy toward the Dagomba, necessary for the success of their policy of Indirect Rule. Though oral narratives have been criticised for their lack of consistency, they are nonetheless of immense value (Vansina 1989:54–61) in understanding the Dagomba and their neighbours, who remain predominantly non-literate.[7]

3.2.2 Written sources

The written sources used in this work include the Hausa *Ajami* chronicles in Arabic script, the *Ajami*, archival materials and both published and unpublished literature on the Dagomba and other related peoples.

The Ajami literature

The *Ajami* manuscripts are an important written source of Dagomba history. These comprise Muslim chronicles in Hausa written in Arabic script (Oppong 1973:13). Some of the *Ajami* manuscripts date as early as the 1800s. According to Stanislaw Pilaszewicz of the University of Warsaw (2001), it was the Hausa Muslims who initiated and developed this literary

---

[4] PRAAD Accra. ADM 56/1/91.
[5] Institute of African Studies Library, DP/DT 507.7.
[6] PRAAD Tamale. NRG 8/2/1:1.
[7] The 2000 Population & Housing Census: Summary Reports of Final Results, Accra: Ghana Statistical Service, 2002. The report reveals that whereas Greater Accra Region has an illiteracy rate of 20.6% the three northern regions have: Northern (78.7%), Upper East (78.1%) and Upper West (75.5%).

tradition with help from a Dagomba Muslim cleric. This literature was written in the Arabic and Hausa languages at the expense of the Dagomba language. The Islamic undertones of these manuscripts made production of literary work in Dagbani redundant since they guaranteed the use of Arabic, the holy language for all Muslims, in their worship of *Allah* (God). The accounts in these scripts have an Islamic slant to them and their objectivity is questionable, especially where issues relating to non-Muslim peoples such as the Konkomba are concerned.

Colonial records

Colonial records abound in information about colonial agents' dealings with the Dagomba and other peoples. These records include annual reports, correspondence, native affairs reports, ethnographies, memoranda on certain issues and survey reports. These varied sources help to document aspects of Dagomba history. By contrast, written sources for non-centralised ethnic groups such as the Konkomba are sketchy and more-often-than-not appear as footnotes on accounts of the Dagomba. Robin Horton notes that "there are scarcely any contemporary written records covering the stateless societies in pre-colonial times" (Horton 1985:87–90).

These colonial records are more dependable than the traditional oral history. First, there are not different versions of the same account. Second, they document the socio-cultural life of various ethnic groups in the colonial period. The relative reliability of the colonial records notwithstanding, they tend to marginalise the non-centralised or stateless peoples especially with the introduction of the British policy of Indirect Rule that favoured the centralised or chiefly societies.

3.3 History of the Dagomba

Dagomba history deals with their identity, that is, who they claim to be, where they came from, their social organisation, their relationship with other ethnic groups and how all these have shaped them as a people. To do this, primary sources such as oral traditions and interviews as well as secondary sources have been consulted. Certain aspects of Dagomba life which have contributed to the translation of the Christian Scriptures into Dagbani are what we discuss in this section.

3.3.1 The jihads

According to historians, the early 19th century jihads in northern Nigeria displaced many people. Those rulers who did not want to give up their traditional way of life faced the choice of migrating or submitting to forcible conversion to Islam. Tohajie, the founder of the Dagomba, Mamprusi, Nanumba and Mossi, is believed to have been among those who ran away from such forced conversion. Tuurey comments on the state of affairs then:

> ...a politically advanced people somewhere in Hausaland, in what is now northern Nigeria, were finding it difficult not only to accept but also to tolerate and co-exist with the prevailing state of affairs then obtaining in the region. Islam, like bush fire, had engulfed the whole region, thus threatening to blot out the age-old traditional way of life [sic]. Those of the pagan rulers who were tied to the worship of the ancestors could not possibly subscribe to Islam. In the given circumstances some of the pagan rulers decided to leave the area. One such pagan ruler was Tohajie, the Red Hunter. Tohajie left his home state of Zamfara, one of the seven Bastard Hausa States, with a large following into self-imposed exile. (Tuurey 1982:26)

The harsh policies of the jihad thus led to massive migrations of peoples to more peaceful areas. The human quest for peace, which the earlier form of Islam in West Africa reflected, had given way by this time to a radical form of Islam. The jihads changed an otherwise peaceful West Africa and introduced a militant and an intolerant Islam.

The migration of Tohajie and his descendants from Zamfara to present day Ghana was a consequence of the Muslim jihads. Though they ran away from militant Islam and settled among non-Muslim peaceful people, they were later to encounter peaceful and a non-threatening Islam in their new homeland through the Dyula Muslims.

3.3.2 Possible origins

Martin Staniland, writing on kingship in Dagomba, modifies the myth of their origin. He speculates that the Mole-Dagbani may have been of pagan Hausa origin, possibly coming from Zamfara in northern Nigeria with their legendary great grandfather the "Red Hunter" Tohajie. (Staniland 1975). The common ancestry shared by these peoples might explain the existence of so many similarities in their calendars, customs and institutions with those of the Hausa (Naden 1996). In another interesting legend, Emmanuel Tamakloe basing his works on Dagomba oral tradition, traces Tohajie's ancestry to Noah (1931:1–3).[8] However, there is no concrete historical evidence to support this claim. Similarly, Ibrahim Mahama attempts to trace Dagomba ancestry to Ad of ancient Arabia (Mahama 2004:4).

---

[8] Tamakloe was a colonial clerk and also served as a catechist for the then Ewe Presbyterian Church.

The Dagomba, Mamprusi, Mossi and Nanumba agree about their common kinship because they all trace their origins to a common ancestor, Tohajie (the "Red Hunter"). According to the Ghanaian historian, F. K. Buah, Tohajie's putative grandson, Gbewaa (Gbewa) or Bawa, had descendants who subsequently founded the Dagomba, Mamprusi, Mossi and Nanumba kingdoms. These peoples are believed to have first settled at Pusiga in the present Upper East Region from where they later dispersed to their present locations following a power struggle among the princes (Buah 1980:32ff.).

The Dagomba trace their descent through Nyagse[9] (Levtzion 1997:461), a reputable warrior, who reigned from 1476–1492. He is believed to have conquered the ethnic groups east of Dagomba and in the process adopted a merciless policy of wiping out the *ten'danba*,[10] the 'priests of the earth' who were the spiritual leaders of the conquered non-centralised people, and destroyed their shrines (Buah 1998:33ff). A *ten'dana* (singular) is described by the British anthropologist Rattray (1932), as a "king-priest" because of his political and religious role in non-centralised societies. However, in centralised societies his role became restricted to religious matters while the *na* 'chief' assumed his political functions. By executing the *ten'danba*, the Dagomba began a process of marginalising the Konkomba politically and socially.

In 1908, R. A. Irvine, the Acting Chief Commissioner of the Northern Territories, wrote that the Dagomba kingdom of Dagbon "lies approximately between Latitudes 10° N and 9° N and between Longitudes 0° and 10° 15' E."[11] Forty years later in 1948, A. W. Davies indicated that the Dagomba kingdom covered an area of about 8,000 square miles[12] or 11,900 square kilometres (Barker 1986:129) and lies in what is now the north-eastern part of the Northern Region of modern Ghana.

Most historians of the Dagomba agree that Dagbon is a "blend" of *autochthones* (indigenes) and an immigrant ruling class (Oppong 1973:13). Buah notes that the Dagomba belong to the Mole-Dagbani group, comprising the Mamprusi, Mossi, Dagomba and the Gonja (Buah 1980:32). Most other scholars however exclude the Gonja from the Mole-Dagbani group. The former is usually classified under the Mande family and the Guan cluster of peoples. Buah's reason for including the Gonja in Mole-Dagbani group may be because they are close neighbours of the Dagomba. The Dagomba have the Mamprusi, their kinsmen, as neighbours to the north, the Nanumba

---

[9] The name Nyagse is sometimes spelt Nyaghse.

[10] The *ten'dana* is spelt differently by different writers. Two other spellings are *tindana* and *tengdana*. *Ten'danba* is the plural form. Tamakloe recounts the slaughter of these *ten'danba* of the vanquished people in the expansion of Dagbon in the Dagomba history (Tamakloe 1931:2).

[11] PRAAD Accra. ADM 56/1/91.

[12] PRAAD Tamale. NRG 8/2/1:1.

3.3.3 The colonial era

In 1892 during the reign of *Na* Andani, the kingdom of Dagbon was divided between the British and the Germans. However, in 1914 the kingdom was reunited as part of the Gold Coast (Oppong 1973:15). In chapter five, these events will be shown to be significant in the introduction of Western Christianity and at a later date, in the discovery of mother-tongue Christianity, with the introduction of Dagbani Christian Scriptures.

The division of Dagbon occurred as a result of a treaty concluded between the British and the Germans in London without consultation with the Dagomba themselves. Under the treaty, eastern Dagbon was assigned to the Germans as their sphere of influence whilst the western part went to the British. Western Dagbon formally came under British rule on 14 November 1899.[13] This partition of Dagbon led to the artificial separation of kinsmen; consequently, families, villages and resources were divided. In 1914 the traditional kingdom was reunited. Under the Treaty of Versailles of 1919, Germany renounced all her rights over her overseas possessions including Togoland.[14]

The relationship between the Dagomba and the British colonial authorities after 1914 was mixed. Some colonial officials saw the Dagomba as civilised and co-operative, while others thought they were rather lazy and exploitative (especially in their dealings with the Konkomba).[15] Generally however, the British colonial powers tended to side with the Dagomba whenever they had a conflict with the Konkomba because the British used Dagomba *naanima* 'traditional rulers' to implement their policy of Indirect Rule.[16]

One of the goals of the British colonial authorities for the introduction of the policy of Indirect Rule was to use the existing indigenous structures to empower the peoples of the Northern Territories.[17] Through this policy they subjugated non-centralised societies under the authority of chiefly societies to facilitate colonial administration, thereby leading to the marginalisation of non-centralised societies. This policy sowed the seed of future problems

---

[13] PRAAD Accra. ADM 56/1/91.
[14] See C. N. P. British Sphere of Togoland's Order by Frederick Gordon Guggisberg, Governor of the Gold Coast.
[15] PRAAD Accra. ADM 56/1/204 (Case No. 78/15 Acct. No. 1390).
[16] The policy of "Indirect Rule" was the brainchild of the colonial official, Lord Luggard, whose father was a missionary. Luggard however was not sympathetic to the Christian missionary cause. The policy sought to co-opt traditional rulers into the British administration with the sole purpose of cutting down cost and mobilising indigenous structures for effective political ends.
[17] PRAAD Tamale. NRG 8/3/46.

between the chiefly groups and the non-centralised ones (Katanga 1994b:24). Justice Katanga quotes Tait to illustrate the far-reaching transformative effect of the policy of Indirect Rule on the relationship between the two types of societies exemplified by the Dagomba and Konkomba respectively:

> With the imposition of British rule, the power of Dagomba chiefs in eastern Dagbong was strengthened and the claim of the Dagomba to rule the western Konkomba was upheld. It is very doubtful if their claim had much validity. As recently as the 1920s there was sporadic fighting between Konkomba and Dagomba adjacent villages. In this sort of fighting the Konkomba could more than hold their own and today, man for man, it is hardly too much to say the Dagomba fears the Konkomba. But Konkomba had no form of regimental system, no cooperation of segments on a wider than tribal scale and could put nothing into the field comparable to the Dagomba cavalry. Equally, the Dagomba had no administrative system or standing army with which to control those Konkomba whom they neither absorbed nor expelled. The eastern chiefdoms of Zabzugu, Sunson and Demon are, even today, Dagomba outposts in a predominantly Konkomba territory and Sunson village, at least, is still separated from Konkomba settlements by a stretch of empty bush. (Tait 1961:9)

Backed by British rule, the Dagomba tended to view the Konkomba as a reservoir of cheap slave labour and providers of cheap farm produce. No wonder the former tended to look down on the latter, souring their relationship. The siting of the administrative capitals was another source of friction, as was the establishment of Christian missions.

3.4 Administrative capitals

The siting of political and administrative headquarters was determined by a number of factors such as location on trade routes, availability of water and centrality. R. B. Bening argues that these factors influenced the relocation of the Northern Regional Headquarters from Gambaga in Mamprugu territory to Tamale in Dagbon. This relocation raised the status of an otherwise traditionally insignificant town to a prestigious and socio-economic power (Bening 1973:7–20). Tamale is now the nerve centre of northern Ghana. This development has made the city home to numerous ethnic groups and religions and predisposed the Dagomba to look down on other ethnic groups, especially the non-centralised ones. It is common to hear the Dagomba retort at the least provocation by a non-Dagomba in Tamale, *a ya mbognon?* 'is this your town'? Or to use the insult, *grundoo* or *grungna* 'slave' (Pul 2003:40).

The traditional capital of the Dagomba is Yendi whilst Tamale is the modern administrative headquarters. This situation is not unique to the Dagomba, for the Mamprusi Nalerigu is the traditional capital and Gambaga is the district administrative seat. Bening explains that economic and political considerations led to the siting of administrative stations away from ethnic capitals. He elaborates:

> With the introduction of indirect rule and the increased importance of chiefs in local administration traditional capitals regained their lost prestige as Native Authority headquarters. However, the earlier capitals have consolidated their importance as economic, political and cultural foci of higher order administrative divisions in spite of the proliferation of local councils since 1952. (Bening 1975b)

3.5 Demographic data

In the Mole-Dagbani family, the Dagomba are the demographically dominant group. The Population and Housing Census for 2000 estimate the population of the Dagomba at 746,924 representing 4.3% of the national population. The figures for the Mamprusi and Nanumba are 200,393 representing 1.1% and 78,812 representing 0.5%, respectively.[18] According to that same census, these people are adherents to traditional religion in the main and have a primal worldview even though about 53% of the Dagomba claim to be Muslims.

3.6 Dagomba relationships with other ethnic groups

3.6.1 The Mamprusi

Buah and Barker note the reciprocal relationship between the Dagomba and the Mamprusi. This relationship is based on the seniority of the Mamprusi *na yiri* 'overlord or king', to those of the Dagomba, the Mossi and the Nanumba. They argue that this seniority is partly based on the belief that Mamprugu was the centre of dispersion for the Mossi-Dagomba kingdoms (Buah 1980:33–34). More importantly it is based on the fact that the Mossi and Dagomba rulers continue to look to the *na yiri* for guidance in the settlement of traditional governance problems and other related traditional issues (Barker 1986:120). Recently, the *na yiri* was one of the three Eminent Chiefs the government of Ghana appointed as mediators between the feuding Dagomba factions.

---

[18] 2000 Population and Housing Census of Ghana: Summary Report of Final Results, Ghana Statistical Service, March 2002, p.23. The National population figure is put at 18,912,079.

The Dagomba and Mamprusi have a common traditional military formation known as the *kambonse*. Established after the Asante model in about 1830 during the time of *Na* Gariba, the *kambonse* was intended to deal with the threat of common enemies. The Asante helped in the building of these more sophisticated armies for the Dagomba and Mamprusi. The *raison d'etre* of the *kambonse* was warfare,[19] and the military formations have helped in no small way to project the Dagomba and Mamprusi as belligerent people *vis-à-vis* their non-centralised neighbours.

3.6.2 The Mossi and Nanumba

Apart from the Mamprusi, as previously mentioned, the Dagomba claim a common ancestry with the Mossi and Nanumba. They all have as their ancestor *Na* Gbewaa, the grandson of the Red Hunter, Tohajie. Gbewaa's daughter is believed to have run away northwards to marry her lover and then founded the Mossi kingdom. In due course, Gbewaa's other children founded the Mamprusi, Dagomba and Nanumba kingdoms. The similarity in language and culture of these ethnic groups attests to this traditional interrelationship (Barker 1986:120).

It was the Dagomba campaign against the Konkomba that subsequently led to the creation of their sister kingdom of Nanumba in the territory vacated by the Konkomba who were forced southward. The consequences of Dagomba pressure on the Konkomba will be discussed in chapter four.

3.6.3 The Gonja

Dagomba influence on trade in the Northern Territories posed a threat to Gonja interests, particularly in relation to the salt mine in Daboya. The protection of Gonja interests necessitated the recruitment of Mande soldiers from Mali. Under the able leadership of Sumaila Ndewura Jakpa Lanta, the Gonja were successful in forcing the Dagomba to relinquish their hold on Daboya and move their capital eastwards to present day Yendi, east of Tamale, in about 1660–1675 (Fage 1969:393–404). Traditionally, the Gonja of northern Ghana are deemed to be the "playmates"[20] of the Dagomba. The relationship between the two can best be described as a "love-hate" relationship. Each tries to outwit the other in the quest for economic and political control of the northern region (Oppong 1973:14).

---

[19] PRAAD Tamale. NRG 8/2/1.

[20] Their traditional relationship allows them to make jokes or tease each other without either side taking offence.

3.7 The impact of the Asante empire on the Dagomba and the Asante decline

The Asante embarked upon hegemonic rule in the 18th century and were able to make both the Dagomba and Gonja of northern Ghana their tributaries (Fage 1969:393–404). Asante subjugation of the Dagomba and Gonja occurred in the wake of a major raid on the two in 1730. That raid was enough to force the Dagomba king to acknowledge the suzerainty of the *asantehene* 'king of the Asante'.[21] Subsequently, there has been a long and symbiotic relationship between the Dagomba and the Asante.

In the eighteenth-century the Asante helped reorganise the Dagomba army through the introduction of guns and *kambong naaneme* (Asante) 'warriors', where there had been only archers and spear-wielding cavalry. *Asantehene* Opoku Ware I is reported to have invaded the Dagomba in 1744–1745 and concluded a treaty with them. The treaty granted the Dagomba access to Asante markets. In return, the Dagomba were required to pay an annual tribute in goods and slaves.[22]

Slave raiding was common in the nineteenth century and was the main source of supply of slaves for the Dagomba payment of tribute to Asante and for their own domestic use. Slaves were military captives mainly from the Konkomba, Basare and Grushi (Oppong 1973:14–15). Even today the natural reaction of the Konkomba towards these former slave raiders is strong resentment.

The British historian Ivor Wilks (1975) asserts that the Asante had a deep influence on the Dagomba, not only politically but more importantly, in the economic, military and social spheres. He explains that the Asante's fourth trade route passed through important towns like Mampong and Atebubu (Bowdich 1819) in the Ashanti Region to link Salaga and Yendi in the Northern Region with Kumasi (Wilks 1975:21). The Asante monitored the route to rid it of bandits. Wilks explains that Dagbon became part of Greater Asante, which extended to Gambaga in Mamprugu.[23] He further points out that the incorporation of the Chamba, a subgroup of the Konkomba, into Dagbon in the time of *Ya Na* Andani Sigili, Dagomba "king" in the first half of the eighteenth century, made them effectively part of Greater Asante (Wilks 1975:21).

To support his assertion of Asante hegemony, Wilks cites a Dagomba narrative that records "the tribute to Asante which was paid at Kpembe where the *ya na* was represented by his *wulana* 'linguist' and the *asantehene* by one Akyampon." The Dagomba also adopted some aspects of Asante culture, like the use of Asante day names (e.g. *Kofi* 'Friday, *Kwadwo* 'Monday' and *Kwasi* 'Sunday'), army formations (e.g. *kyidom, gyasefo,* etc.) and the

---

[21] PRAAD Tamale. NRG 8/2/1.
[22] PRAAD Tamale. NRG 8/2/1.
[23] Mamprugu is the Mamprusi kingdom.

Asante stool instead of the traditional animal skin used by northern chiefs (Wilks 1975:247–248).

Although Dagomba traditional narratives tend to portray the Dagomba people as invincible, the reality was that they lost and won battles just like the other ethnic groups.

3.8 Post-independence developments

> Traditional leadership has played an indispensable role in the planting of Christianity in Dagbon. The populace has a high regard for chiefs, and one cannot do anything in the community without their support. The high esteem enjoyed by *naanima*, that is, traditional rulers, naturally makes *naam* attractive to the Dagomba and they will go to any lengths to secure it. (Staniland 1975:13)

In northern Ghana, the royal seat of authority is an animal skin; the type of animal skin one sits on indicates the rank in the royal power structure. For instance, the king of the Dagomba, the *ya na*, sits on a lion's skin. "Enskinning" refers to investing a sovereign with authority by installing the king on his skin. Among southern Ghanaian ethnic groups, a chief sits on a stool, and his installation is referred to as "enstoolment," similar to enthronement. In Dagbon, all "terminus *naanima*," that is, those who have reached the terminal point of their line of authority, are entitled to be seated on a lion's skin. They are enskinned in the evening to signify that they have no further opportunity for ascent on the royal ladder. Being a patrilineal society, Dagomba royal succession is along patrilineal lines. The first category of royal chiefdom is *doo bihi nama* 'men's sons', chiefdom reserved for patrilineal ascendancy. "Non-terminus *naanima*," a lower category of *naam* 'chieftaincy' provides opportunity for the incumbent to move into higher ranks of *naam*, provided they do not overtake their own fathers. They are installed during daylight hours (Oppong 1973:21) to signify that opportunities exist for them to rise to a higher position.

The *naanima* are regarded as custodians of traditional culture and resources and perform their duties with the help of certain functionaries. Not only do they ensure the preservation of their ethnic identity, they are also the focal point of mobilisation for development. *Naanima* were associated with traditional religious practices such as sacrifices to ancestors and gods, which deterred committed Muslims and Christians from seeking those positions. Today, however, Muslims and Christians are accepting *naam* because of the developmental role it can play. Traditional rulers in Ghana today are assuming important roles in maintaining peace and mobilising their people for development.

3.8 Post-independence developments

3.8.1 Recent history

Hippolyt Pul, an anthropologist and writer on the northern Ghanaian conflict, has observed that by appealing to ethnic pride, Dagomba leaders have been able to solicit commitment of their people to embark on expensive tasks such as war from which they have nothing to win materially. This has been possible because of what Pul terms "elusive pride in the glories of the past." He comments:

> Every Dagomba person walks round with a sense of pride that derives from being a member of the ruling tribe that had a glorious past. That pride translates in daily interethnic interactions into a superiority complex that makes members of every other tribe, especially the non-chiefly ones, inferior. Land and chieftaincy are the symbols of that pride and greatness and the term "grundoo" or "grungna" is pejoratively used to label all those who do not belong to one or the other of the ruling ethnic groups. It is therefore the highest level of insult for a Dagomba to imagine that a "grungna" will claim equal status with him or her in any field, especially in the arenas of traditional authority. Their pride of place had already been invaded and threatened by the rise of education among the "grungnas", who by virtue of educational attainments now occupy positions of authority in the civil and public services – positions that give them power and authority over less educated Dagombas. That is already more than those labelled "grungna" can take. To ask for paramountcy and land is to add insult to injury; it amounts to an invasion of the collective privacy of the ruling ethnic groups. Chieftaincy and the land that goes with it, is their preserve. If war is the answer to keeping the "grungnas" out of chieftaincy and in their place of inferiority, so be it, as long as it preserves the pride of place of the Dagomba. This is the source of the collective commitment of the Dagomba people to the war effort of their ethnic group. (Pul 2003:64–65)

The Dagomba high self-estimation is evident in their treatment of other ethnic groups as inferior and undeserving of respect. The derogatory word, *grungna*, is a Dagomba term denoting a slave. Other ethnic groups naturally tend to resist this superior attitude of the Dagomba in the modern democratic state of Ghana where all citizens have equal status. The Bible in Dagbani, like the Ghanaian constitution, espouses the equality of all persons. The superiority attitude exhibited by the Dagomba has been a major stumbling block to peaceful relationship between the Dagomba and the Konkomba throughout their long history of contact. For a harmonious relationship to be established between the Dagomba and other non-chiefly groups, mutual respect is indispensable.

The obsession of the Dagomba with the institution of *naam* has been the bane of their unity. The royal "gates," or "houses" of the Yendi skin, that is, the royal families that can ascend to the paramountcy of Dagbon, have been at the centre of Dagomba conflicts. Only recently an impasse between the Abudu and Andani royal gates was resolved. This impasse resulted from the murder in 2002 of the then incumbent *Ya Na* Yakubu II and forty others in what was a long-running controversy concerning chieftaincy matters.[24]

3.8.2 Urban Dagomba and rural Dagomba

The urban Dagomba, especially those in the Tamale and Yendi areas, wield much economic and political influence and tend to influence the direction of development in Dagbon. Most of these urban elite exhibit an attitude of superiority and, consequently, marginalise the rural Dagomba. The urban Dagomba tend to look down on the rural people because they assume they are *zugsabla*, that is, uneducated and therefore unsophisticated.

3.9 Language

As we showed earlier, the Dagomba speak Dagbani *(Dagbane* or *Dagbanli)* (Wilson 1972) [25] and are closely related culturally and linguistically to the Mossi of Burkina Faso, and the Mamprusi and Nanumba peoples, also of northern Ghana (Oppong 1973:13). Dagbani is a member of the Mole-Dagbani (sometimes called Moore-Dagbani) sub-group of the *Gur* family of languages (Wilson 1972:Introduction), as noted from the oral accounts of the origins of Dagomba, Mamprusi, Nanumba and the Mossi Dagbani group of people. The other reason why many non-Dagomba speak Dagbani is that Tamale is home to many non-Dagomba who have to use the language daily in their social interactions. For instance, there are many schools, commercial houses and government agencies where many non-Dagomba interact with the Dagomba. Furthermore, many Dagomba engage in trade and all these have kingdoms, their founders are descendants of a common ancestor, Tohajie. This explains the similarity and mutual intelligibility of their languages: Dagbani, Mampruli, Nanun and Mossi. Nabdam and Tallensi and the other members of the *Mabihi* language family also show interrelatedness (Wilson 1972:Introduction). Dagbani is spoken widely because of its affinity

---

[24] The government's White Paper on this tragic event which occurred between 25 and 27 March 2002 is contained in *The Daily Graphic* (Ghana's highest selling newspaper), Tuesday, 24 December 2002. No. 148705, pp. 7 and 11.

[25] According to Wilson, Dagbani is pronounced and written differently because of regional difference, e.g. eastern Dagomba pronounce it *Dagbani* whilst the western Dagomba, that is, in Tamale area, pronounce it *Dagbanli*.

with the languages of the other *Mabihi* of the Mole – which helped to spread the Dagbani language.

Dagbani is among the six Ghanaian languages spoken on the Ghana Broadcasting Corporation's radio and television service. It is taught as a subject in school and is examinable by the West African Examination Council. All these make Dagbani a prestigious language and the only northern Ghanaian language of its kind. Though Islam has been with the Dagomba for the past three centuries, Dagbani was not available in written form until the advent of Christianity in Dagbon in the twentieth century. The Christian missionaries developed an orthography for the language and vigorously promoted Dagbani literacy. By contrast, Islam pursues Arabic education in their Qur'anic schools in Dagbon. Sanneh's claim that Christian missions enhance vernacular development is therefore borne out in the Dagomba context.

3.10 Social organisation

The quest of every Dagomba is for a life of dignity and nothing less. Towards this end, the society is well structured from the household level to the state level. Males are more highly valued than females. Every Dagomba desires his firstborn child to be a male to guarantee continuity of the family line. In this patriarchal society men wield significant power and demand total submission from their wives. The District Commissioner of Tamale responding to the Chief Commissioner's enquiries on the subject of "Christianity and Native Custom" in 1937 had this to say about Dagomba attitude toward women: "The Dagomba already say that the white man has spoiled their women through a misguided regard for their feelings. They quote the Dagomba proverb "a weeping bride makes a happy marriage." Women to them are "chattels."[26]

The subservient role a woman plays in Dagomba society is manifested at both the domestic and communal level. For instance, in a typical Dagomba home, when a woman brings food to her husband, she must kneel down until her husband permits her to get up, that is, when he says *gafara*.[27] The women and children are also expected to kneel down and greet their fathers and older males as well as elderly females. Respect and the courtesies are very much cherished among the Mole-Dagbani people. It is therefore a great offence to pass by somebody in the community without greeting.

As described in an interview by Pastor Moses Yahaya of Tamale, the Dagomba family is composed of the living and the departed ancestors. Proper reverence is required to be shown to all the elderly to attract

---

[26] PRAAD Tamale. NRG 8/19/7.

[27] *Gafara* is a Dagomba word for "excuse me." It is used when asking for permission to enter a room or used by elderly person asking a younger person to arise after kneeling in greeting.

blessings and avoid curses. The young are expected to honour their elders, and it is incumbent on the elders to adequately cater for their young. It is a disgrace when a man is unable to manage his household well. The *yidana* 'head of household' has absolute authority over the whole of his household and his word is law. Beyond the household level, sectional elders help to maintain law and order. They assist the *na* to oversee the village or town. The village or town ruler is also responsible to a ruler of superior rank on the higher hierarchy of the Dagomba traditional royalty. The *ya na* is the supreme authority in Dagbon. All the other categories of rulers are expected to pay him homage. It is this hierarchical arrangement of chiefly authority that undergirds political centralisation in Dagomba.

Gender roles assigned to members at family level transfer to the larger community. In early times it was the men who fought the wars and did the farming and hunting. The women supervised domestic chores, fetched water and firewood and bore children. Dagomba children are socialised to see certain tasks as female ones and others as male ones. The social organisation of traditional Dagomba, however, has been challenged in modern times through contact with Christianity and education and this will be shown in later chapters.

3.11 Rituals governing traditional life

Pastor Daniel Wumbee, one of the Dagomba Bible translators, described the group as a people with a primal worldview who are keenly aware of their closeness to the divine and to nature. They therefore strive to be in harmony with the divine and their environment for a life of fulfilment through the observances of certain rituals and taboos. The *ten'dana* controls all ritual functions related to the land and to community life.

In Dagbon the land is divided into a series of ritual areas or parishes, each with its own taboo animals (Goody 1954:17). These animals are considered sacred and are symbolic of the mystical aspects of the earth. The lion, for instance, is the sacred animal or totem of Yendi as well as the symbol of Dagbon kingship (Oppong 1973:17). The title, Lion of Dagbon for the *ya na* (Staniland 1975:viii) will strike a familiar note when we remember that Jesus is also described as the Lion of Judah. Could this be an indication that Dagomba culture anticipated the coming of Jesus Christ? For the Dagomba reader of the Dagbani Scriptures the traditional title for the Dagomba king resonates with Christ's title.

3.11.1 Marriage

Poga kpagi bu means marriage in Dagbani. It is the normal and expected goal of every Dagomba young man and woman. Rituals, rules and regulations exist to guide this important institution. Amongst the Mole-Dagomba, for instance, close relatives are forbidden from marrying each other. However, when getting a spouse outside the family is difficult due to a handicap, a man can be permitted to marry his mother's brother's daughter. Betrothal, arranged marriages, often of infant girls, used to be the mode of marriage among the Dagomba, but it is uncommon now due to external religious influence like Islam and Christianity. Religion now plays an important role in the choice of a partner among the Dagomba. Though Dagomba parents have enormous influence on the choice of a spouse for their child, they do consider their child's feelings sometimes. Various traditional methods were employed in taking a bride. Prior to weddings, which were introduced by Islam and Christianity, three of the methods as identified by Madeline Manoukian were: elopement, arranged marriage and betrothal (Manoukian 1951:36, 37).

The Tallensi of northern Ghana mostly practised elopement. It involved a period of courtship and later, with the connivance of the girl's mother or sister, the capture of the girl by the husband-to-be. This method did not favour the bride in most cases because she was not given time to prepare for her place in the bridegroom's home. This practice tended to treat women like men's chattel since their consent was not sought before their capture.

Among the Dagomba, Mamprusi and Nanumba arranged marriages were common. These were agreed upon between responsible heads of the respective families of the bride and bridegroom after a period of courtship. As a formality, the girl's consent was sought. Some heads, however, often resorted to coercion if the girl was reluctant to give her consent to the arranged marriage. Comparatively, girls enjoyed more freedom in this system than elopement or betrothal.

In chapter four, a detailed discussion on Konkomba marriage demonstrates that they mostly practised the third method whereby a young girl was betrothed to a man and after a long period of courtship, marriage took place. This system undermined the girl's free choice, because these betrothals were often done when the girls were infants, or later without their consent. Sometimes the age gap between the man and girl was very wide, as much as twenty years. With more enlightenment, many girls now resent this practice.

Marriage among the Dagomba is not just between the bride and bridegroom but a corporate agreement involving their families (Manoukian 1951:38). The consent given by the heads of the families has both religious and psychological significance in that it reassures the young couple that their families, including both the living and the dead, are prepared to support them. Divine guidance through divination by *baga* 'soothsayers' or *mallams,* mystical 'Muslim clerics', is done to ascertain the viability of the marriage before it is embarked upon. When everything is certain, divine blessings are sought through prayers or sacrifices. This process has been described in interviews with Christian pastors in Tamale.

Among the Dagomba, *poga kpagi bu* has seen a great transformation because of the increasing influence of Islam. Prior to Islamic influence, all that was needed to make marriage legal was the payment of *sandane,* that is, placation consisting of some 4,000 cowries. Madeline Manoukian explains the form traditional marriage takes:

> There is no marriage-payment, but during courtship,[28] from betrothal to marriage, the girl's parents receive gifts from her suitor at each of the five great festivals. The marriage ceremony is performed by a Mallam in the presence of the fathers of the bride and groom: they themselves are not present. (1951:41)

However, with the Islamisation of the Dagomba, *amilia,* or wedding, has become the vogue. This situation has changed very much because the celebration involves the bride and groom. The celebration includes Qur'anic recitals, music, dancing, sharing of gifts and meals, and this has assumed a communal dimension.

The Dagomba treasure the institution of marriage very much and frown upon sex outside marriage in congruence with Christian teaching. In an interview with the pastors in Tamale, elderly Dagomba Christians with immense knowledge of the Dagomba culture, they explained that it was considered a virtue in traditional Dagomba society for a young woman to marry as a virgin and this was considered a great honour to her family. To test for virginity, a white sheet was laid on the couple's bed for the first night of their marriage. In the event that it was stained with blood, the young girl was deemed a virgin and, consequently, honoured by her husband with gifts. The man would then be expected to pay the bride price and all other expenses the would-be in-laws demanded of him.

As long as an unmarried woman is with her parents she is under their authority. However, when she marries she comes under her husband's authority and lives with him in or near his parents' house. Most Dagomba men exercise authority over their wives and expect to be obeyed unquestioningly. Household chores are the responsibility of the woman, and if she has daughters they assist her. Males are not expected to be around the kitchen because it is seen as the preserve of females. Dagomba men, like most northern Ghanaian men, are like lords in their homes. They do very little work. It is even perceived as a sign of weakness for a man to do what is deemed woman's work.

---

[28] Note that "courtship" in Ghana is different from the Western understanding of the term. The courtship period extends from the proposal to the day the woman comes to the man's home. In some cases it did not include the young woman; only the suitor and the girl's parents were involved.

3.11.2 Beliefs around pregnancy

Among the Mole-Dagomba people, the ceremony marking a woman's first pregnancy is called *prisigu*.[29] With the help of the diviner, the family head, *yidanaa*, is able to discover the reincarnated ancestor whose name the baby should take. Being a patrilineal society, it is usually the baby's paternal aunt, *pribaa*, who first announces the pregnancy and later the *yidanaa* names the child and prays to the ancestor after whom it is named to be responsible for its well-being. The ceremony might involve animal sacrifice or libation at a time prescribed by a diviner (Oppong 1973:33–34 and Barker 1986:131). With the coming of Dagbani Scriptures, in later chapters this practice is shown to be undergoing modification by Dagomba Christians.

3.11.3 Birth

Among the Dagomba, the circumstances surrounding the birth of a child sometimes determine the name the baby should be given. For instance, where earlier siblings died, the name of an ethnic group or a humorous name might be given to the new baby to prevent its premature death. It is believed that if the child bears an unfamiliar name, death will not recognise it and will therefore not claim it. It is therefore not uncommon to have the Dagomba name their children after the gods or people of neighbouring ethnic groups in order to solicit their protection (Barker 1986:172).

The birth of a child, especially a boy, is a happy occasion. Prior to the naming ceremony the baby is considered a stranger until a name is chosen for it. Before the naming ceremony, the baby is called *Sandow* 'stranger-man' or *Sanpoga* 'stranger-woman'. There is usually one week waiting to be certain that the baby is destined to stay and not return to God. Taking the baby outdoors for the first time is done on the eighth day and it is on this occasion that a name is given to it. Due to Muslim influence, a *suuna*[30] or naming ceremony attracts many relatives and well-wishers. Muslim Dagomba are abandoning their indigenous Dagomba names for Arabic ones. Since names are crucial for identification, the implication of the trend whereby indigenous names are discarded in favour of Arabic ones amounts to an erosion of Dagomba identity.

3.11.4 Circumcision

Circumcision is playing an identification role amongst the Dagomba and the other chiefly societies that have had Islamic influence. It is now a norm

---

[29] The Mole-Dagomba practice this custom which is an occasion for pre-natal education and spiritual protection of the expectant mother and baby.

[30] *Sunna* is a term in Hausa for name. *Mallams* are usually called to come and pray for the baby and family, and an Arabic name given to it. Cola nuts used to be given out to invite well-wishers but now some give out invitation letters or cards to invite well-wishers to the naming ceremony.

among the Dagomba to circumcise their male child on the eighth day and it is inconceivable to have an uncircumcised male baby a month after delivery (Barker 1986:172). The circumcision is usually carried out by the *warizam*[31] but now it can be carried out in hospitals also. For fear of exposing those who are circumcised to AIDs infection, the Ministry of Health has been teaching courses for Traditional Birth Attendants (TBA) and *warizams*.

3.11.5 Death and burial

The Dagomba honour their dead and are meticulous in the way they send them on their journey to the other world. They bury their dead promptly on the day of death, in contrast to the Akan who can keep a corpse for several months. The corpse is usually bathed with herbs and then the nails cut, and hair trimmed. The trimmings, which are considered sacred, symbolising the person's spirit, are put into a calabash in which they are stored (Barker 1986).

The Dagomba have a mixture of the traditional and Islamic mortuary practices. The traditional Dagomba, or *Dagban daba,* normally perform rituals to determine the cause of a person's death (Barker 1986:175). They usually call on the diviner immediately after death occurs and then again on the third day, to determine finally the cause of death. Islamic influence on some Dagomba however, has led them to discard some of these practices deemed "pagan." The Muslim Dagomba tend to be resigned to death as a natural event, for they attribute everything to Allah.[32]

The performance of funerals for one's parents among the Dagomba is mandatory, according to one pastor interviewed. Failure to give a befitting funeral to one's parents or chief is deemed a disgrace and a great dishonour, both to the one who has died and to the family. Libations and sacrifices are performed during funerals. Whether sheep or cattle or other animals are used for sacrifice depends on the status of the one who died and also on the economic means of the person overseeing the funeral, usually the firstborn son. Assurance of thus being honoured in death is one of the reasons why the Dagomba prefer sons to daughters.

3.11.6 Festivals and celebrations

Festivals are an outward expression of a people's worldview, that is, the re-enactment of their rituals and ceremonies, which express belief systems and deep meaning beyond being merely innocent celebrations. The historical roots often lie in a desire to display power and re-assertion of identity.

Dagomba festivals are called *chugu* (singular) or *churi* (plural). The traditional beliefs of the Dagomba and their kinsmen, the Mamprusi and

---

[31] The *warizam* are traditional barbers who also perform circumcision.
[32] The Dagomba Muslims of the Wahabian tradition will not engage in the traditional practice of consultation to find the cause of death.

Nanumba, are often fused with Islamic ones (Sanneh 1989:236). The four main traditional festivals are: *Konyuruchugu, Damba, Kpini* and *Bugum* (1989:137). The *Konyuruchugu*, which literally means 'water drinking festival', is observed on the first day of the tenth month of the Dagomba calendar and coincides with the end of the Muslim fast of Ramadan.

A second festival is *Damba* which Muslims claim is Muhammad's birthday. The date varies according to when the moon is sighted. It can be celebrated on either the tenth, eleventh or twelfth day of the third month of the Dagomba traditional calendar, which corresponds to the Islamic lunar calendar. It is a traditional festival that has been politicised, as subordinate traditional rulers dance to affirm their allegiance to the regional or ethnic overlord (Barker 1986:137). The other northern chiefly ethnic groups like the Mamprusi, Gonja, Nanumba and Wala also celebrate the Damba.

The *Kpini* or Guinea Fowls Festival, which has roots in Islamic belief, is observed on the ninth day of the seventh month of the Dagomba calendar. This festival involves the whipping of guinea fowls to commemorate the alleged wickedness of the guinea fowl to Muhammad when he was thirsty. During this festival, husbands are expected to send guinea fowls to their in-laws to celebrate. It is also an occasion for husbands to buy new clothes for their wives. In contrast to festivals in southern Ghana, Dagomba festivals are not usually used as occasions to mobilise support for development of such projects as schools or clinics.

The fourth festival, *Bugum* or 'fire', is observed on the ninth day of the first month of the Dagomba and Mamprusi calendar. This celebration is to honour the ancestors by offering them food. After the evening meal, torches are lit and drumming, chanting and dancing continue until the people finally throw the torches into trees, cursing their enemies. The throwing of the burning torches is meant to drive Satan into the west (Barker 1986:137) and by implication, one's enemies also.

It is obvious that the observance of Dagomba festivals has taken on some Islamic colouring. During the celebration of these festivals *imams* and *mallams* are active participants in the performances of the rites associated with the festivals. This approach is not unique to the Dagomba but is a feature of West African Islam that is seen to take pragmatic steps to combine traditional customs with Islamic ones (Hostetter 1975:7).

3.12 The Dagomba response to Western education and development

The Dagomba response to Western education from the time they encountered Westerners has been poor. A colonial ethnographical investigation report revealed that there were only two government schools in Dagbon in June

1933.[33] Recruitment of children was still a very big problem, as the people of the Northern Territories did not yet appreciate the full benefits of Western education. Some parents hid their children, and others thought they were doing the government a favour by sending their children to school.

At a Dagomba conference in 1934 the District Commissioner strongly urged the Dagomba chiefs to send their boys to school.[34] In fact, he promised to pay for the first boy and prompted other Europeans to offer to pay for an additional boy. If convincing the chiefs to send their boys to school was a difficult proposition, asking them to send their daughters to school was an even more daunting task. The reason for the disinterest in sending children to school may be inferred from the complaint of the *ya na* that when he sent his boys to school at the request of the government, the majority of them did not return to him. Other Dagomba rulers shared the concern of the *ya na*.[35]

The Dagomba find themselves in a fast-changing world which challenges their traditional position as rulers. They are also confronted with protracted chieftaincy disputes that invariably become violent. Dagbon in the modern state of Ghana is faced with poverty, illiteracy, environmental degradation and lack of potable water, as well as with diseases and superstition. These challenges tend to create self-doubt and helplessness (Boi-Nai and Kirby 1998:535) in spite of their characteristic self-assurance. This prevailing situation in Dagbon has attracted many non-governmental organisations (NGOs), Christian and non-Christian alike. They seem to have contributed significantly to the well-being of the people.

Though the Dagomba have now realised the need to change with modern times they have yet to embrace formal Western education enthusiastically (Bening 1990:87). A reason for their reluctance could be their fear of conversion to Christianity. They are however sympathetic to Qur'anic schools, which they see as a valid alternative that meets their religious aspirations (Oppong 1973:66–71). They fear that Western education might alienate the educated from their traditional roots, whereas the traditional Qur'anic education almost invariably reinforces them. The exception to this is the threat of the jihadists, who are calling for the repudiation of Dagomba traditional cultural practices from current Dagomba Islam.

Formal education for girls among the Dagomba is not enthusiastically embraced; in fact, female enrolment is lowest in northern Ghana, particularly in Dagbon (Oppong 1973:21) compared with the rest of Ghana. Women work mostly at the domestic level in northern Ghana helping on the farm with the harvesting, petty trading and planting vegetables. The traditional expectation of girls is that they will ultimately get married and have children. Bearing children is desirable while childlessness is despised.

---

[33] PRAAD Tamale. NRG 8/3/46:38–40.

[34] PRAAD Tamale. NRG 8/2/25.

[35] PRAAD Tamale. NRG 8/2/25:7.

Most Dagomba are peasant farmers who endeavour to provide adequately for their dependants. Among the Dagomba there is no distinction between adult and child labour. What matters to them is strength, not age. With the urban promise of material wealth, many children are now abandoning both their traditional domestic roles and school. The lure of paid labour has led many children, young men and women to towns in the south to earn money (Bening 1990:19–20). This is one of the contributing factors to the growing phenomenon of street children in our towns and cities. This influx of the northern people into southern Ghana has necessitated the emergence of the Northern Outreach Programme. The programme has embarked upon various interventions such as literacy classes and the use of mother-tongue Scriptures as well as provision of vocational skills to give the young people meaningful lives. These vulnerable people are more open to change brought about by the interventions mentioned.

In Dagbon, riches are not openly displayed, and personal property is often kept secret for fear of envy, witches and demands from the family (Bening 1990:19). This, however, does not mean they encourage laziness and selfishness; rather it is intended to promote humility and modesty. Indeed, in Dagbon, industry and generosity are counted as virtues.

3.13 Dagomba Religion

Almost all Dagomba are believers in *Naawuni* 'God', whether they practice traditional worship or are Muslims or Christians. Traditional Dagomba have allegiance to several deities in addition to *Naawuni*, including a number of different totems. Those notwithstanding, the Dagomba have a common reverence for *Naawuni*. The primal traditional religion influences the beliefs of Dagomba including Muslims and Christians. With respect to Muslim grouping in Dagbon, there are three main sects: the Wahabians, the Tijahnians and the Ahymadists. The Christian denominations that are effectively evangelising the Dagomba include the Assemblies of God mission, the Catholic Mission, the Presbyterian mission, the Baptist mission and the Bible Church of Africa.

3.13.1 Effect of migration on religions

There has been an influx of non-Dagomba into the Tamale metropolis with their various religious affiliations. Although the majority of Dagomba in Tamale city claim to be Muslim, there are other Dagomba who are traditional worshippers or Christians. In addition, although there are African-instituted churches in the Tamale metropolis, the Dagomba do not attend them. The reason might be that they have not heard or seen the mother-tongue Scriptures being used by them.

3.13.2 Dagomba primal religion

The worldview and beliefs of the Dagomba can be surmised from their practices, their attitude towards the supernatural, and their observance of various rituals and ceremonies. The Dagomba have a primal worldview and do not draw a line between the spiritual and the physical or between the secular and the sacred. This outlook necessarily affects how they respond to their mother-tongue Scriptures.

The Dagomba believe in the Supreme God and Creator whom they call *Naawuni*, a term which literally means, 'king God'. Although their belief in this God is strong, they do not know of his specific geographical location but refer to him as abiding in "heaven" otherwise known as *Naawuni yili* 'God's home' (Lidorio 1999:135). A Dagomba myth, similar to one among the Akan, suggests that God was once close to humans but when a wicked old woman offended him, he withdrew (Kofi Opoku 1978:23). This belief has an affinity with the biblical account of human sinfulness that caused a separation between God and human beings. This affinity between traditional beliefs and the biblical stories would make the Scriptures appealing to the Dagomba when related in their mother tongue.

According to their traditional religion, Dagomba think the 'king God' cannot be approached directly in ordinary circumstances, just as they cannot approach their own *naanima* directly. For this reason, the help of supernatural intermediaries is sought in the relationship between God and human beings. Although the Dagomba did not know the language God speaks (Barker 1986:135), they did know they could call on him in their mother tongue in times of crisis. Just as with many other ethnic groups in Ghana and the Urhobo of Nigeria (Kofi Opoku 1978:32), the Creator has no shrine or priest in Dagbon.

Buga '(lesser) divinities' and 'nature spirits'

The *buga* or *wuna* '(lesser) divinities' of the Dagomba are viewed as God's children and therefore act as intermediaries between humans and God.[36] They are essentially spirits and can inhabit streams, trees, rocks and taboo animals. They are also found in the groves of trees, tall baobab trees and mud moulds. Other divinities are associated with natural phenomena like rain and thunder (Barker 1986:54, 67).

The chief is normally expected to provide sacrifices so the priest can perform rituals for the prosperity of the earth. Prayers are offered to the deities and the Supreme Being to bless not only the human beings but also economically important trees such as the shea butter, dawadawa, baobab, kapok and mango trees (Oppong 1973:17).

---

[36] God is presented as a hospitable God in contrast to the intolerant God preached by missionaries.

As a society that attaches great importance to hierarchical status, it is understandable why the Dagomba will approach God through the ancestors and *buga* or *wuna*. Just as it would not be appropriate for a commoner to approach the king directly, so God cannot be approached directly in their view. Islam has however modified some of these earlier perceptions of God and therefore has paved the way as well as placed obstacles for the Dagomba's understanding of the Christian God in relation to the *buga* or *wuna*.

Baga 'diviners' or 'soothsayers'

The *baga* 'diviners' serve as the spiritual guides of the communities because they are believed to be in constant touch with the spiritual world and know the will of the divine. Thus, the *baga* play an important and an indispensable role in the daily life of the Dagomba. For this reason, no misfortune or crisis is taken lightly or at its face value; the spiritual cause is often sought from the diviners (Barker 1986:136).

The earliest form of Islam introduced into Dagbon by the Dyula, 14th-century merchant traders, found a home with the Dagomba for it accommodated Dagomba culture (Hostetter 1975:3). Traditional cultural practices such as divination had affinity with the Dyula Islamic occultic practices by some *mallams* who also prescribed sacrifices and provided amulets and charms to ward off evil just like the traditional diviners do (Hostetter 1975:4). However, the more orthodox Muslims denounce these *baga* and *mallams* who play these traditional roles of spiritual guidance and protection.

Son-nya 'witchcraft' or 'sorcery'

Belief in witchcraft is widespread among the Mole-Dagomba people. The belief is that some people have evil powers and can use them for destruction. Generally, it is dreaded; where ill will and envy abound, witchcraft accusations are rife. In some Dagomba communities where there is hostility towards Christians, *son-nya* 'witchcraft' accusations are often used as a way of persecuting Christians (Boi-Nai and Kirby 1999:148). A witchcraft accusation is like blackmail; it can be used to destroy an enemy. The stigma associated with witchcraft accusation often leads to the accused being ostracised from the community.

Though men are believed to practice witchcraft too, it is usually old ladies who do not have prominent or wealthy children to support them who are the victims of such accusations. Witches are feared because they are believed to possess powers to fly and to subtly attack their victims (Barker 1986:177). A visit to the witch camps in Gambaga and Gyani in the Northern Region reveals that almost all the victims of witchcraft accusation are old women. Most of these are poor and this tends to suggest that the vulnerable and social rejects are more at risk of others making witchcraft accusations aimed at them than are the rich and powerful in society (Boi-Nai 1997).

However, the Dagomba believe that not all witchcraft is destructive, and it can be bought or inherited. Like the Akan of southern Ghana, the Dagomba believe in *son-nya sung* 'good witchcraft' (Kofi Opoku 1978:140) which is employed not to catch and eat people but rather to fight to protect their families against the evil ones.

Witch camps

In former days, persons accused of witchcraft were tortured and killed. With modernisation and the emphasis on the rule of law, this practice has been stopped. However, extradition to witch villages or homes is still in vogue. Upon a successful de-witching event, the so-called witches are settled in a camp or a secluded community (Boi-Nai and Kirby 1999:148). In Dagbon the witches are taken to a shrine where the witchcraft is believed to be neutralised by the keeper of the shrine. Witchcraft accusation has a functional role in the community in that it provides a society with the means to externalise ill will.

The Dagomba seek protection from witchcraft and witchcraft accusations through *mallams* and traditional priests. Wealthy people may behave as though they are of ordinary means for fear of being targets of a lurking witch. This worldview influences Christians too but they use different resources to handle witchcraft or sorcery. Some Christians would normally fast and seek deliverance and exorcism (Boi-Nai and Kirby 1998:538–542). From a Western perspective, witchcraft mentality is self-destructive and tends to stigmatise others unjustly.

Tam and *tiima* 'traditional medicine'

A critical analysis of Dagomba life suggests that the society is governed by fear, hence the Dagomba's longing for spiritual protection in *tam* 'medicine'. Whereas some *liliga* 'medicines' are for protection against accidents, others known as *kosalegu* protect against bullets or cutting metals. Still other medicines, *yurilim tam,* serve as love potions (Boi-Nai and Kirby 1998:542). Aware of visible and invisible enemies, the Dagomba invoke the supernatural to confront these life-threatening entities or circumstances.

Harmful medicines, *tiima,* also exist and are used to fight enemies. One such harmful *tam* is *sambo*, which behaves like a spiritual mine. It is buried in the ground along the path where an enemy walks or sits and, when operational, can cause a lingering disease to afflict its victim who passes over it or sits on it (Hostetter 1975:136, 178).

The primal worldview of the Dagomba, which recognises the reality of the power of spirits and bad medicines, causes the Dagomba live in perpetual fear and suspicion of neighbours. Consequently, they take all necessary precautions to avoid falling victim to harmful medicine.

Saba 'amulets'

The Dagomba, like many primal societies, use amulets in a "search for ways of controlling or balancing the forces and powers that encircle man" (Sanneh 1976:86). The Dagomba universe is populated by a host of spirits, benevolent as well as malevolent, hence the need for amulets. In this context, amulets provide a solace for the possessor and make him feel secure. As Sanneh observed, "Amulets are not religious offerings; rather they are the cautious, calculated steps a man takes so that he may not stumble obliviously over life's precious gifts" (1976:94). The Dagomba are keenly aware of the unpredictable universe of their existence and therefore do not take chances with their security.

Amulets assume some of God's functions, in that they are perceived to provide security in time of danger and preserve against hazards. Thus, the Dagomba who use amulets see them as more than just a convenience for, from their perspective and, as Sanneh also observed, "*jujus*[37] were a companion of man in his journey through life, preventing slips which could add up to a denial of the very goal towards which he was travelling and therefore in that way contributing to the value of that crown which their guiding light had made worth pursuing" (1974:95).

Amulet users see no contradiction between their faith in *Naawuni* and the amulets; they complement each other. This perspective, of course, conflicts with the stand of orthodox Christians and Muslims who owe total allegiance to God, or *Allah*. For, as Sanneh pointed out, "Trust in God goes far beyond our need of someone to snatch us out of difficulty. It relates us in a very human way to the object of our worship and trains us in a relationship of encounter and response" (1974:96).

Thus, real faith in God is compromised by the use of amulets. Most Dagomba have not yet attained maturity in their faith to realise this implication. The reality today is that they believe in *Naawuni* and use amulets concurrently.

3.14 History of Islam in Dagbon

A number of factors led to the Islamisation of the Dagomba. One source says that the most crucial event was the conversion to Islam in the 1750s of one of their kings, *Na* Zangina, to save his kingdom (Barker 1986:137). Through that initial act, Muslim influences were introduced into the Dagomba society. J. S. Trimingham demonstrates how every aspect of traditional Dagomba life had Islamic features superimposed upon it. These include Muslim offices, festivals, calendar and ceremonies at naming, marriage and death (Oppong 1973:14).

---

[37] The term *juju* refers to spiritual powers, including the effect of amulets. Thus, *juju* is all-encompassing, including both tangible objects and intangible spiritual force.

Na Zangina therefore became the first Dagomba king to adopt the Muslim faith. In spite of the help from the Muslims, *Na* Zangina could not hold back the Gonja advance militarily. He abdicated in favour of his elder brother *Na* Andani Ziblim who succeeded in driving back the Gonja. Muslims honour *Na* Zangina for introducing Islam into the Dagomba royal house. Many Dagomba Muslims hold the view that no other *ya na* has since identified himself quite so closely with Islam (Barker 1986:137). Most Dagomba chiefs are primarily adherents of traditional religions even though they might regard themselves as Muslims. The term *Dagban doo* literally means 'Dagomba man' and refers to a traditionalist which indicates the dominant role of traditional religion even in a seemingly Islamicised Dagomba society. Generally, however, the term is used for a Dagomba who is neither a professing Muslim nor a Christian. In other words, it is reckoned that a person who does not belong to either of the two faiths can be nothing other than a traditionalist in Dagomba thinking.

Another source credits Hausa and Wangara traders in the seventeenth and eighteenth centuries as being instrumental in introducing Islam into Dagbon. These Muslim traders settled among the indigenous people and with persuasion gradually won some of them. The indigenous people were attracted to these Muslims because they complemented the traditional functions of the diviners and medicine men (Hostetter 1975:5-6). They provided talismans, concoctions from Qur'anic writings and amulets for the royal as well as the common citizens in Dagbon (Oppong 1973:14). The Dagomba royalty are quick to admit that they owe most of their victories to the help of the Muslim charms and spiritual protection.

Islam in Dagbon has been propagated not through jihad, but through the commercial activity of three trading groups. Over time, Muslims have monopolised certain jobs such as butchery. Tamale is presumed to have the highest percentage (about 65%) of Muslims in any town in Ghana. Jon Kirby maintains that about 85% of the Dagomba in Tamale would claim to be Muslims (Boi-Nai and Kirby 1999:124). At present the Dagomba constitute the largest Muslim community (53%) in the Northern Region. Although Islam is seen invariably as the Dagomba state religion, Barker argues that it would be a mistake to conclude that Dagbon is solidly or even predominantly Muslim. The erroneous notion of Dagbon as a Muslim state goes back as early as the 1800s (Barker 1986:137-138). Other ethnic groups regarded the Dagomba as Muslims because of their outward expressions of Islam, in terms of their clothes, naming ceremonies, practice of circumcision and burial rites, as well as the Islamic overlays of Dagomba chieftaincy and festivals (Staniland 1975:6). A reason suggested for the spread of Islam in Dagbon is its willingness to compromise with Dagomba traditional beliefs and practices. A. W. Cardinall argues that by doing this it acted as a firm bulwark against the influence of pure Islam and he thought that Dagomba adoption of Arabic names and keeping Ramadan were merely outward trappings. In his view, "semi-Islamization was not a step towards full commitment to Islam, but an inoculation which prevented the mass of the people from catching the real thing" (Hostetter 1975:139).

As mentioned earlier, Muslim influence in the palaces attracted Dagomba adherents to Islam for pragmatic reasons (Hostetter 1975:7–9). Muslim leadership was incorporated into the chieftaincy structure. A case in point is the appointment of an imam who then becomes part of the social and political structure. Muslims seem to feel at home in Dagbon and are easily integrated into the chieftaincy system by creation of other Muslim officials at the court of the chief.

For a long time, Islamic presence in Dagbon was peaceful. Muslims and non-Muslims have lived together in the same house and as a family without any problem. Thus, Christians and Muslims have lived together peacefully and enjoyed mutual respect. The situation is changing now, however, especially in Tamale. Justice Katanga observes, that "signs of Islamic fundamentalism are present and anti-Christian sentiment is rising – something previously unknown in Ghana" (Katanga 1994a). There has been an influx of Muslim missionaries from Pakistan and Arab countries. In Tamale now there is even a Muslim mission house called "Jihad House."

The transformative effect of Islam on Dagomba society has been immense and will become evident in the examination of the translation of the Christian Scripture into Dagbani. Arabic and Hausa terminologies have found their way into the Dagbani Bible because of the pervasive influence of Islam.

3.15 Dagbon chieftaincy and religion

At the performance of the succession rites of chiefs, the different estates and professional groups are linked together. For instance, diviners, drummers, land priests, imams, court officials and *naanima* all have their roles to play. Another remarkable feature is that the ancestral cult and Islamic prayers are mingled to form the context of royal Dagomba belief. Oppong explains that after a week's confinement of the king, the Yendi imams and *mallams* recite prayers. The king grasps the Qur'an and asks God's help in the tradition begun by *Na* Zangina (Oppong 1973:23).

It is clear, then, that *naanima* among the Dagomba are held in high esteem, and there is thus an obsession to become a *naanima*. Islamic influence on Dagomba chieftaincy is also immense. In fact, Boi-Nai and Kirby suggest that "the core of Dagomba belief and practice is shifting from its traditional base and moving toward Islamic orthodoxy – if not fundamentalism" (Boi-Nai and Kirby 1998:535). To these writers the Dagomba people who are gravitating towards Islam are losing their cultural identity and increasingly assimilating Arabic culture. For instance, one group of Dagomba Muslims is advocating for the repudiation of some aspects of Dagomba cultural practices, such as funerals, deemed pagan. On the other hand, Dagomba Christians are now striving to make Christianity more Dagomba in outlook.

Early Western Christianity that was inherited had not shown great enthusiasm for chieftaincy because of the perception that practices not compatible with Christianity accompany the institution. There has recently been a shift in attitude on the part of Dagomba Christians who, in light of emerging African Christianity, are accepting the chieftaincy institution. There are now Dagomba Christian chiefs symbolically conveying the idea that there is another way of being Dagomba without being an adherent of traditional Dagomba religion or Islam.

The Dagomba have played an important role in the politics of Ghana as far back as colonial times. Analysing the Dagomba political hegemony over the other northern ethnic groups, Boi-Nai and Kirby point out the polarisation it has fostered in terms of religion, ethnic identity and land tenure system (Boi-Nai and Kirby 1998). They note that the acephalous peoples, otherwise known as stateless peoples, are now asserting their rights to rule themselves, control their land and to repudiate Dagomba hegemony (Boi-Nai and Kirby 1998:123). In their quest they have found an ally in the Christian church, particularly the Catholic church. This is one explanation for the significant conversions of these acephalous peoples to Christianity as compared with the Dagomba. It will be shown later how the Bible in the vernacular has *conscientised* (borrowing a verb invented by Freire 1970:186) and facilitated the process of conversion.

A contentious aspect of Dagomba political rule involves land tenure and the resistance of these stateless peoples, particularly the Konkomba, against their subjugation by the Dagomba. With the abolition of slave raiding and indentured labour, Boi-Nai and Kirby observe that the flow of resources that used to come to the rulers has stopped. This tension-ridden relationship can be likened to a time bomb that successive governments have glossed over but which a Catholic Bishops Conference in 1999 drew attention to. For political expediency, successive governments have sided with the Dagomba because of their considerable influence. The bishops, however, perceive themselves as God's agents to fight all forms of injustice, exploitation and subjugation by one group of people against another. In a previous conference the Catholic Bishops gave a prophetic warning that was captured in unambiguous terms "against resurrecting old historical grudges" and against "return to systems of 'old tribal hegemony.'" They concluded by warning against "attempts to keep one ethnic group in vassalage to the other" (Catholic Bishops Conference 1984:536).

3.16 The Dagomba of Northern Ghana: Conclusion

The Dagomba have rich traditions that are being passed from one generation to another by their traditional institutions such as the *lunsi* and *gunji*.

3.16 The Dagomba of Northern Ghana: Conclusion

Furthermore, many major history books on northern Ghana focus on the Dagomba and their kingdom. Early writings such as colonial treaties, reports and ethnographies give more prominence to the Dagomba than to any other northern Ghanaian ethnic group.

The creation of Tamale as the capital of the Northern Region of Ghana has boosted the image of the Dagomba, as they see themselves now as both a political and an economic power in northern Ghana. The consequence of this is the widespread use of Dagbani in northern Ghana. On the religious scene, the recent adoption of a more radical form of Islam by some urban Dagomba is making them now less tolerant of non-Muslims whom they regard as *kaffir*[38] or pagans. The Dagomba exhibit a sense of superiority and tend to look down on others, especially the Konkomba. This is the context in which the Dagbani Bible has been translated.

To conclude, the Dagomba have been shaped by their past heritage and their identity has been moulded by their historical circumstances. In addition, their beliefs and worldview determine how they respond to other peoples as well as to new experiences. The Dagomba encountered Islam about three centuries before the Christian faith came to Dagbon. The Dagomba have a rich traditional, cultural past and so this has prepared them for eventual Christian mission, especially the translation of the Bible into Dagbani.

---

[38] A Hausa term for a non-Muslim.

4

The Konkomba of Northern Ghana

4.1 Introduction

Chapter three gives an overview of the history and cultural institutions that helped shape the identity of the Dagomba. This helps explain the Dagomba people and the context in which Bible translation into Dagbani took place. Chapter four explores the shaping of Konkomba identity and context. The Konkomba, neighbours of the Dagomba, have experienced subjugation, with the devastating consequence that they have had limited opportunity to articulate their own story.

The origins of the Konkomba and the shaping of their worldview, their cultural practices, their contact with their neighbors and colonial authorities, and the effect of Islam on their society will be discussed in this chapter. These factors affect their attitude toward education and development and their response to Christianity.

The Konkomba belong to the class of societies that are described as not having a centralised political authority. Their socio-political system is clan-based as opposed to hierarchically administrated; hence they are called an acephalous, stateless society. Robin Horton spells out the four essential features of a stateless society. First, there is little concentration of authority, by which he means one cannot pinpoint an individual or limited group of men as ruler or rulers of that society. Second, in his view, the authority roles that exist affect only limited aspects of the lives of the persons under that authority. The third feature he identifies is that the authority exercised is neither full-time nor specialised. Finally, he points out that "the unit within which people feel an obligation to settle their disputes according to agreed rules and without resort to force, tends to be relatively small" (Horton 1985:87).

Because of this loose societal organisation, the Konkomba have not had a stable environment; conflict was common among themselves as well as with their neighbours. The lack of central authority made the Konkomba vulnerable to enemy attacks and intra-clan fighting. Consequently, other people feared the Konkomba and considered them wild. It seems that early historians did not take the Konkomba seriously and therefore wrote little about them.

The Konkomba of northern Ghana now hold some fascination for social scientists and politicians as a typical example of the acephalous society. The Konkomba had also been the subject of ethnographical studies in the colonial era with the aim of assisting the colonial authorities to know how to handle them. From the colonial era to the present, the Konkomba have agitated the political scene, the root cause being their desire to shake off Dagomba domination. Media reports on these agitations have tended to blame the Konkomba as aggressors (Katanga 1994b:19). In this chapter we attempt to give an objective account of the Konkomba history, particularly their religious encounter with Islam and later with Christianity, in order to determine the effect of Bible translation on them.

4.2 Sources

Primary and secondary sources have been consulted in writing this chapter. Primary sources were in the form of oral interviews and archives; secondary materials included books and published articles. Because Konkomba culture and worldview influence how they respond to the translated Scriptures in their mother tongue, we will examine those areas.

Writing on the Mole-speaking community, Gabriel Tuurey observed that, though Arab writers have written and documented facts about events in the medieval African kingdoms that lay in the Sahelian region immediately south of the Sahara, not much has been written about the large groups of peoples who inhabit the Voltaic region. The reason for this neglect, according to Tuurey, is that the peoples of this area lacked gold, the commodity that the Arabs and Europeans eagerly sought. He notes further, "Historians generally dismiss this area and its peoples in a page or half a page and even in some cases in an expanded sentence" (Tuurey 1982:11, 12).[1] The available sources now are colonial reports, ethnographies and recent literature on the Konkomba after their 1994 war with the Dagomba, Gonja and Nanumba. Another source consists of gleanings from Dagomba history.

---

[1] The Voltaic Region is home to the Brifor, Senufo, Gurma, Busansi, Gurunsi, Sissala, Vagla, Lobi, Bobo, Bimoba, Konkomba, Tampulma, Dogon, Gonja Fulani, and the Mole-Dagomba peoples.

The impoverished nature of oral source material on the stateless societies also stems from the fact that they lack, in Horton's words, "specialist historians" (Horton 1985:88). Among the Dagomba drummers and fiddlers found in the royal courts fill this role. Even where there are oral traditions amongst the stateless societies they are inferior in depth and in publicity. Thus, the sources of Konkomba history are limited in comparison to the Dagomba discussed earlier.

The Konkomba seem not to show keen interest in their history according to Jean-Claude Froelich, an ethnographer. He offers the following reasons for this seeming lack of interest: first, he argues that they are more committed to their families and therefore tend to ignore the history of the larger social groups. Secondly, he reasons that the old men knowledgeable in Konkomba history have either died or lost their memories. According to him the Konkomba believe they are the earliest inhabitants of their area because their old men told them that *"Woumbor* [God] created man in the regions of British Togo which they still inhabit." Thus, the diverse Konkomba groups have a common ancestor, and through him the clans spread out to occupy the "countries of the east, which abounded in game" (Froelich 1954:13).

4.3 History: Origins of the Konkomba

In his book, *The Konkomba Tribe of Northern Togo*, Jean-Claude Froelich outlines five motives that have guided Konkomba choice of settlements. The first was their quest for good soil in the Oti plain. Secondly, they fled earlier settlements to escape from invasions by their enemies and slave raiders such as the Dagomba. The third factor in choosing settlements was the desire for safe watercourses that had no *glossinas* or flies that caused blindness. Very close to this is the fourth that had to do with their pursuit of permanent water places for comfortable human habitation. The fifth reason was the avoidance of settling along European routes, in order to escape European interference in their lives (Froelich 1954:3). The prejudice and harsh treatment suffered among the Konkomba at the hands of the colonial authorities, created resentment in them and resulted in their desire to avoid Europeans.

The Konkomba homeland straddles the border between Togo and Ghana.[2] According to the ethnographer, Madeline Manoukian, the Konkomba belong to the Gurma language group and call themselves *Bekpokpam* (sing. *Okpokpandja; Okpokpampi*) and their land *Kekpokpam*. Geographically, "they inhabit the area between 0° 20'W and 0° 50'E and between 10° 15'N and 9° 25'N, that is, the Oti plain between the Ngkpe [Oti] River and the Togo hills" (Manoukian 1951:5).

---

[2] See PRAAD Tamale NRG 8/2/70 Konkomba.

The Konkomba in Ghana believe that the whole of Yendi district originally belonged to them. Legend has it that nine generations ago, the Dagomba king, *Na* Luro, founded Yendi as his capital, compelling the Konkomba to migrate eastward.[3] The Konkomba have laid claim to Yendi, the traditional capital of the Dagomba, as their town because one of their historic shrines is located there.

Within Ghana the Konkomba are found also in the kingdoms of the Dagomba, Mamprusi, Nanumba and Gonja, whilst others have migrated to the northern part of the Volta Region (Barker 1986:170). They consist of five subgroups (Lidorio 1999:5). These subgroups are the Gimba, the Nafeba, the Chemba, the Konmba and the Monkpimba. The first three are perceived to be well organised under Dagomba jurisdiction. The fourth, in Martison's view, is difficult to classify. However, he describes the fifth one in uncomplimentary terms as the "bad Konkomba" (Martinson 1994:37).

Lidorio calculates that the various Konkomba groups speak twenty-three dialects of Likpakpaaln (1999:5). Although they speak multiple variants they consider themselves one ethnic entity that shares a homogenous culture with only minor differences in customs and practices (Manoukian 1951:5). In peaceful times they generally mind their own business and show unflinching support only to those who are members of their families. Yet they gather for reinforcement when there is an imminent threat to the larger ethnic group.

The Konkomba are settled mainly on the eastern edge of the Dagomba kingdom. As noted earlier, they are described as stateless because they did not have a centralised political system. The Konkomba, however, claim ownership of land (Tamakloe 1931:II), though some territory was lost to the Dagomba through conquest (Oliver 1977:460–461). Some Konkomba, however, do not accept that the Dagomba conquered them. Rather, they claim that they were displaced by the Dagomba invasion to avoid being conquered.[4] The Gonja also invaded the Konkomba and imposed their rule (Tamakloe 1931:18–19). The Konkomba resented that the colonial policy of Indirect Rule legitimised Dagomba and Gonja subjugation of them (Tait 1961:11).

Dagomba rulers were imposed on the Konkomba, but eventually Konkomba leaders, who submitted to Dagomba suzerainty, were enskinned as chiefs by the Dagomba. The Dagomba continued to appoint chiefs to Konkomba towns and villages until 1981 (Barker 1986). Whereas the Dagomba history portrayed the Dagomba as conquerors with a history of showing dignity, Konkomba history portrays the Konkomba people as marginalised and despised by others.

---

[3] The *Palbas* (*Kpalbas*), a subgrouping of the Konkomba, explain that a taboo against eating crocodiles was due to the kindness it showed them on this occasion as they were escaping from the Dagomba.
[4] PRAAD Accra. ADM 56/1/91.

As stated earlier, the Konkomba call themselves *Bekpokpam*, their language *Likpakpaaln* and their homeland *Kekpokpam*. The standard name, Konkomba (in English), is derived from the Dagomba term *Kpakpamba* (Tait 1961:11). When David Tait points out the political tension between the Dagomba and the Konkomba, he notes that, although Konkomba land falls under Dagomba jurisdiction administratively, the Konkomba themselves consider the land they now occupy to be independent of Dagomba rule, hence their use of *Kekpokpam* to describe their geographic domain (Tait 1961:1).

4.4 The Konkomba under colonial authority

The British colonial authorities did not easily administrate the Konkomba. A letter from the French Republic Governor at Porto Novo to the governor of the Gold Coast, dated 3 March 1935, demonstrates that the French had faced the same difficulties administrating the Konkomba as did the British. Colonial authorities failed to find solutions to the numerous difficulties that confronted the Konkomba. They described the Konkomba as extremely quarrelsome people who did not like colonial control. Seeking the reason for Konkomba resistance to colonial rule, this colonial French governor blamed the location of the Konkomba homeland. He noted that, "their country favours independence because of the Oti River – inundated during six months of the year."[5]

The records show that the Konkomba suffered at the hands of the colonial authorities. The Yendi Diary for January 1918 states that Konkomba villages were burnt and a number of Konkomba killed as punishment for fighting the Dagomba. Part of the account from a colonial official, reads, "They told me they had burnt and laid waste more than twelve villages, confiscating all the cattle, sheep, goats and pigs, the last if not eaten by their push were killed and left, they also destroyed any grain and, so far as possible, the yam farms."[6]

Rather than leave to chance that the injustice against the Konkomba be addressed, the Konkomba were often killed and their property destroyed. Thus, the force used by colonial authorities to subdue the Konkomba undoubtedly aggravated their administration of the Konkomba. A colonial Inspector General of Police reported on 15 September 1935: "...we collected and destroyed upwards of 19,000 arrows from the Konkombas...our mission is to disarm the Konkombas who were too frequently killing one another in settlement of village and boundary disputes."[7]

---

[5] PRAAD Tamale. NRG 8/2/70.
[6] PRAAD Accra. NAG Yendi Diary for January 1918.
[7] PRAAD Tamale. NRG 8/2/70.

Whereas the colonial authorities' aim was to bring about law and order, the Konkomba resented the colonial encounter as an intrusion into their lives. However, the introduction of locally recruited police to regulate Konkomba life was not so negative. In fact, they helped to transform an otherwise chaotic environment into a more harmonious one.

Colonial records reveal that perceptions of the Konkomba were generally unfavourable. The colonial officials and other ethnic groups that share common borders with the Konkomba often blamed the Konkomba for anything that went wrong. In 1940, when the war broke out between the Dagomba and Konkomba, the latter were blamed for being the aggressors who were prone to violence and savagery.

However, a few dissenting voices countered that generally-held view as some persons testify. Explaining the circumstances behind the so-called Cow War, the then Director of Veterinary Services reveals some of the remote causes for the perennial conflicts between the Dagomba and Konkomba in this testimony:

> I have worked as a Veterinary Officer in Konkomba and know them and their villages. Neither my Veterinary Officers, my African staff nor myself have encountered any opposition nor hostility and I append notes by members of my staff. The Konkomba must at times regard us as a nuisance because although a keen and competent arable farmer, he is an apathetic cattleman; however, he has never opposed us although his lack of interest is seen in his slackness in bringing cattle to the Demon immunisation camp but on the other hand, our pleuro-pneumonia vaccination teams, who inoculate at his home villages, receive every help.[8]

The then Yendi district Veterinary Officer who knew and had worked with the Konkomba absolved them from the blame of being the aggressors of the Cow War. Contrary to the prevailing stereotype, he explains further the hospitable nature of the Konkomba as witnessed during his stay with them:

> My experience and that of my staff is that the only people who are not well received are the Dagomba overlords and their servants. The Dagombas regard the Konkombas as serfs, as beasts of burden to catch all the Dagombas' cattle at immunisation camps and if possible, to be exploited. The Konkomba is a finer physical specimen, a harder worker and a better type than the eastern Dagomba. I do not think that the Segbiri riot is an isolated incident caused by the innate savagery of the Konkomba but that it, the 1939 Kugnau

---

[8] PRAAD Tamale. NRG 8/2/88.

4.4 The Konkomba under colonial authority

trouble and other cases, are part of a coherent whole, of a smouldering resentment against the Dagomba, which blazes into sudden flame after long provocation.[9]

Long-standing unresolved exploitation and lack of respect for the Konkomba on the part of the Dagomba had become like gunpowder that was ready to explode at the least provocation. The conclusion of this Veterinary Officer is instructive: "I feel that the trouble is due to the Dagomba and that increased repressive measures [of the Konkomba] will eventually yield greater trouble. It is easy to understand the horror and anger at the spectacle at Segbiri, but it may have blanketed the fundamental cause."[10]

It is significant that some colonial agents, such as the one above, were bold enough to defend the Konkomba at critical moments against the prevalent opinion. Another senior Veterinary Officer tried to disabuse the Konkomba of blame when he testified at colonial official investigations into the causes of the Cow War. He argued that:

The behaviour of the Konkombas at these camps compares very favourably with that of the people attending the camps of any other area in the Gold Coast. Their discipline at the camps has been excellent and I have never seen any incidents of quarrelling or violence in which they were concerned. My impression at these camps is that the Konkombas were imposed upon to some extent by the few Dagombas who also come to the same camps. All the work seems to be done by the Konkombas while the Dagombas take it as a natural right that the Konkombas should do their work for them, especially when there is Govt. authority to shelter under.[11]

This senior Veterinary Officer's observation is not an isolated incident but applies to a series of events. The Konkomba, as he noted, were kind not only to Westerners but also to other Africans. He recounts the experience of his African staff: "The African Veterinary Staff are constantly trekking Konkomba country and in all my time I have had no complaints of molestation or threats by the Konkombas."[12]

The policy of Indirect Rule meant that the colonial officials tended to channel their policies through the Dagomba chiefs. Since the Konkomba were under Dagomba chiefs they were more easily exploited, as exemplified in this report by the same senior Veterinary Officer:

The Dagomba chiefs are suspected of taking advantage of the immunisation regulations to extort; e.g. this year at

---
[9] PRAAD Tamale. NRG 8/2/88.
[10] PRAAD Tamale. NRG 8/2/88:2.
[11] PRAAD Tamale. NRG 8/2/88.
[12] PRAAD Tamale. NRG 8/2/88.

Gushiago an old Konkomba explained he had not brought the listed number of cattle to the camp was because the chief of Gushiago had taken two of them as 'fine' for not having his cattle immunised the previous year. This incident was investigated by the D.C. on my representation, and the chief was ordered to return the cattle.[13]

Although the colonial authorities had an inkling of the uneasiness between the Dagomba and Konkomba, they did not have the political will to find a lasting solution to the impasse. Thus, the relationship between the Dagomba and Konkomba ethnic groups has been fraught with hostilities, resulting in the outbreak of violence in 1914, 1917, 1940 (the Cow War – over cattle immunisation), 1946 (the Fish War – over fishing rights), and 1994 (the Guinea Fowl War – which began as a quarrel over a guinea fowl) (Martinson 1994:53–73). The immediate causes of conflict were trivial matters, as the names suggest, but the root cause originated with the Dagomba intent to exercise authority over the Konkomba, as in times past.[14] Contemporary Konkomba youth regard the continuing exercise of power over them by the Dagomba as contradicting the letter and spirit of the constitution of Ghana.[15]

Perhaps the most serious root of hostility between these two groups stems from sporadic raids the Dagomba made on the Konkomba to obtain slaves, both for their own domestic use and for annual tribute [to the Asante empire] (Der 1998:1). Although these armed raids on the Konkomba ceased after the 1870s, other forms of raids continued, with collectors sent to Konkomba territories to forcibly gather corn to sell, raising income for the chiefdom. Tait cites one such raid in 1950 when, in the Saboba region alone, more than two lorry-loads of sorghum were collected. He recounts another occasion when, on a Yendi market day, Konkomba new yams were seized as tribute to the king of the Dagomba. Tait notes further that the Konkomba, out of humiliation and anger for this extortion, occasionally take revenge on Dagomba communities. To forestall attacks and counter-attacks there are no-man's-land gaps between settlements of the two peoples (Tait 1961:9–12).

Notwithstanding the general Konkomba hostility toward the Dagomba, some Konkomba have a good relationship with the latter. Though the majority of Konkomba reject Dagomba rule, those in the chiefdom of Gushiego accept them. For this reason, the Konkomba in the Gushiego chiefdom are most closely integrated into the Dagomba system. Tait supports his claim of the paradoxical relation of love and hate between the Dagomba and Konkomba by citing the scenario in which the Konkomba serve as the

---

[13] PRAAD Tamale. NRG 8/2/88.
[14] PRAAD Tamale. NRG 8/2/88.
[15] The Konkomba Youth Association's stance.

kambonsi, that is, the infantry of the chiefdom, alongside the Dagomba. The Konkomba constitute a significant proportion of the army. At the time of Tait's writing, of the thirty-one titles of the traditional army, the Konkomba held twenty-one (Tait 1961:10).

The Dagomba-Konkomba relationship is a complex of hostilities and harmonies because they inter-marry, trade together and relate on other socio-political spheres. The complexity in their relationship is evident in that, whilst the Konkomba strongly resist cultural borrowing from the Dagomba on the one hand, on the other hand, intermarriage between the two groups is high.

4.5 The Konkomba after Ghanean independence as a republic

After Ghana's independence in 1957, justice and equality for the Konkomba did not improve significantly. The Saboba Town Developmental Committee Chairman outlined the representative frustrations of the Konkomba on the occasion of an extraordinary meeting held 23 August 1968. He catalogued the items they requested that the government enact in order to improve everyday life for the Konkomba. First, they solicited a health facility. Second, in the area of transport and communication, they wanted the government to bridge the River Oti to link them to the republic of Togo. Third, a thorny issue was their request that the local government council seat be returned to Saboba from Zabzugu (a Dagomba town). Fourth, they requested that water dams and wells be dug for potable water to serve nine villages in the district. Finally, they wanted the government to listen to their request for tractors to boost agriculture in that area, which had fallen on deaf ears.

The Konkomba have been fighting for justice and recognition, particularly in the area of representation in government circles. They also had hoped that issues of land ownership and the system of traditional rule would be addressed after national independence was granted, but that was to be elusive. This situation is attributable to what Hippolyt Pul terms, "wavering state policies on chieftaincy and land ownership rights," which have contributed to the marginalisation of the Konkomba and other acephalous people (2003:40).

4.6 Recent history

The Konkomba stand against Dagomba hegemony has been possible mainly because they have maintained their own social structure and religious system. In addition, David Tait is convinced that this has been possible because their beliefs and culture have been maintained throughout the centuries. He supports his conviction by arguing that the Konkomba are "infinitely loyal to a fellow clansman, instantly aggressive to an outsider." In light of this, Tait argues, "they [Konkomba] have been able to preserve their own way of life to this day" (1961:12). In a 2005 interview with some Konkomba from Accra, it came out that some other Konkomba have adopted Dagomba lifestyle, especially those around Yendi. The motivation for this being to court favours from Dagomba so that they can be accepted as equals in pursuit of their goals in commerce or political power. Thus, some of them make themselves Dagomba by converting to Islam and marrying Dagomba women.

4.7 The Konkomba and their neighbours

The most important neighbours of the Konkomba in their homeland are the Dagomba not only because they reside in the same geographical location but also because they have had a long-standing relationship that can best be described as a love-hate relationship. The colonial officials, though aware of this, did not help matters because they took sides, and there is abundant evidence of stereotypes of the Konkomba and the Dagomba in their writings and pronouncements to support this. As shown in his Handing Over Report, the Yendi District Commissioner acknowledged that the Dagombas and Konkombas occupied the Yendi District even though there were other ethnic groups within the District besides the two. Though the colonial officials knew the Dagomba were exploiting the Konkomba, they did nothing to halt it.[16]

The colonial officials' responses to the Dagomba-Konkomba were sometimes ambivalent. An example of this is captured in the Handing Over Report:

> Twenty years ago, the Dagombas were a masterful and warlike tribe and who, except by the Ashantis, had never been conquered, of late years their characteristics have entirely changed, and they are now lazy, effete, passive resisters of the worst description and in my opinion are dying out. If any race required the German method of coercion the Dagombas do.[17]

The above assertion is not wholly true because the Gonja have defeated the Dagomba in the west, sacking their first traditional capital located in Diari Dapare.[18] Again, there are accounts detailing how the Asante raided

---

[16] PRAAD Accra. ADM 56/1/204:1.
[17] PRAAD Accra. ADM 56/1/204:2.
[18] "Dapare" refers to the ruins of an old town; Diari Dapare is a location in present day Diari town. Yendi, the original seat of the Dagomba king, was first situated in old Diari. It was later moved to its present location in the east after it, too, was destroyed by the Gonja.

the Dagomba and forced the latter to pay tribute to them.[19] This colonial officer continues with his perception of the Dagomba and Konkomba:

> The Konkombas are the reverse, and you will find them most interesting to deal with. They are industrious, merry and prolific. Whereas in Dagomba towns the number of old men and cripples is astonishing, in Konkomba villages the large population of children and well set up young men in [sic] is most remarkable. They are impetuous, seldom separated from their bows and arrows, and like the Irish always ready for a scrap. A brush between two villages is common and a few casualties on either side seem to worry them not at all. In my opinion this is a better trait than inertia and immovability.[20]

A third quotation from the report of colonial perception of the Dagomba and Konkomba also shows lack of neutrality on the part of colonial authorities:

> The DAGOMBAS give little trouble but they are a lazy and dirty lot of people. The KONKOMBAS are a better type but are a source of anxiety on account of their quarrelsome nature when under the influence of drink. They will fight on the least provocation and it has been found necessary to station constabulary in certain villages in order to keep the peace.[21]

This colonial official acknowledges the Konkomba as hardworking. However, he jumps to the usual name-calling, describing them as quarrelsome when drunk. Naturally, the Konkomba tend to resent cheating. They do not just enjoy fighting, as the colonial official seems to suggest, yet when they feel cheated they will seek instant justice which might result in a fight.

4.8 Language

A significant portion of the Konkomba people speak other languages in addition to Likpakpaaln. This is possible for two reasons: They migrate and settle among other ethnic groups to farm and many traders from other ethnic groups trade with these industrious Konkomba farmers. It is estimated that about fifty percent of Konkomba in their homeland speak Dagbani. This might be explained by the fact that Dagbani is imposed on Konkomba children in schools. Very few Dagomba, however, try to learn

---

[19] See the Kanbonse of the Dagomba and Ivor Wilks' (1975) account on the Dagomba and Asante.
[20] PRAAD Accra. ADM 56/1/204.
[21] PRAAD Accra. ADM 56/1/204.

the Konkomba language (Barker 1986) as if they might find it degrading to learn their subjects' language.

The Konkomba organise themselves under a system of clanship. This creates a strong sense of ethnic loyalty and powerful unity, which is manifested especially in times of war or crisis where they are easily mobilised. The Konkomba people are largely unstructured; a collection of geographically separate, loosely related, scattered groups. The language of this people group, *Likpakpaaln*, has three distinguishable subgroupings: *Lichabol*, *Limonkpeln* and *Likuln*, with twenty-three dialects (Lidorio 1999:9).[22]

4.9 The Konkomba and related ethnic groups

David Tait explains that the Konkomba are closely related to the Basare, who can be found in the Republics of Togo and Ghana and speak a dialect of the Gurma cluster. The cultures of the Basare and Kabre of Togo are very much like the Konkomba and their compounds are of a similar architectural design, although the Basare live in much larger settlements than the Konkomba. He further notes that there are cultural differences among these people: Konkomba diviners are all men whereas Basare diviners are women. Also, the Konkomba practise infant betrothal of girls and exchange sisters in marriage, but the Basare do not. Their kinship terminology, in Tait's observation, is very much the same (Tait 1961:2).

With respect to the settlement pattern between the Konkomba and the Kabre, Tait describes them as similar both in terms of pattern and scale. He remarks that the number of medicines and shrines are the most striking features of their compounds. In view of the close similarities between them, Tait claims it is hard to talk of distinct boundaries separating them (Tait 1961:3).

4.9.1 The Mamprusi kingdom

The Konkomba, or the Komba as they are also called, have as their neighbours to the north the Mamprusi kingdom (Mamprugu) and the Bimwaba (i.e. Bimoba). The Mamprusi are overlords whereas the Bimoba are co-settlers with the Konkomba. Apart from occasional skirmishes there has been peaceful co-existence amongst them. There is similarity in architecture among the Mamprusi, the Konkomba and the Bimoba. Well-built houses with circular compounds surround courtyards at the centre. There are circular rooms with conical roofs for the women; low walls of about five feet in height join rectangular rooms for the men.[23]

---

[22] The *Ethnologue* lists seven dialects (Eberhard, Simons, and Fennig 2019): https://www.ethnologue.com/language/xon; OLAC gives nine known names and dialect names: http://www.language-archives.org/language/xon.

[23] PRAAD Tamale. NRG 8/3/22.

4.9 The Konkomba and related ethnic groups

Regarding marriage, the Mamprusi and Bimoba consider pre-marital sex disgraceful and shun it, whilst the Konkomba condone, even celebrate, it. Amongst the Konkomba, to have a baby before marriage increases the marriageable value of the woman.[24] However, the Konkomba and Bimoba, as well as the Kusasi, practice exchange-marriage. In exchange marriage, if someone marries a man's sister, then, within four days, he should give his own sister to that man in marriage.[25]

Generally, the Konkomba are perceived of by the Mamprusi as primitive, industrious farmers who live in broken, hilly country; a people who do not move about much and keep to themselves. They are considered a happy and friendly people who live privately and mind their own business.[26]

The relationship between the Mamprusi and the Konkomba is generally friendly. The Konkomba live along the southern slope of the Gambaga escarpment in the kingdom of the Mamprusi. Although the Mamprusi hired the Tshakosi[27] to assist the Nalerigu *na* in his wars, they never attacked the Konkomba (Tait 1961:4). Their amiable relationship may explain why the Mamprusi declined to help their kinsmen, the Dagomba, fight the Konkomba in the Guinea Fowl War of 1994.

4.9.2 The Nanumba

The Nanumba claim ownership of the land farmed by the Konkomba and, like the Dagomba, exercise authority over them. However, the Konkomba resent what they consider exploitation. They perceive of the Nanumba as arrogant usurpers of their land.

The Konkomba find even more objectionable the Nanumba's practice of settling Konkomba marriage disputes. According to Tait, the Konkomba's main objections to marriage settlement by the Nanumba is in regard to harsh fines that the Nanumba have imposed on the Konkomba and their lack of appreciation of Konkomba cultural marriage practices. These issues led to bloody clashes in April and June 1981, in which many hundreds of the Nanumba and the Konkomba died (Brukum 2001:9, 173). A number of wars have been waged as a result, the worst of them being the Guinea Fowl War of 1994 when the Nanumba were allied with the Dagomba and Gonja against the Konkomba and their allies (Tait 1961:4).

---

[24] PRAAD Tamale. NRG 8/3/34. Annual Report of the Mandated Area South Mamprusi District, January–December 1930.

[25] PRAAD Tamale. Report on the mandated area of Togoland under the Kusasi District for the year ending 30th November 1927.

[26] PRAAD Tamale. Report on the Mandated area of the District of South Mamprusi for 1925 and 1928.

[27] The Tshakosi are thought to have originated from Akan mercenaries.

4.9.3 The Gonja

The Konkomba's relationship with the Gonja cannot be described as cordial. However, it is not as hostile as their relationship with the Dagomba and Nanumba. In the recent past the Konkomba fought alongside the Nawuries against the Gonja and then in 1994 against the Gonja, the Nanumba and the Dagomba. (Brukum 2001:1) The Konkomba are settler farmers in the vast east Gonjaland and for a long time they lived in peace with their Gonja host. However, those two wars brought about a deep rift which is yet to be healed.

4.10 The stigmatisation of the Konkomba

The mention of Konkomba carries with it certain derogatory connotations from pre-colonial times which persist to the present, conjuring up uncomplimentary words and making the people victims of vicious stereotypes. Stereotyping robs us of objectivity and therefore tends to make us blind to the good in the victim. The mass media, which ought to thrive on objectivity, can sometimes be sucked into stereotyping. The Konkomba are treated like the Devil, who is blamed for every conceivable evil. History, it seems, has not been fair to the Konkomba.

A number of factors have contributed to this state of stigmatisation according to the findings of the Tamale-based Catholic anthropologist, Jon Kirby. These include sporadic raiding of the Konkomba by the Dagomba for slaves prior to colonial rule. Under Indirect Rule, the Konkomba sent women to the Dagomba as wives. As noted earlier the Konkomba have had to learn Dagbani and some even gave up their Konkomba identity for Dagomba identity. Expatiating on this Kirby writes:

> As more women were fed into the system more Konkomba began calling themselves 'Dagombas.'... The grandmother of the current *ya na*, the paramount chief of all Dagombas, for example, is a Konkomba, and his first son, who fled to Accra during the recent Northern Conflict, is by a Konkomba woman. Intermarriage was and still is so great that when the conflict broke out in February 1994, many Yendi Dagombas did not know who the enemy was. There was hardly a person who could claim pure Dagomba parentage or ancestry. (Kirby 1996:2)

Pressed against the wall, some Konkomba could no longer countenance their past inferior status and had to fight. The late *Ya Na* Yakubu II's mother was a Konkomba, as was one of his wives whose son is the eldest. However, although he shared the blood of the two peoples and could have been a peacemaker between the Dagomba and Konkomba, he did little to give Konkomba any recognition.

4.11 The Konkomba and ethnic pride

When analysing the motivation of the 1994 Northern Conflict, Hippolyt Pul, another anthropologist, identified ethnic pride on the part of the Konkomba and their acephalous allies. His findings among the Konkomba and their allies confirm that:

> Ethnic pride is also the core motivator for Konkomba mobilization to fight. This time, however, it is not the pride of the past that is at issue. Konkombas fight for the right to be respected and treated as equals under the laws of the modern state. They resent the past in which they were collectively treated as inferior. They want to be recognised as a major ethnic group in the region; they want to [re]claim their status as equals with other tribes in the region and in the country as a whole. If chieftaincy is the route to gaining this equality of place, so be it. They will ask for it, they will fight for it, even though traditionally they have never had a pan ethnic paramount chief. (Pul 2003)

In the eyes of Konkomba neighbours, especially the Dagomba, the Konkomba "occupy the lowest rung on the social scale and were viewed as labourers to be hired." Thus, the Konkomba in earlier times "occupied the position of the underdog" (Gaskin 1986:iv).

As observed earlier by Kirby, a Konkomba woman raised in Yendi points out that there is much intermarriage between the Konkomba and Dagomba, to the extent that it is increasingly difficult to find a person in Yendi without a trace of mixed blood. However, it is the Konkomba who desire Dagomba identity who embrace these intermarriages and these same people who adopt Islam. On the contrary, those who retain their Konkomba identity remain adherents of traditional religion or become Christians. Islam has intertwined itself with the Dagomba culture (Tait 1961:11) and is perceived as the oppressor's religion.

The Konkomba have no past to be proud of since they were victims of conquest and slave raiding and were also disunited. To have their rightful place among the peoples of Ghana, the autonomous Konkomba clans had to mobilise themselves to fight for their common interest, hence the formation of the Konkomba Youth Association (KOYA). The preamble to their constitution unequivocally states,

> We the Konkomba Youth: Having realised the need for coming together as a body; conscious of our responsibility to harness the human and natural resources of our people. Inspired by a common determination to promote understanding among ourselves. Believing that we are capable of being a vital force in our society as a group. Determined to

safeguard and consolidate unity among ourselves; dedicated to the general progress and welfare of Konkombaland in particular and Ghana in general. Desirous that all Konkomba should henceforth unite so that our welfare and well being can be assured; resolved to reinforce our unity by coming together. (Talton 2010:152)

From the preamble one can surmise that their central purpose is the quest for unity. The appeal for, and the value of, unity cannot be missed from this introductory statement of their constitution. The aims of the constitution echo the Konkomba's desire to affirm their identity and to mobilise all their resources for their well-being and that of the wider society. The translation of the Bible into the Konkomba language coincides with this search and thus furthers the Konkomba cause, that is, their ethnic pride.

4.12 Education and literacy

Serious formal Western education among the Konkomba did not take off until in the 1950s when the Evangelical Presbyterian Church (EPC) and the Catholic church, who each have education as part of their missionary strategy, came to the Saboba area. With the coming of these two missions into Konkombaland, a lot of schools were opened. Though the AG church was the first to be stationed in Konkombaland, they concentrated on their clinic at Saboba rather than schools. In the area of education, therefore, the Catholics and Presbyterians have empowered the Konkomba even though they began work there later than their first missions to the Dagomba. One of the setbacks for the Konkomba in relation to formal education is the use of Dagbani instead of Likpakpaaln in Konkomba schools. That the Konkomba language was not developed in these schools may have been because this was not permitted by the government, or perhaps for other reasons.

4.13 Social organisation

The social structure of the Konkomba consists of the extended family, the lineages and the clans. As a patrilineal society, the Konkomba usually trace their genealogy through their patrilineal extended family and then to their patrilineages among their ancestors (Tait 1961:72). These lineages compose the clans, which are seen as the building blocks of their society. It can be argued that the key to understanding the Konkomba society lies in how clanship works.

Each clan has its totems such as the *Lipaar* 'gorilla', *Unpin* 'crocodile' and *Ku* 'snake', each with its own *liyajakubi* 'taboos' (Lidorio 1999:9). With this knowledge, communicators of the Christian message were guided on how to transmit the Good News message appropriately through the social structures of the Konkomba. In chapter six we will see that the expatriate Bible translators lived among the Konkomba and studied their social structure and that the knowledge of that structure informed them in their translation work.

Traditional Konkomba decision-making processes involve many consultations, in which all those who have a stake in the issue are included (Lidorio 199:113). Decisions are collectively taken and owned. Consensus-building amongst the Konkomba makes them united and strong in crises and enables them to repel external aggression. In addition, since external religious influence (Islam) on the Konkomba was not as pervasive as it was among the Dagomba, Konkomba traditional structures and practice remain more apparently intact and influential today.

4.14 The traditional beliefs and worldview of the Konkomba

4.14.1 *Uwumbor* 'supreme God'

In his "Some Random Notes on the Customs of the Konkombas," A. W. Cardinall records that the Konkomba "have no idea what he [God] was or is."[28] However, Cardinall's perspective of the Konkomba perception of *Uwumbor*[29] could not be accurate, for the Konkomba were not, by any means, ignorant of God.

Froelich, also writing on the Konkomba, concluded that: "We discerned the belief in a creator, monitor and source of life whom we call 'God.'" He goes on to state the testimony of the Konkomba themselves: "There is somebody who made us, something which is stronger than we are, this is *Woumbor*." In Konkomba language there is no gender differentiation in the use of the pronoun. *Uwumbor* is neither male nor female but because of the use of English language there is the problem with using the male pronoun. *Uwumbor* is perceived as the supreme God and Creator.

Froelich's text below bears ample evidence that God is well known to the Konkomba, for to them

> *Woumbor* is the Creator who made the earth, heaven and men, nobody knows exactly how he did it. Nobody can see him nor represent him; his dwelling place is unknown, it is the place of the dead, or rather of their *ouwins*, it is perhaps in heaven. *Woumbor* is constantly watching over his creation; if not, people would all die. When God is strong, people too are vigorous and have many children. God has in mind

---

[28] PRAAD, Accra. ADM 56/1/91 Cardinall, A. W.
[29] The name of the Konkomba traditional God is spelled variously by different authors: *Woumbor*, *O-Wun-bour*, or *Uwumbor*. Except when directly quoting an author, we will use *Uwumbor* as the standard spelling.

what is good and not what is evil, he punishes the wicked by sending sickness to them, often it is leprosy. People pray to *Woumbor* to ask for children, food, long life, cattle herds, many wives and even drink and silver. *Woumbor* punishes the murderers: if a man has killed your son and you are too weak or old to revenge yourself, then you take a white fowl, and addressing God directly without calling the ancestors, you ask of him the death of the murderer....

It is God who gives the rain.... The sacrifices made to the Creator are transmitted by the *loual* one prays to; in order that he will transmit the victim it is necessary to operate according to his wishes and offer a victim whose feathers are convenient to him in colour. Thus, it is possible to pray to the Creator himself and offer a white victim whose colour is pleasing to him, or else pray through the intermediary of a *loual* which is more frequent, and in this case the victim has to be pleasing to the *loual*.... We do not know *Woumbor*, we have never seen him; it is he who made everything, the rain and the heat; when it is hot we used to say: "*Aba Woumbor!*" We think he lives in heaven, but perhaps he lives elsewhere. (Froelich 1954:132)

The Konkomba are very clear in their minds of the distinction between *Uwumbor* on the one hand and the *louar'k* 'spirits' and *kenjaa* 'gods' on the other. The latter derive their authority from the former. Thus, the spirits and gods cannot act on their own volition without the permissive will of *Uwumbor*. The latter are therefore seen as conduits and the former as the source and ultimate decider of every action. In very critical situations these intermediaries are by-passed and *Uwumbor* addressed directly. Thus, whereas *loual* 'spirit (singular)' and *kenjaa* can be dispensed with when it is necessary, *Uwumbor* cannot because he is ultimate. Even where *Uwumbor's* name is not specifically mentioned in prayer, it is assumed that all answers to prayer emanate from him.

For the Konkomba, religion is not abstract but practical and pervades the whole of life. It must have immediate relevance in solving life's problems. In other words, religion is essentially utilitarian and problem-solving in nature. Thus, when the Konkomba embrace the gospel they expect it to transform, guide and bless their lives here and now. In his study of the Konkomba traditional religion, Ronaldo Lidorio concludes that man is at the centre of Konkomba religion. He argues that their prayers indicate that they are geared to promoting human welfare (Lidorio 1999:10).

In spite of the fact that human concerns feature prominently, it is too simplistic to conclude that Konkomba religion is man-centred. The will of the divine is sought in order to live in harmony with him and other spiritual beings in their delicately balanced socio-cultural environment. A critical examination of the Konkomba will refute the idea that religion is purely utilitarian. It is a religion that combines utilitarian function with that of worship of the divine. The fact that the Konkomba do not make a distinction between their spiritual and physical life attests to their holistic perception of worship and the quest for material well-being.

4.14.2 The *kenjaa* 'lesser gods' and 'nature spirits' of the Konkomba

The Konkomba cosmology, which is similar to that of the Dagomba, has a place for *kenjaa* 'lesser gods'. They believe *Uwumbor* is the source of all good *kenjaa*, for he has created them. However, he is opposed to a *kesuo* 'general evil'. To the Konkomba therefore, "the good that comes from *Uwumbor* is conveyed to man through shrines of the earth, of water, of fertility, through the ancestors and through animal sacrifice." Therefore, the gods and ancestors are not rivals of God, but rather part of God's family, where *Uwumbor* is the father or ruler and they are but his children or messengers (Barker 1986:175).

Tait sees a distinction between rites of sacrifice and of prayer in Konkomba. These are religious and depend on the will of the ancestors and of *Uwumbor,* in contrast to the making of medicine or magic, which involves the manipulation of objects. Because of the hostile and unpredictable spiritual and social environment, medicines or magic are cherished amongst traditional Konkomba, for they act as protection against one's enemies (Tait 1961:226).

4.14.3 *Bininkpieb* 'ancestors' of the Konkomba

The Konkomba have a special role for *bininkpieb* '(their) ancestors' because they serve as a vital source of authority (Lidorio 1999:52). They often invoke the ancestors whenever important decisions are being made or when conflicts need resolution. Just as with the Dagomba, it is the diviners who determine the will of the ancestors and prescribe solutions. In Lidorio's analysis of the Konkomba and the ancestors he concludes, "[The] lives of the living are subject to the present will of the ancestors" (Lidorio 1999:43). Thus, the ancestors serve as invisible "police" ensuring that the Konkomba live rightly and act appropriately towards one another. The ancestors promote morality in that they punish the deviants and reward the morally upright in society. Also, because the living Konkomba aspire to join the ranks of the ancestors when they die, they strive to live upright lives on this earth in order to be eligible for ancestorship. Lidorio's conclusion that the lives of the living are subject to the will of the ancestors is, however, debatable. If the ancestors themselves are subject to *Uwumbor,* their powers are necessarily limited to the level of intermediary roles and therefore *Uwumbor* himself can overrule their pronouncements.

4.14.4 *Oubwa* 'diviners'

Konkomba soothsayers, otherwise known as diviners, play an important and indispensable role in the daily living of the community. These *oubwa* are perceived to be close to the supernatural beings and can determine their wishes. For this reason, any misfortune or crisis is not taken lightly or at its face value; the spiritual cause is often sought (Barker 1986:136). Thus, they do not only provide guidance, they equally provide avenues to securing protection. Security is fundamental to the Konkomba who are very much aware of an array of enemies they have to contend with daily.

Being keenly aware of the universe with both benevolent and malevolent spiritual beings, the Konkomba patronise the *oubwa's* services in order to navigate safely to their destination in this complex environment. The coming of other religions among the Konkomba has brought challenges to these *oubwas* because these religions also provide parallel services of guidance and security. For instance, Christian pastors and Muslim *mallams* also carry out these functions for their members and the general society.

4.14.5 *Njog* 'sorcerer's medicine'

The Konkomba term *njog* literally means 'sorcerer's medicine' (Tait 1961:232). *Luul*, for example, is for vanishing and for protection against bullets and sharp metal edges. As warriors and hunters, the Konkomba would need protection against wild animals and enemy soldiers. Vanishing medicine that is believed to enable people to vanish from their enemies and dangerous situations would therefore be attractive to the Konkomba as it addresses their need for protection. *Njog* protects the person who possesses the medicine but can be harmful to others.

In the light of the Konkomba primal worldview, which recognizes the reality of the power of spirits and bad medicines, the Konkomba live in perpetual fear and suspicion of their neighbours. For this reason, they take all the necessary precautions not to fall victim to harmful *njog* medicines.

4.14.6 *Kesuo* 'witchcraft/sorcery'

The Konkomba believe that witchcraft *kesuo* is not inherited but acquired, unlike the Dagomba who hold the view that it can be both inherited and acquired. Furthermore, the Konkomba believe that witches or sorcerers can kill for many reasons, including pleasure. Very much aware of this reality, the Konkomba are careful when receiving nuts or drinks from other people, as they might be potential suspects with respect to witchcraft (Tait 1961:233). Witchcraft is very much feared, and as a result, witches are isolated and camped in designated villages of Gnani near Wapuli. The shrines in these villages are believed to have the power to de-witch those accused.[30]

The majority of Konkomba hold the view that witches do not operate entirely in the spiritual realm; they also operate through physical objects and animals. They are believed to fly in the night in the form of a ball of fire. Furthermore, they believe witches operate in disguise and work through animals such as snakes, cats and others in order to harm people. Although either men or women can be witches, it is usually the women who are accused of witchcraft. When it was suspected that a witch had killed somebody in traditional society, that person's corpse was carried round the village to find the culprit (Manoukian 1951:93, 94).

4.15 The Konkomba and Islam

The Konkomba tend not to be attracted to Islam. As we noted above, those Konkomba who desire to be Dagomba adopt both Islam and the Dagomba lifestyle. Most Konkomba, however, have perceived Islam as the oppressor's religion because of its association with the Dagomba.

The Reverend Moses Mulingna Bakar, a Konkomba and minister of the EPC, Ghana, notes that the Konkomba encounter with Islam coincides with the Islamisation of Dagbon in the seventeenth century. Muslim clerics who accompanied traders were the initial propagators of Islam in Dagbon, which includes Kikpapkan (Konkombaland). These Muslim traders and clerics settled in Yendi, the traditional capital of Dagbon, for protection under the Dagomba king. From there they spread out to other parts of the kingdom including Konkombaland.

Muslim traders such as the Hausa, Wangara and Mossi settled and traded among the Konkomba. Though these Muslim settlers did not systematically reach out to convert the Konkomba to Islam, they maintained their Muslim identity in their quarters and portrayed Islam as superior to the traditional religion (Bakar 1988:15ff.). Thus, the battle lines were drawn between Konkomba traditional religion and Islam. A social gulf as well as a spatial one was created between the Konkomba and the settlers. The implication for this is that few Konkomba would embrace Islam, as it was seen as a religion of aliens and particularly those who had connections with slave raiders and slave traders in whose hands the Konkomba suffered immensely.

Bakar further observes that the Muslims did not underrate or deny Konkomba traditional religion even though they felt their religion to be superior. On the contrary, the Muslims have similar beliefs and adopt magical rituals to confront a rather hostile world, which is in consonance with the Konkomba traditional approach. Some of the rituals Muslims adopt to ward off evil include "amulets, charms, recitation from the Qur'an." In this

---

[30] PRAAD Accra. ADM 56/1/91.

last case, verses from the Qur'an are written on a wooden slate which is then washed, and people drink the washing water "to prevent evil forces as well as offer good luck for trading" (Bakar 1988:19).

4.16 The Konkomba traditional festivals

The Konkomba have fewer festivals than the Dagomba and these have no links with Islam. The reason might be found in Ross Gaskin's explanation that "the Konkomba developed a hatred for and a parallel resistance to the advances of the Islamic culture, a dislike which has passed down the ancestral line" (Gaskin 1986:11). Thus, the Konkomba festivals are spared the onslaught of Islamic interpretations of what are traditional festivals. In Konkomba festivals therefore, we experience unadulterated traditional celebrations.

Peter Barker (1986:36) explains that Konkomba festivals tend to be celebrated at the clan level, rather than at the larger ethnic group level. He identifies only the yam festival and a simple form of the fire festival known as *Namisei*, which are celebrated at the Konkomba ethnic group level. Sacrifices to the ancestors are commonplace in the Konkomba festivals. The celebrations are not political in nature but are for the preservation of the clan. In the Konkomba traditional festivals, the traditional priests, *ten'danba*, take predominant roles.

Ross Gaskin, who lived among the Konkomba, mentions two other important festivals which are communal and involve the whole ethnic group. These are the Six Day Market festival and the Saboba Easter festival. These two more recent festivals appear to have been developed by the Konkomba in an effort to overcome what they perceive as their marginalisation. Gaskin provides evidence from a letter written by a Konkomba pastor that outlines the objectives of the Saboba Easter festival:

1. To make Konkombas aware that they have a home town and the need to develop that town.
2. To make sure they have not forgotten their traditional dance and also to entertain strangers. In order to see another form of modern dance.
3. To bring Konkombas to the national level whereby their ethnic group will be recognised by the government and also to look back into the past to see what their forefathers were able to do and the mistakes they did and what corrections they can do. To make them aware that whatever disturbs, it does not matter, they are one.
4. To help Konkombas be able "to read and write and through this be able to read the Word of God for themselves, to be able to settle their own cases without taking it to any other tribe...". (Gaskin 1986:36)

In this letter, one can see glimpses of Christian influence on the Konkomba, which we shall examine later. The Bible in their mother tongue and Konkomba literacy are now integral parts of their social life. These are seen as the means of affirming their identity and promoting their empowerment.

Kwame Bediako appreciated the deeply spiritual value of traditional festivals and challenged Christians to embrace them, though not uncritically. He spoke persuasively at a Ghana Institute of Linguistics, Literacy and Bible Translation (GILLBT) seminar in 2000, that vernacular Christianity will have to consider seriously the deeply rooted cultural events, in order to attract mother-tongue speakers into the Christian faith. This conviction is based on the belief that every culture has been uniquely prepared to receive the Christian message of salvation.

4.17 Traditional ritual and belief

4.17.1 Marriage

The Konkomba place a high premium on marriage, hence their practice of infant betrothal. This practice involves the giving of infant girls to young men in their early twenties in marriage. Another aspect of this is that families practice exchange marriage of girls. The traditional bride price includes corn which is paid yearly during the courtship. In the event a marriage does not occur as a result of death or marriage to another man, the bride-price corn is not repayable (Manoukian 1951:101–112).

The effect of infant betrothal of girls is that men delay their marriage to about the age of forty. Also, since the girls were given to men in their infancy, their consent was not sought which can bring about conflict later between parents and children. Trends in the last couple generations are challenging this practice because many young people want the right to choose whom to marry. In 1986 Barker reported the following social change in this regard: "in 1977 the Konkomba chiefs meeting in Saboba accepted a proposal from the KOYA that girls of 14 years and over should no longer be forced to marry the husbands to whom they were betrothed in infancy" (Barker 1986:175).

Fornication is not an issue among the Konkomba, for a young woman is allowed to enjoy sexual freedom and it is even expected of her to carry a pregnancy to her husband's home. However, as soon as she is married she must renounce all her lovers, for adultery is abominable. Konkomba men jealously guard their wife and will not hesitate to fight for their right as a husband. The mother-tongue Scripture brings a counterpoint view regarding the Konkomba practice of premarital sexual liberty enjoyed by the unmarried (Manoukian 1951:42).

As described by Barker, most traditional Konkomba marriages are polygamous. Desire for more children, traditional family planning, religious taboos and economic reasons are often cited for this tradition.

From the time a Konkomba man marries he ceases to take meals from his mother (Barker 1986:172–175). Thus, he begins a sort of independence analogous to the biblical injunction of "leaving father and mother and cleaving to his wife" (Genesis 2:24).

4.17.2 Circumcision

Again, according to Peter Barker, the Konkomba do not practice circumcision in their homeland (Barker 1986). Others explain that circumcision is considered a breach in Konkomba traditional thought, for it is not expected of a man to lose any part of his body except through war or accident. It is not that the Konkomba do not practice circumcision at all, rather they do not circumcise babies as Islamicised groups do. According to Ross Gaskin, some Konkomba are circumcised as a rite of passage when entering into adulthood (Gaskin 1986:35).

The likelihood of the Konkomba circumcising their children outside their homeland now is high because of cultural borrowing. For instance, Konkomba students in boarding houses in schools will be tempted to circumcise to avoid being ridiculed by Dagomba and other Islamicised students who look down on the uncircumcised.

4.17.3 Death and burial

As described by Barker, the Konkomba honour their dead and are meticulous in the way they send them on their journey to the other world. Like the Dagomba, the Konkomba promptly bury their dead on the day of death. Different rites are observed for men and women. Whereas Konkomba men are buried in their own villages, the women are buried in their husbands' villages. Another difference is that whereas a Konkomba man is buried naked, a woman is clothed. Like the Dagomba, a Konkomba corpse is usually bathed with herbs. Then the nails and hair are cut and put in a calabash in which they are stored, symbolizing the person's spirit. The calabash is kept in the home town of the deceased person.

The main difference between the two peoples is that the Dagomba have a mixture of the traditional and Islamic practices whereas the Konkomba observe strict traditional customs. Though the Konkomba people view the death of a person as inevitable they nevertheless think somebody might be responsible, so they call on a diviner to determine why the person died (Barker 1986:175).

4.18 Conclusion

The Konkomba share much in common with their neighbours, but also have widely divergent experiences from them. They share a similar worldview,

4.18 Conclusion

attitude to education, ecology and economy. Also, they initially encountered Christianity through Western missionaries, Yoruba traders from Nigeria or southern Ghanaian Akan and Ewe-speaking Christians who went to work in northern Ghana.

The Konkomba history of origin, however, differs remarkably from that of the Dagomba. Whereas the Dagomba claim to be overlords and legitimate owners of Dagbon, the Konkomba perceive them as intruders and claim that they themselves are the indigenes. This victor/victim relationship between the Dagomba and Konkomba is conflict-prone. The former always try to exercise hegemony, which the latter in turn resist with all the might they can muster. The Konkomba have been victims of stereotyping and stigmatisation. Therefore, to reclaim their dignity, the Konkomba have had to fight several battles for recognition and for their rights.

The Konkomba have a primal worldview that embraces a universe where the physical and spiritual are inseparable. They have maintained their identity and belief system even in their encounter with other people and new religions. Although Islam has heavily influenced the Dagomba culture, its influence on the Konkomba is minimal. The socio-cultural context of the Konkomba we have observed has largely influenced the Bible translation into Likpakpaaln. Consequently, it has also determined how the Konkomba interpret aspects of the biblical message that deal with historical matters such as slavery, oppression, exploitation, marriage, peace and the indigenous religious vocabulary.

5

Christian Mission in Northern Ghana: The Dagomba Story

5.1 Introduction

In discussing Christian mission to the Dagomba, certain contributory factors come to the forefront. Among them are Islam, colonialism, the introduction of Western Christianity and translation of the Bible into Dagbani. According to the Right Reverend Philip Naameh (personal communication by interview), the Catholic Bishop of Damongo, denominational rivalry has also influenced the development of this mission. These factors have, in diverse ways, contributed to the conversion story of the Dagomba. Colonial powers in northern Ghana were not wholly allies of Christian missions, as is popularly assumed. In some instances, the colonial authorities were obstacles to the spread of Christianity and instead, enhanced the spread of Islam (McCoy 1988).

This was particularly the case in the introduction of British Indirect Rule. For instance, a colonial policy initially shielded Muslim enclaves in northern Ghana such as Tamale and Wa from Christian missions (Naameh 2001:15). The colonial authorities had this lingering perception that all northerners were Muslims and could speak Hausa. They gave preferential treatment to them because they thought the northerners were good fighters. This might have accounted for their action of getting Muslim "priests" and securing lands for them for their mosques.

5.2 Colonial authorities and Christian mission in the Northern Territories

In looking at the role of the colonial authorities in the Northern Territories we can appreciate the dynamics that influenced the communication of the Christian message among the Dagomba and other northern peoples. The British colonial authorities preceded Western missionaries in northern Ghana, signing treaties of friendship to facilitate trade after making initial contact with the local people. The British policies and relationship with the various missionary bodies in the Northern Territories influenced the evangelisation of the indigenous peoples. Prior to the introduction of colonialism, when the British interest in the Northern Territories was simply to engage in trade, the British had no authority over the peoples of the Northern Territories, so they had to compete with other European nations to win the friendship of the indigenous rulers or chiefs and their peoples. It was in this context that the Fanti surveyor, George Ekem Ferguson, initiated a treaty between the Dagomba and the British, which was signed on 12 August 1892 at Yendi, the seat of the Dagomba king. The Dagomba trusted the British so much that they turned down treaties with the Germans and the French (Arhin 1974:89). The treaty signed sought to give the British some monopoly in matters of commerce among the peoples of the Northern Territories prior to the introduction of full colonial rule in 1898 (Bening 1975a:65–79).

The colonial contact with the Dagomba of northern Ghana was apparently a peaceful one, accomplished through a process of persuasion and friendship. The colonial authorities relied on the surveyor, Ferguson, to initiate the process of signing treaties between the peoples of the Northern Territories and the colonial authorities. There were no colonial wars for the control of the Northern Territories and this situation augured well for the introduction of Christianity later. However, by the time Christianity was introduced in northern Ghana, the colonial authorities had gained power and regulated missionary activities.

In northern Ghana, the relationship between the colonial authorities and missionaries was ambivalent. At the beginnings of Christian missionary work in northern Ghana, although in most places Christian missions were working hand in hand with the colonial administration, the administration started introducing the policy of Indirect Rule, a process which tried to increase the powers of the traditional rulers or chiefs. This was a strategy to channel colonial policies through existing traditional political structures with the purpose of reducing colonial expenditure. To a large extent this policy was successfully implemented in northern Nigeria. Traditional rulers or chiefs were made to carry out the policies of the colonial authorities among their people. Ethnic groups that did not already have chiefs, for instance, had some imposed upon them and in some cases, ethnic groups

5.2 Colonial authorities and Christian mission in the Northern Territories

were brought under other ethnic groups. With this experience, the British set out to replicate policy in the Northern Territories of the Gold Coast. This policy facilitated the spread of Islam which had entrenched itself in the courts of the traditional rulers of the Dagomba. The Dagomba language also assumed a dignified status among many non-Dagomba people.

Initially, the colonial authorities thought that northern Ghana was a Muslim area like northern Nigeria and Christian missions were restricted for fear of courting disturbances from the people. However, the colonial authorities quickly realised that the situations were not the same; whereas northern Nigeria was strongly a Muslim area, northern Ghana was not. Though there were some Muslims, the majority were non-Muslims. As Trimingham explained, the traditional royal courts in West Africa were heavily Islamiscised on the one hand but on the other, they were surrounded by "a sea of pagans" (1962). In other words, the influence of Islam in the royal courts was immense, but it was not wholly embraced by the subjects.

Generally, the colonial attitude toward the peoples of the Northern Territories and the rest of the Gold Coast was to leave the peoples there in their natural environment without Christian missions. From the perspective of the Reverend A. L. Kwansa, a former Synod Clerk of the PCG, the colonial authorities feared that the message of Christian missionaries with its accompanying education, would make the northern people aware of their rights and they would then rebel against colonial rule, as happened with their counterparts in southern Ghana when missionary work created awareness of their dignity and rights. One of the groups doing this work was the Aboriginal Rights Protection Society which was made up of the Christian intelligentsia and activists in the Gold Coast (Kimble 1963:161). Also, the disturbances that erupted between Christians and traditional rulers of the Akyem Abuakwa State might have contributed to this reluctance to support Christian missions in the Northern Territories by the colonial authorities (Debrunner 1967). Furthermore, conflicts between Christians in the Dagaaba traditional area in the north-western part of the Northern Territories could have also prompted the colonial authorities to regulate the activities of Christian missions so that the peace of the area would not be breached.[1]

Another reason colonial authorities restricted Christian missions in the Northern Territories of Ghana is that they feared and thus tried to avoid, possible Muslim resistance and violence. The Nigerian theologian, Yusufu Turaki, recounts a similar situation of colonial restrictions of Christian missions in northern Nigeria as a result of the introduction of the colonial policy of Indirect Rule.[2] Apart from these reasons the colonial authorities believed that Islam was suited to the African because of its civilising role. The fighting spirit of the Muslim was also appealing to the colonial powers.

---

[1] PRAAD Tamale. NRG 8/19/7.

[2] Turaki explained the implications of colonial policy in northern Nigeria in his book, *The British Colonial Legacy in Northern Nigeria.*

Other colonial policies, such as the economic ones, have had an influence on the development of northern Ghana. The most devastating of all the colonial policies in the Northern Territories was the one that sought to exploit the north as a reservoir of cheap labour for the southern Ghanaian mines and plantations (Prah 1975:306). This colonial economic policy led to a massive migration of peoples from northern Ghana to the southern regions of the country, and this migration had implications for Christian missions. In southern Ghana, the northern people were either attracted to the Christian faith because they found good treatment or resented it because the opposite was the case. In this regard, a perception was created that Christianity was the religion of the colonial masters or the southern Gold Coasters or both. Commenting on this colonial economic policy towards the peoples of the Northern Territories, historian Professor Benedict Der noted that it triggered the increasing number of migrants to southern Ghana. He buttressed his argument by citing the following colonial reports: In 1922, the figure of northern migrants was 21,452; then, from 1924–25, it rose to 38,514 and by 1928–29 it increased to 69,486 labourers (Der 1983:316). Its effects have been profound and have contributed to the current *kayaye*[3] phenomenon in Accra and Kumasi.

Analysing the deep effect of British colonial rule on the peoples of northern Ghana, R. B. Bening writes that the region was "condemned to a protracted slumber economically and educationally while the rest of the country was rapidly advancing in all fields of development." Bening cites W. J. A. Jones, a colonial governor, to buttress the fact that there was colonial neglect of the people of northern Ghana. He writes that Jones perceived the people "as an amiable but backward people, useful as soldiers, policemen and labourers in the mines and cocoa farms; in short, fit only to be hewers of wood and drawers of water for their brothers in the Colony and Ashanti" (Bening 1975a:79).

The activities and policies of the colonial authorities produced a negative attitude among the Dagomba towards the Christian faith. For instance, by refusing to allow Christian missions to the Dagomba, the colonial authorities were indirectly telling the Dagomba that Christianity was not good for them. This might have been reinforced by the fact that Islam had been with the Dagomba for about three centuries before the introduction of Christianity.

Relations between colonial authorities and Christian missions

Some of the colonial authorities arrogated to themselves the right to direct missionaries where they could evangelise and where they were restricted from evangelising. As we noted earlier, when missionary bodies applied

---

[3] *Kayaye* is a Hausa term for a porter or load carrier. This is mainly undertaken by females who live in slums in the cities.

for permission to establish work among a particular group of people, the colonial authorities would decide whether it suited colonial interests. They also showed preference for certain missions rather than others. A case in point was A. W. Cardinall, who wrote in 1927, "The Colonial gov't [sic] wished to station missionaries near Lawra but not to open schools since that is at the present reserved by the government for the English Church mission" (Hostetter 1975). There were always some conditions mission bodies had to fulfil in order to gain permission and support from the colonial government, as the minutes by the government dated 14 April 1927 reveal. The minutes stated that the government was prepared to reserve the Lawra-Tumu District of the Northern Territory for the English Church mission on the following conditions:

(i) No education work shall begin until government is satisfied that the mission has sufficient trained teachers to enable it to comply with the Education Ordinance of the Northern Territories.
(ii) The English Church accepts that any government control of its educational activities may be made law in the future.

The District was to be reserved until the 1st April 1930.[4]

Another case was when the White Fathers expressed interest in working in the Tamale area. They were not allowed in that area until the late 1940s.

Ironically, no such restrictions were extended to Muslim missionaries. They could go anywhere they wanted to do their evangelisation. The colonial authorities argued that they had a duty to protect the Christian missionaries and so, when they felt that they could not guarantee their safety, they stopped them. In part this may have been an excuse because there was no apparent threat to the lives of the missionaries, at least as far as the records show. No missionary was ever murdered in the then Northern Territories.

To be clear, there were conflicts between the mission bodies and the indigenous people. On certain issues, the colonial authorities acted as mediators when conflicts arose. In spite of the fact that those authorities fought for more freedom for Christian missions, they nonetheless restricted them when they felt their missionary activities could disturb the peace of the wider society. The nagging question in the minds of Christians still remains, why were there no restrictions on Muslims too?

The perception of the colonial authorities as pro-Muslim attracted international attention to the extent that it was on the agenda of the World Missionary Conference in Edinburgh in 1910. Since there was no single colonial policy on religion as far as the records show, it could have been that colonial policy was most informed by the perception of prevailing circumstances rather than anything else. The colonial authorities defended

---

[4] PRAAD Tamale. NRG 8/19/3.

their policy explaining that they wanted to ensure freedom of worship and to respect existing agreements with local authorities.

Though the colonial authorities did not want to appear antagonistic towards Christian missions, in practice they restricted Christian mission involvement for their own convenience. As one of them remarked to Debrunner: "It has been our policy to make the Northern Territories mission-proof" (Debrunner 1967:216). Lamin Sanneh concluded: "Perhaps colonialism was an obstacle to the growth of Christianity, so that when colonialism ended it removed a stumbling block" (2003:18).

5.3 Beginnings of Christian mission

Several missionary bodies in northern Ghana had embarked upon Christian mission to the Dagomba prior to Bible translation into their mother tongue. The Acting Chief Commissioner of the Northern Territories in an ethnological investigation covering the year 1932, referred to the number of Christian missions operating in the area in these words:

> The Christian missions operating in the Protectorate are three, the White Father mission [Catholic], the Trans Volta mission [Bremen] and the Assemblies of God mission. During the year the Wesleyan mission sent up the Reverend Mr. Wood who has been carrying out investigations on language and customs in the western side of Gonja.[5]

The Reverend Father Oscar Morin, vicar of the White Father Mission for West Africa, articulated the ethos of the Catholic Mission when he wrote to Major Walker Leigh, Chief Commissioner of the Northern Territories about their holistic mission involving the provision of education, health and other socio-economic services.[6]

Father Morin was speaking for what most of the Christian missions believed in his letter to the Chief Commissioner. Mission outreach was more than the mere proclamation of the Christian message. Mission was seen as the proclamation of the gospel and civilisation, that is, social services and westernisation. The missionaries thought that the indigenous people were illiterate, poor and uncivilised; thus, the gospel proclaimed by the missionaries was based on their conviction that Christianity was arbiter of both salvation and civilisation.

Let us turn now to Christian missionary bodies that had made a significant effect on the Dagomba prior to the translation of the Scriptures into their mother tongue. This includes the missionary activities of the Basel Mission/PCG, the Wesleyan/Methodist church, Ghana, the AG church, the

---

[5] PRAAD Tamale. NRG 8/3/46.
[6] PRAAD Tamale. NRG 8/3/46.

5.3 Beginnings of Christian mission

Catholic church and the Baptist church amongst the Dagomba. We will also see that the colonial authorities played an integral role in the missionaries' quest to execute their Christian activities among the Dagomba.

Whenever a missionary could not speak the mother tongue of the recipients of missions, initially preaching was carried out in that missionary's language followed by an interpretation. However, some of the pioneer missionaries from the outset began to learn the language of the indigenous people, and thus began a contribution to the development of those languages.[7] The ultimate goal of these missionaries was to be able to communicate the gospel directly in the mother tongue of recipient communities. As there were no vernacular Scriptures and preachers had to rely on instantaneous translation, there were bound to be a number of problems of faithful rendering of the Scripture in the peoples' mother tongues. This made apparent the need for Bible translation.

Ethnographic studies of the peoples of the Northern Territories were commissioned by the British government. These studies influenced the British colonial authorities' perception of the indigenous religion as well as the relationship between cultural groups. The studies, then, both informed of and dictated colonial policy towards, the northern peoples. What had begun on the basis of partnership with the local people became one of master-servant.

For the indigenous people, initially all *sulinminsi* 'white people' were one. There was no distinction in the Dagomba mind between politicians, traders or missionaries. Christianity of that time was perceived to be a white man's religion. However, attitudes towards and adoption of, the indigenous language eventually helped to distinguish the missionaries' attitude and approach from that of the colonial authorities.

5.3.1 The pioneer missions amongst the Dagomba

The Basel Mission

The Basel Mission, founded in 1815, came from a pietistic Swiss background. Inspector Josenhans of the mission in 1885 verbalised the motivation of the Basel Mission for coming to Africa. He notes:

> For thousands of years black Africa, the slave of all slaves, was lying prostrate on the ground. Crumpled together, she did hide her true face from her tormentors and the traders. We stand under the impression that this Africa now raises her head, unveils her maltreated face and hurries, pouring tears of sorrow and hope, towards Him who delivered her from servitude, shame and death, and who will lead her children to earthly and heavenly freedom. (Debrunner 1967:103)

---

[7] This was the case with the Basel missionaries, the White Fathers and the Assemblies of God missionaries working in northern Ghana.

The motivation for the coming of Western missionaries to Africa was to bring freedom in its entirety to the African. This missionary vision for Africa was also articulated by Sir T. F. Buxton in his famous saying: "Let missionaries and schoolmasters, the plough and the spade, go together. It is the Bible and the plough that must regenerate Africa" (Debrunner 1967:103). With this motivation, the missionaries came well armed, not only to preach the gospel but to improve the lives of Africans.

The Basel Mission was involved in the first missionary venture among the Dagomba. An exploratory trip to Yendi in northern Ghana in 1897 began to lay early groundwork (Berinyuu 1997:5). It was about this time when Ferguson began to establish treaties with the peoples of the Northern Territories on behalf of the British colonial authorities (Arhin 1974).

Soon afterward, on 29 April 1909, Governor Watherson invited the Basel Mission to establish a factory in Tamale, southern Ghana. According to R. Fisch, a few craftsmen were trained by the Basel Mission in Tamale and, along with some government clerks, they constituted a congregation of about seventy. Thus, the Basel influence in the south was already known before their official mission venture moved to Yendi (Debrunner 1967:214).

Holger Weiss, writing on the Basel Mission's work in Yendi, points out that this was possible because of a sudden change in policy by the German colonial authorities in 1911. This enabled the mission to prepare to establish their work in Yendi which was still under German control. He traces the pioneer Basel missionary work to Yendi, as follows:

> Otto Schimming and his wife Julia, Hans Huppenbauer and Immanuel Kies. Schimming and his wife had been on the Gold Coast for some years and had also visited the mission field in Kamerun, whereas Huppenbauer and Kies were studying African languages, among others, Hausa, in Germany. In autumn 1912, the group was ready for departure and arrived on the African coast in December 1912. On the 13th of January 1913, the group arrived at Yendi. (Weiss 2005)

These pioneer missionaries were not total strangers to Africa and were therefore well prepared to embark upon their task. They had some knowledge of African people and their languages. When they settled in Yendi they took to the study of not only Dagbani but also the languages of the neighbouring peoples. Unfortunately, this noble initiative could not be sustained and is one reason for the present low literacy rate among the northern peoples.

As has been noted, the Basel missionaries pioneered their missions in the Dagomba traditional capital, Yendi, in 1913 upon the recommendation of Dr. R. Fisch (Debrunner 1967:215). This attempt was, however, short-lived due to the First World War which brought it to an abrupt end. As a natural reaction, the British could not trust the missionaries who were German and thus perceived as sympathetic to the German cause. In fact, the

5.3 Beginnings of Christian mission

British took four of them, Mr. and Mrs. Schimming, Mr. Huppenbauer and Mr. Kiess, as prisoners of war.

Even though this early pioneer missionary effort left no sustained concrete signs of Christian witness among the Dagomba, a lot was accomplished within their short missionary enterprise. Weiss enumerates some of these:

> Despite the restrictions, Huppenbauer was able to collect an enormous amount of data on Dagbanli and other languages: among others, a card index of 3,000 Dagbanli words, one collection of some 110 Dagomba stories, one collection of Dagomba proverbs as well as an outline of a Dagbanli grammar, a card index of of some 1,800 Basari, some 1,200 Konkomba and some 1,200 Moba words in addition to outlines of Basari Konkomba and Moba grammars. (Weiss 2005)

The Basel Mission's teaching could have had an attraction for the Dagomba whose oral history links them to the patriarch Noah of the Bible. (Tamakloe 1931:1–3). It is interesting to note, however, that a Dagomba Muslim, writing on the history the Dagomba, also claims that the people group comes from Arab ancestry, that is from Shem, Noah's son (Mahama 2004:4). Though this claim cannot be supported with concrete historical evidence, it nevertheless might have facilitated the Dagomba acceptance of the missionaries. This tradition could have also served as a cultural key that the missionaries used in the evangelisation of the Dagomba to show them that they were no strangers to God's covenant. The historicity of the myth notwithstanding, it is in congruence with God's covenant with Noah, which essentially stresses God's desire to save all mankind. Working from this premise, we can argue that Christian mission to the Dagomba had been anticipated by their history.

At first the missionaries thought of using the trade language, Hausa, for evangelisation. Fortunately, they were quick to realise the inappropriateness of Hausa and so adopted the indigenous language, Dagbani. By that action, these pioneer Basel missionaries adhered to their missionary language policy of employing the mother tongue of recipients of mission and this led to the study of Dagbani (Smith 1966:143–145). Around this period the German-speaking linguists developed the written form of the Dagomba language and later came out with a German-Dagbani Dictionary in 1912, credited to R. Fisch. Within a short period of time these missionaries had made much progress. They could deliver sermons in Dagbani and proceeded to translate the Gospel of Mark (Kwansa, cited in Berinyuu 1997:3–10). Thus, from the outset, the will to translate the Scriptures into the mother tongue existed among the Basel missionaries. Dagbani was studied first and then an attempt was made to investigate its relationships with other local dialects. According to Smith, at the end of 1915 Huppenbauer was able to read a portion of the Christmas story for the first time in Dagbani.

In general, the Dagomba response to the Christian message was discouraging and could be traced to the influence of Islam in Dagbon royal courts and in society generally which created suspicion towards Christianity. Consequently, it took much effort to win the trust of the Dagomba. At the inception of the Christian mission, Islam had already gained a prestigious status; it was an honourable thing to become Muslim in Dagbon. Even a superficial adherence to Islam was sufficient to create a formidable barrier between the Dagomba and Christian preaching. Because of this attitude of the adult Dagomba, the hopes of the missionaries for future outreach to the Dagomba rested in the small school that was begun in January 1914 with a few boys (Smith 1966:145). As the Basel Mission was ministering in eastern Dagbon, the Wesleyan Mission was seeking permission from the colonial authorities to work in western Dagbon.

The Wesleyan Mission

According to a letter from the Acting Commissioner, Southern Province, on 16 May 1913, a Wesleyan Mission had been started at Tamale. This was after some heated arguments between the colonial authorities and the missionary Reverend H. G. Martin. When the colonial authorities finally gave permission for the Wesleyan Mission to be stationed in Tamale, stringent rules had been laid down demanding that "the religion of pagan boys at Tamale school must not be interfered with until the permission of parents is given in the presence of a Commissioner." In spite of these initial restrictions, the pioneer school children showed some interest in the Christian religion. A colonial report states, that "20 boys attending Tamale Government Primary School received permission from their parents and through the court to receive religious instruction."[8] Two of the Dagomba children who showed interest in the Christian religion were from the village of Zugu in the Tamale area. They had had their parents' permission to attend religious classes and the Provincial Commissioner's office attested to this from the letter dated 15 February 1915. Apart from the children getting permission from their parents, the Provincial Commissioner also required them to see him for the final permission.[9] Continued opposition to the mission from the Chief Commissioner was finally resolved by the Colonial Secretary in 1913, in a letter pointing out that the "[g]overnment has no power to prevent the establishment of a mission in the N. T. Therefore, the Secretary of State has approved the establishment of a Wesleyan Mission in the N.T."[10] This intervention helped tremendously in the establishment of the Wesleyan Mission in the Northern Territories.

---

[8] PRAAD Accra ADM 56/1/160, Case No 7/1913.
[9] PRAAD Accra. ADM 56/1/160.
[10] PRAAD Accra. ADM 56/1/160, Case No 7/1913.

5.3 Beginnings of Christian mission

When the final permission was granted, the Wesleyan Mission was given a plot of 400 feet by 400 feet in Tamale on the Yapei road, on 11 June 1913. Buildings were subsequently constructed by the mission for work among the Dagomba in the Tamale area. Apart from preaching, the missionaries also engaged in social activities to make life more bearable for the indigenous people.[11] However, a letter from S. N. Nash, Acting Commissioner, South Province, reported that these Wesleyan Methodist Mission buildings were in a deplorable state, prompting the Provincial Medical Officer to ask for them to be pulled down in September 1916.[12]

One wonders why the mission's buildings only survived three years while the eventual cessation of work amongst the Dagomba took a much longer time. Still, the brief duration of Wesleyan missionary activities among the Dagomba did not enable them to formulate a lasting mission strategy to reach the Dagomba. In particular, they did not embrace the use of Dagbani as a focal missionary strategy. Even to the date of this writing the Wesleyan Methodists have not been able to win the confidence of the Dagomba people because the denomination is perceived to be a foreign *Kambonga* church.[13]

5.3.2 Role of southern Christians

Though southern Ghanaian Christians did not make much progress with respect to converting the Dagomba, there were a few successes chalked up by the church which later Christian bodies would build on to establish the church in the Tamale area. Civil servants who were Christians from southern Ghana were to become the nucleus of a United church out of which several denominations eventually emerged. The colonial records support the existence of this Christian community for there was a request from the Chief Commissioner's office on 17 January 1921 for baptism of children of native officials of the Public Works Department. In response, the Reverend Robert Fisher accompanied the Governor to baptise the children in Tamale.

5.3.3 The challenges to the Christian mission enterprise

There were several reasons the early Christian mission outreach did not accomplish their goals among the Dagomba. The first phase of missionary outreach to the Dagomba was met with a lack of enthusiasm on the part of the colonial authorities, especially in the Tamale area.[14] Another challenge had to do with the outbreak of the First World War in 1914 and then its aftermath. The more formidable challenge to Christian mission success, however, was the entrenchment of Islam in Dagomba life and culture.

---

[11] It is reported that a certain woman who was being "hounded" because of a witchcraft accusation, took refuge in the Wesleyan Mission in 1913.
[12] PRAAD Accra. ADM 56/1/160, Case No 7/1913.
[13] *Kambonga* is a northern Ghanaian term for a southerner, especially the Asante.
[14] PRAAD Accra. ADM 56/1/160, Case No 7/1913.

These challenges notwithstanding, fresh attempts were made by Christian organisations to bring Christianity to the Dagomba after a fallow period of about two decades.

5.4 Another phase of the Christian mission to the Dagomba

In the second phase of Christian mission to the Dagomba, the AG took up the challenge. They were followed by the Catholics, the EPC, the PCG and the Baptists (Smith 1966:146).

5.4.1 The Assemblies of God mission to the Dagomba

In this phase of missionary outreach to the Dagomba, the AG Mission comes to the fore. In her account of their mission in British West Africa, Elizabeth A. Galley Wilson, a former missionary in north China and the Philippine Islands, Instructor and Director of Missions, Southwestern Bible Institute, Waxahachie, Texas, writes about the increasing cooperation from the colonial authorities:

> The governments in British West Africa are on the whole friendly toward Protestant missions, although some difficulty has been experienced in entering territory that is strongly Moslem in religion because the British government feared that the introduction of Christianity into strong Moslem areas would cause a break down of the established political system due to the interrelation between Islam and politics. This difficulty has been largely overcome and Protestant missions have been permitted in some areas without causing any serious difficulties. (Wilson 1955:67)

Thus, the British colonial authorities permitted the AG to start their missionary work in Dagbon without the restrictions the early missions had experienced. Ms. Wilson reported that in January 1931 the Governor of the Gold Coast granted them permission to work in the country.

The AG church came into Ghana in 1931 by way of Burkina Faso. The pioneer missionaries were Reverend Lloyd and Margaret Shirer. Wilson elaborates that in October 1931, Reverend and Mrs. Shirer, together with Miss Beulah Buchwalter and Reverend Guy Hickcok, began work at Yendi. Both Miss Buchwalter and Reverend Hickcok died in 1932, he at the Tamale hospital while in service (Wilson 1955:73). It is baffling that a colonial official record reports only the death of Hickcok without any mention of Miss Buchwalter's passing, even though they both died the same year, and both were buried in Yendi. It is plausible that the colonial officials did not want to recognise female missionaries in the Northern Territories at that time.

5.4 Another phase of the Christian mission to the Dagomba

In an interview with the Reverend Wumbee in 2004 the author learned that the Shirers' initial intention was to settle in Tamale, the capital of the then Northern Territories. However, upon the advice of the *gulkpena*, the Tamale chief, they settled in Yendi, the Dagomba traditional capital. The rationale behind this advice was that he, the *gulkpena*, did not find it expedient to receive the missionaries without the appropriate traditional protocol. He saw himself as the son of the *ya na*, and therefore should accord to the king the dignity of first hosting the missionaries. The acceptance by the *ya na* of the missionaries then paved the way for subsequent settlements of Christian workers in other parts of Dagbon.

To facilitate missionary work among the people in Yendi, the Shirers immediately erected two dwelling houses and a school. They then began to study the local language. Within a year, they had baptised five converts (Wilson 1955:74). They also introduced the plough to improve efficiency in agricultural pursuits. Very quickly thereafter they were able to go round the surrounding villages within a ten-mile radius of Yendi to provide first aid and to preach the gospel.[15]

In February 1932, missionary H. B. Garlock and his family arrived in the Gold Coast from a previous work in Sierra Leone. When they came to Tamale in 1933, they built a residence and then began to work (Wilson 1955:74). These Western missionaries did not begin in a vacuum since there were already southern Ghanaian Christians who had organised themselves to worship. The records show that the AG missionaries took over the management of the group, known as the Tamale Christian Church.[16] It is worth noting that Africans initiated this church comprising various denominations from the colony. Most of these people were government officials or employees. This fact confirms the point Sanneh made about the primacy of indigenous initiative with respect to missionary activities in Africa (1983:244).

The onset of the Second World War seriously affected white missionary work in the Gold Coast. According to Wilson, there were only two AG missionaries, Mr. Arnold Weston and his wife, who were left in the Northern Territories of the Gold Coast in 1944 (Wilson 1955:74). Once more, it is baffling that Wilson omits the name of Weston's wife. It seems to be another case of female marginalisation in Christian mission history.

In an interview, the northern superintendent of the AG church, the Reverend Solomon Nyaba, related that the missionaries came from the north, specifically from Burkina Faso, instead of along the traditional missionary route, which was from the coast to the hinterland. He explained that they came from the eastern border and settled first in Bawku in the upper east and then moved to Yendi. Prior to settling in Yendi, they had already been using the route when traveling from the coast to what is now Burkina Faso. It was on one of these occasions that they were convicted to embark

---

[15] PRAAD Tamale. Colonial report for Yendi District, 1932.
[16] PRAAD Tamale. Colonial Annual Report, 1932.

on a missionary outreach to the Dagomba. The Reverend Nyaba explained further that because the missionaries did not use the Paga border, they started the AG church in Yendi, Tamale and up to Walewale before going up to Bolgatanga to do the same. Another AG minister of the Bilpela AG church near Tamale elaborated. He related how the Reverend Shirer and his wife brought the church from Ougadougu, via Gambaga, to Yendi and how Shirer won the hearts of the Dagomba people. He was known for having been sensitive to, and for identifying with, the Dagomba to the extent that the *ya na* enskinned him, that is, gave him the chiefly title, *malgu na* 'development chief'. He endeared himself to the traditional rulers by helping with development projects such as schools, night school or adult education, mass education and clinics.

When in 1932 the AG opened its station in Tamale, they embarked upon literacy and medical work. Dagbani primers and other literature were produced, and the world of the Dagomba expanded with many more of them gaining access to the literate community. It was the graduates of this literacy programme who formed the initial crop of indigenous AG church pastors – who subsequently facilitated the rapid spread of the gospel to other parts of the Gold Coast. Though the need to have Dagbani Scriptures was realised as the bedrock upon which their work was to succeed, this did not materialise until four decades later with the completion of the New Testament translation.[17]

Dagbani was used as the medium of instruction in both the AG church and its seminary at Kumbungu, near Tamale. The Reverend Nyaba explained that the missionaries were losing the graduates of their literacy programmes to the secular government. To forestall this, they promoted the use of the vernacular to retain the young people in the church's ministry. Furthermore, though sociological and political expediency contributed to the use of the indigenous language, there was also a theological reason: the fact that God desires all people to hear His word in their mother tongue.

When several local Christians were interviewed to find out why many Dagomba do not respond very enthusiastically to the Christian message, though they were the first in the Northern Region to host the missionaries, they laid the problem on the doorstep of the influence of Islam on the traditional politics and life of the Dagomba. Muslims are involved in every sphere of Dagomba life. As noted earlier, the immense influence Islam has had on the traditional rulers who wield a lot of power over their subjects tends to make the Dagomba resist Christianity.

The influence of Muslims on the social aspects of Dagomba life includes the naming ceremony of babies, funerals and sorcery in the form of equipping traditional fighters with magical powers, marriage and Qur'anic schools. Ironically, whereas the AG missionaries encouraged the use of the mother tongue, they imposed certain prohibitions which tended to

---

[17] The Dagbani New Testament was completed and launched in 1974.

undermine Dagomba cultural practices. For instance, the chewing of kola by its members was prohibited even though it is the symbol of friendship in social functions such as marriages, funerals, festivals and others. By such a prohibition, the Dagomba converts were being alienated from their people. Kola was prominent in traditional religion and other functions, hence, the missionaries' prohibition of it, as they were suspicious of any practice or objects associated with the traditional religion.

To local Christians, the Dagomba situation in relation to Christian mission is not a hopeless one. There is a Dagomba proverb that says, *"jangbiog yi kuli waggi, di maal la gbabo shee"* 'a long walking stick always has a place to hold', to the effect that God has made it possible for some Dagomba people to respond to the Christian gospel. One Dagomba pastor took consolation in his belief that the Holy Spirit has opened the eyes of the Dagomba to see the truth of Christianity. This is in agreement with Jesus that "by its fruit you will know the tree," and attributes the recent positive response of rural Dagomba communities to Christianity to an increased number of Dagomba preachers. Many up-and-coming young Dagomba are now receiving literacy and formal education and most significantly, theological training.

The situation in Tamale, however, does not seem to suggest that Muslims are abandoning their religion for Christianity, as there has been a revival of Islam in the Tamale metropolis. What is even more worrying is the emergence of militant Islam that tries to halt the growth of Christianity. That challenge notwithstanding, there has been faithful Christian witness in Dagbon with positive results. For instance, thousands of young Dagomba have enrolled in a Bible correspondence course under the auspices of the Ken Radach Memorial Centre. It is not known how many secret Christians there are among the Dagomba who fear Muslim persecution.

A Dagomba Christian recalls the persecution he suffered at the hands of his Muslim family and friends. He was consoled that his father did not oppose him until he decided to go to the Bible School. He explained that his father's hostility was not on a doctrinal basis, but rather, it was on an economic basis, fearing that he was leaving his more lucrative teaching career for a poorly paid pastoral ministry with the AG church. His father's fears were understandable because the pastors of that church in northern Ghana are poorly remunerated. With time however, he was reconciled to his father who proved to be even more supportive than his siblings. His father's tolerant attitude was partly due to the accommodating nature of West African Islam that characterised the early Dagomba Islam (Sorkpor 1967).

The general apathy of the Dagomba towards Christianity notwithstanding, God's word among them has not been in vain. Conversions had taken place during the early years of mission work and continue to increase with every passing year. Some prominent church leaders have been Christians for over fifty years. For example, the Bilpila-*Naa*, Abukari Tiah, is a devout Assemblies of God Church member.

5.4.2 The Catholic church

Although there were early deliberate attempts to evangelise northern Ghana by the Basel Mission, it was the Catholics who actually made significant headway in the evangelisation of the northern people, as early as 1906 (Berinyu 1997:1). The Society of Missionaries of Africa, also known as the White Fathers, who brought Christianity into northern Ghana that year (Der 1974:41). This coincided with the assumption of British colonial rule of the then Northern Territories.

According to available records, the colonial authorities initially hesitated to grant the missionaries permission to operate in the northern part of the Gold Coast. The colonial policy was at variance with that of the missionaries, whom the colonial authorities threatened to expel in 1907 (Der 1974:41, 42). When the authorities finally did authorise the missions, they still tried to curtail their movements and activities (McCoy 1988:29). For instance, the missionaries, as noted earlier, were not given approval to evangelise Tamale and Wa, places perceived to be Muslim strongholds.

Another area where the colonial powers did not agree with the missionaries was language policy. Whereas the authorities wanted English to be the lingua franca, according to McCoy, the missionaries preferred that the native language be developed and used for evangelisation. The White Fathers had to face this opposition from the British as they resorted to the study and use of Kasem, the language of the people of Navrongo where they were permitted to settle. This conflict over language policy is understandable. Whereas the colonialists were eager to establish control and train the local people to service their political goals for the colony, the missionaries wanted to achieve deep conversion, which was far more likely with the use of the native language. In another vein, the colonial government officials feared that with the use of the mother tongues, the missionaries would gain more favour and power among the local peoples (Howell 1997:114).

The missionaries' nationalities and mission orientations were also contributory factors in determining their acceptability by the colonialists. Since denominations and missionary bodies held allegiance to their countries of origin, the colonialists were wary of entertaining just any mission body. They had to ascertain where the loyalty of the mission bodies operating under their jurisdiction lay. This explains why the British were reluctant to grant permission to French and German missionaries to operate in the Gold Coast. This is not to say that the British colonialists supported all the missionary bodies from their own country. Benedict Der cites cases in which Wesleyan missionaries had conflicts with their British compatriots (1974:41–61). The White Fathers were compelled to replace their Superior, who was French, with a British subject (McCoy 1988:30).

According to Fr. Olivier Lecestre, a former missionary to the Dagomba, Catholicism was introduced to Tamale in 1927 by a Fanti young man, Kwasi

5.4 Another phase of the Christian mission to the Dagomba

Abakah. He discovered other Catholics who had moved into the area, and they started meeting on Sundays in 1928. By this time there were Catholics from southern Ghana who were civil servants working in Tamale before career missionaries arrived there. In March 1929, the then Tamale chief, Dakpiema Busagri, gave the Catholic Mission a parcel of land to erect their first building. In 1929 around September, the chapel was ready, and priests were invited from Bolgatanga to dedicate it. The first mass was also celebrated on this occasion (Lecestre 1996:2).

From the outset, the White Fathers saw the task of evangelising the Dagomba as a herculean one. Lecestre explains some of the sociocultural barriers they encountered:

> One of the obstacles that the Fathers had to overcome in their early days was the fact that some of the Southerners kept chasing Dagomba children away from the mission grounds. Dagombas even call our church *Kambonsi Jangli* 'the mosque for Ashantis'. Simon Atakora stood out among them by his ability to relate with Dagombas. (Lecestre 1996:10)

Another challenge that Lecestre identified was with the foundation of their mission, working by means of the Dagomba social structure:

> Right at the beginning the Fathers had already felt the need of a foundation in Yendi; Dagombas in Tamale and Western Dagbong, who could not understand why the White Fathers had not opened a mission in Yendi, had asked them: 'if as you say, you are coming to teach us God's path, why do you not go first to our father in Yendi, the *ya na*, and then he himself will tell us?' The fact that there was no foundation at Yendi in the early days of the mission greatly lessened the influence of the missionaries among Dagombas.... But Yendi was S. M. A. territory in the vicariate of Keta, which included the whole of British Togoland; and how could the Fathers explain to the Dagombas that Yendi was S. M. A. [Missionary Society of Africa] territory and not White Father's territory? (1996:11–12)

Mission bodies themselves did not help matters because they were competing against each other (McCoy 1988). Invariably, pioneer missionaries in a given area did not want another competing missionary body there. To avoid confrontations, they resorted to the comity system whereby spheres of influence were determined. The Catholics, for instance, did not want Protestants in the areas they had pioneered. This arrangement did not last long because with the country opening up, many converts had to migrate from their home towns to other places to work in order to earn a living. In the Northern Territories, the Catholics had consolidated their grip on the upper regions. The lower regions of the Northern Territories, however, remained a virgin place with few missions until the 1940s.

As a policy, the White Fathers always devoted time to the study of the language and culture of the people among whom they lived. They therefore adopted the study of Dagbani and translated their mass and scriptural portions into the language. They set up schools and other developmental projects. A night school was established in 1947 and one of its graduates, who learned to read and write English there, is now a prominent contractor in Tamale (Lecestre 1996:12). Benedict Der describes how, also in 1947, the White Fathers in Tamale introduced grinding mills. The new grinding mills particularly lightened the traditional role of women in society, in which they ground flour using mortar and pestle or a stone.

> Their [the grinding mills] introduction in Tamale attracted a large crowd of excited women.... The corn mills helped to take the drudgery out of the lives of women and girls – who had to spend long hours grinding or pounding grains.... This technology affected the domestic life of women in that it has greatly reduced the labour involved in the preparation of food in the home, and women are reluctant to go back to the grinding stones. (Der 1983:361)

Though there are few Dagomba Catholics, the Catholic church has nevertheless done much for the Dagomba and helped transform their lives in the areas of education, health, agriculture, micro credits and relief services. Though Dagomba membership in the Catholic church over the past fifty plus years is not commensurate with their evangelistic efforts, there are at least two Dagomba priests, fruit of their efforts. The Catholic church has reminisced, wondering if the Dagomba would ever embrace Christianity (Boi-Nai and Kirby 1998:533). However, encompassing all Christian efforts, a more optimistic prospect of Christian mission among the Dagomba is that the late start of Christian missions among the Dagomba and other peoples of northern Ghana accounts for the small number of converts. Too much was expected too soon. Mission outreach to the Dagomba, therefore, can be seen with an optimistic view rather than as a failure, especially in the rural Dagomba communities.

Scholars like Vincent Boi-Nai and Jon Kirby do not think the Catholicism offered the Dagomba was utilitarian enough. For example, the Western Christianity that was introduced to the Dagomba did not account for the problem-solving mechanism within the Dagomba culture. Thus, the church did not draw on the indigenous religious resources initially to deal with problems that confront Dagomba Christian converts. In their view, some other issues not addressed by the Catholic church include "problems that involve beliefs and practices concerning fate, dreams, witchcraft, 'bad death,' divination and the ancestors" (Boi-Nai and Kirby 1998:533). Their

5.4 Another phase of the Christian mission to the Dagomba

argument is supported by the fact that these things are not usually the concern of Christian rituals. Yet Christians continue to have these problems. The Catholic church has not adequately helped their members with the tools to solve these fundamental life issues the Christian way. Dagomba response to Christian mission, then, is not so much a case of resistance to the Christian faith itself as its inability to provide them with answers to living meaningful lives. For Boi-Nai and Kirby, "Africans [the Dagomba] are searching for a new unity between faith and culture, and Western Christianity has little to offer unless it can shed its neo-colonial identity" (1998:535). Thus, if the Catholic faith wants to be relevant to the Dagomba, it must shed its Western garb and bring the Dagomba culture on board with their mission.

In the assessment of Western mission to African peoples, Boi-Nai and Kirby concluded that "the official church still carries with it many Western cultural trappings which hinder appropriate responses to their 'African' problems" (1998:546). Drawing their conclusion from their study on "Catholicism and Problem-solving in Dagbon," they seem to echo Der's optimism of the successful conversion of the Dagomba in the not-too-distant future, writing that, "Nevertheless Christianity is having an effect on the lives of Dagombas in deep and lasting ways, especially when it demonstrates God-centred problem solving among village-based Dagomba Christian communities" (1998:546).

Boi-Nai and Kirby do not suggest that Catholic work among the Dagomba was ineffective. They explain that, "despite the initial strong resistance to Catholicism in Dagbon and unsatisfactory attempts to gain converts through schools later on, over the past 25 years the Catholic church has been making some head way with Christian communities" (1998:546).

The Dagomba, especially in the rural areas, are becoming Christians, and many others are also now sympathetic towards Christianity. Dagbani Scriptures will most likely deepen the faith of the Dagomba Christian communities and also help them to evolve Christian problem-solving strategies. The Bible which is the foundational source of Christian beliefs and practices could enable Dagomba Christian communities to cope with pressure from Muslims and traditionalists by helping them to continue to hold on to their identity as Christian and Dagomba.

5.4.3 The Evangelical Presbyterian Church

The EPC worked among the Dagomba in the then Yendi District but has had very little effect on that group. Most of the members of the church in Yendi are Ewe or Konkomba and where the Dagomba are present, they are a negligible number. The Dagomba and Nanumba perceive the EPC as *ayigbe* '(Ewe) church' because of the heavy garb the Ewe church leaders wore. The church's liturgy and music, even in Dagbon, are all Ewe-dominated. Consequently, the Dagomba perceive this church, just as it saw the Catholic church, as one for foreigners and minority ethnic groups. The Bremen Mission did well to develop the Ewe language to the highest level of scholarship (Debrunner 1967:143). This tradition, however, was not continued by their daughter church, the EPC in northern Ghana. Very little was done to develop and use the Dagomba and Konkomba languages.

The EPC set up the Agricultural School and Training College in Bimbilla which have helped the Dagomba and Nanumba significantly, and thus afforded their youth the opportunity to embrace Christianity along with the acquisition of skills. Though the Dagomba and Nanumba have embraced the skills imparted by the mission schools, most of them have turned their backs on Christianity for fear of possible persecution. Mosques can be found on the premises of the schools and Islamic religious rituals are observed. Because of this strong loyalty associated among the Dagomba and Nanumba with respect to Islam, there are few converts to the Christian faith.

The EPC has had more of an effect in other areas like eastern Dagomba and Konkomba with the establishment of developmental projects. According to Ansre, in 1958 the church set up the Yendi Agricultural Station with the support of the *ya na* (1997:219), named Salifu (Billa Billa) III. One achievement of this project, apart from assisting the farmers with extension services, was that it helped to produce the National Farmer (celebration) for 2003.

5.4.4 The Baptist church

The Baptist church in Ghana traces its roots to the Yoruba traders of Nigeria, who carried their faith with them wherever they went, including Ghana. According to historian Marjorie Jones, wherever the Yoruba Baptists settled, they met on Wednesdays and Sundays for worship either in a member's compound or in rented premises. Hundreds of Baptist congregations began that way in Ghana. She notes, however, that these early congregations sent back their tithes and offerings to their home church in Nigeria. Thus, little attention was given to the Gold Coast congregations to build their own chapels (Jones 1967:27, 28).

Continuing in her written history of the Baptist church, *Black Eagle*, Jones recounts how, after persistent requests for missionaries and pastors to the Gold Coast, the Nigerian Baptist Convention responded favourably in 1946. Subsequently, a survey committee was sent to determine the scope of work and recommended that a permanent missionary be stationed there. In February 1947 the Southern Baptist missionary Littleton arrived with his family. Working with Mr. and Mrs. Idowu, they organised congregations and women's groups. Literacy was a great need among church members, so it became an integral part of the church's ministry.

Scrutinising the evangelistic work done so far, Jones reveals that the Baptists' work for some years concentrated only on the migrant Yoruba, and was thus, for a long time, referred to as *Aratafo asore*, 'Yoruba church'. This seemingly inward focus of the Yoruba Baptists might have been because of cultural differences and language barriers. Gradually, the Baptist church of the Gold Coast grew, and in 1956 became independent of the Nigerian Baptist Convention. Mr. Littleton led the Gold Coast Baptists until 1962 when he left the country.

Marjorie Jones traces the history of Baptist work in northern Ghana again to the Yoruba communities and then to the indigenous ethnic groups. In her account, the missionaries Douglas and Sarah Carter settled in Tamale and began a pastors' school. With the help of Mr. James E. Foster, they worked among the Yoruba and began establishing congregations among the Dagomba. Many of the pioneer indigenous northern pastors received their theological training through the literacy programmes, which have been an integral part of the Baptist work in northern Ghana.

Reverend Amo recounts that the Baptists wanted to dismiss the perception that the Baptist church was a White or Yoruba church, and they realised that the future lay in the training of indigenous leaders. With this in mind, Reverend D. C. Cather established the Training Centre in Tamale in 1955. Most of the trainees had very little or no formal education. As adult learners in training for indigenous leadership, their wives were taught along with their husbands, since it was assumed they would work together (Amo n.d.:38).

Apart from the Training Centre, which was meant to disciple and train the would-be leaders, the mission offered the communities medical services. This was in response to the precarious health needs of the northern peoples. Medical doctor George Faile, an American, began this ministry in December of 1956. Nalerigu, in the Northern Region, the traditional capital of the Mamprugu, hosted the Medical Centre which is now renowned for its outstanding medical services. As patients come to the Medical Centre to restore physical health, they are also ministered to spiritually. People from all over the Northern Region of Ghana received help at the Nalerigu hospital. In addition to the curative treatment given at the Medical Centre, they also offer preventative healthcare.

A noticeable shortcoming of the early Baptist Mission in northern Ghana was their lack of providing formal education in the communities in which they served. The Baptists there apparently did not make education a high priority for, not only did they not give formal education programmes to the people in general, they also did not offer higher level theological education for Baptist pastors in Dagbon. Their main strength was that they promoted grass-root churches. With the rapid-paced social changes that were taking place in northern Ghana, they had to respond to the needs of their members or stand the chance of losing their mission in northern Ghana.

The Baptists owe their present day vibrant Dagomba churches to the fact that they have been training the Dagomba whether that was by formal schooling or not. From 1961 to 1984, the Baptist Training Centre in Tamale graduated 46 men and 36 women, all Dagombas. The women were wives of the men who trained to assume Baptist ministry leadership to the Dagomba. Although some of them have died, retired or resigned, a good number of these leaders are still carrying out their ministry to the Dagomba, especially in the rural areas. The first indigenous Dagomba Baptist church was started at Mogla in western Dagbon by a pastor who holds dear both his Dagomba traditions and, equally, his Christian faith.

5.4.5 The second mission of the Presbyterian Church of Ghana to the Dagomba

A renewed attempt by the Presbyterians, the PCG, to evangelise the northern peoples began slowly in the 1940s. But it took many years before northern Christian leaders were recognised by the PCG. The first Ghanaian minister to be ordained in the north was a Gonja man in 1963, the Reverend C. J. Natomah. Northerners were beginning to demonstrate their ability and motivation to assume greater responsibility for the work of the church in their area. Nevertheless, worrisome to the PCG, was the fact that, whereas the Dagomba were the first northern people to be presented with Christianity, they had no minister in the PCG. This was true until after 2007. Currently, three Dagomba ministers have been ordained by the PCG.

To address the needs of the peoples of northern Ghana, the PCG adopted a holistic approach (Kwansa, quoted in Berinyuu 1997:1). The PCG realised early on that leadership development in the north would depend on the educated youth and began a missionary strategy through the schools. Reverend F. Rosingh from the Netherlands volunteered as chaplain in Tamale schools. He began Bible studies, used short dramas, gave personal counselling and encouraged debates on Christianity versus other religions. With lay volunteer workers from the schools and civil servants, a team targeted second cycle institutions. The Dagbani Bible was still not available for these outreach activities. Consequently, all Bible studies were carried out in English, a factor that did not foster indigenous rooting of the Christian faith.

The PCG ministry to the Dagomba began to include formal education. They assumed responsibility for schools in the Tamale and Salaga districts, previously administrated by Local Authority Councils. Nevertheless, the PCG church's impact on education in this area was modest compared to that of the Catholic church. This is evidenced by the fact that comparative conversions among the Dagomba, if any, were negligible. The church, however, persevered in her mission in the face of discouragement and apparent failure.

Thus, the church members did not dedicate themselves only to their mission to the Dagomba, who showed apathy towards Christianity; they moved on to other ethnic groups. As if to make up for an earlier ineffectiveness in their language policy, the PCG undertook to translate into Kusaal,

5.4 Another phase of the Christian mission to the Dagomba

Mampruli and Bimoba, Frank C. Laubach's book, *The Story of Jesus*, Part 1 and Mark's Gospel. With new zeal, a primer was prepared in Kusaal for night school work with the help of SIL's David and Nancy Spratt. Thus, the soil for Bible translation was already being prepared for later major translation and development of northern languages by Bible translation organisations.

By 1966, the PCG in the northern context began to improve in their evangelistic efforts. The PCG Annual Report recorded that there was a steady growth of the church in northern Ghana that year, mostly in the urban centres and among the acephalous ethnic groups (PCG Annual Report, 1966). The stage was being prepared for an enduring evangelistic programme among the Dagomba around the Tamale metropolis.

Mr. A. P. van den Broek, a Dutch agriculturalist, contributed tremendously to the Christian evangelisation of the Dagomba. He and his family arrived in Tamale in 1967. He did not come as a recognised missionary sent by the Netherlands Reformed Church,[18] instead, Mr. van den Broek came by faith that God would provide for his needs. As he was coming into Ghana without the accreditation of the Home Missionary Board of the Netherlands Reformed Church, the PCG had to intervene by sending him a visa on the ship.

Initially, the van den Broeks stayed with the Rosinghs who had worked, as mentioned above, among the students in the Tamale area. The van den Broeks became interested in the student work and joined the Rosinghs in the Tamale chaplaincy work. When he was provided with his own accommodation, Mr. van den Broek initiated the Agricultural Settlement Programme christened "Mile 7" for middle school leavers. The beneficiaries were taught vegetable farming and poultry rearing. The Mile 7 Programme in the Tamale metropolis focused first on the material needs of the target group and subsequently, on its spiritual needs. The programme became so successful that, in 1968, it was fully integrated with the agricultural section of the Christian Service Committee (PCG Report, 1968). Through the van den Broeks other social services undertaken by the PCG included Dagbani literacy and translation of the Old Testament. Ironically, van den Broek was never able to communicate in Dagbani unaided, though his wife learned the language and was the Dagbani reader in the Tamale Unity Church.[19]

The need for literacy and translation in northern Ghana became a recognised need, and therefore embarked upon. The PCG Annual Report of 1968 recounts how delegates from Damongo and Sandema attended the Bible Society Translators' Course at the University of Ghana in Legon. Equally important, missionary initiatives among other ethnic groups were laying the groundwork for Bible translations and the battle against illiteracy.

---

[18] His arrival coincided with a movement in which radical Christian youth groups embraced missions and refused to be held back by orthodox officialdom.

[19] The van den Broeks initially worshipped in the Tamale Unity Church which was nothing but a replica of an urban southern congregation.

Missionary efforts were often fraught with frustrations in the form of disease, poverty, superstition and colonial restrictions. These all affected the training of the indigenous leaders in churches that had been planted. PCG Reports enumerated some of the other setbacks, such as the transfer of southern Christians to northern Ghana. The southern Christians became the nucleus of the PCG in northern Ghana. In fact, in the urban centres, they constituted the majority and therefore exercised some hegemony. Furthermore, the liturgy read, and hymns sung, were in the Twi and Ga languages (Sule-Saa 2000:132).[20] This pervasive perception of southerners' monopoly of the PCG in northern Ghana has given her the label *Kambonga* church. The southern Ghanaian character of the PCG is very pronounced in the urban centres of northern Ghana.

The bane of PCG's missionary work in northern Ghana was the superior attitude of southern Christians over the northerners because of the latter's social and educationally disadvantaged position (Dovlo and Sule-Saa 1999:112–116). For this reason, the PCG appealed to their southern members to interact with the northerners in their mother tongues rather than in Twi, Ga and Ewe. The reasoning for this was that if the southerners considered it appropriate to receive the gospel in their own language, then it was a contradiction for them to deny the northerners the same (PCG Report 1968:129). The church leadership felt that it was only when northerners were made to feel they were in charge that they would embrace the faith as their own and then spread it. Though it took time to change southerners' attitudes, the PCG appeal did not fall on deaf ears, as later reports would show.

The PCG Report of 1968 cites encouraging news of church growth from Gamabaga in the Mamprusi traditional area, Mile 7 in Tamale in the Dagomba traditional area and Salaga in the east Gonja traditional area. The methods of ministry outreach included open-air preaching in the vernacular in compounds and marketplaces, religious instruction in schools and simple Bible talks in hospitals and at clinics. Targeting youth in schools was effective, as the students became the first group of evangelists, lay preachers and ministers. The ministry of the Reverend Rosingh and his team to students in the second cycle institutions in Tamale clearly supports this.

The Reverend Rosingh and his team organised church services and weekend conferences for the Tamale schools. They worked zealously and in a year they had organised twelve weekend conferences with 45 to 50 students, both male and female, at each conference. These conferences consisted of two days of intensive programmes of Bible studies, games, discussions, socio-drama, a panel to answer questions, a special prayer service and thanksgiving with African drumming and dancing. These gatherings were at the cutting edge and were reaching out to the northerners, as the following

---

[20] Although this is still the case in 2017, work is being done to translate the liturgy and hymns into the northern languages.

5.4 Another phase of the Christian mission to the Dagomba

figures reveal: about 60% of the students were northerners of whom 30% were Catholics and the rest from other denominations plus a few Muslims. The weekend conferences were as enjoyable as they were educational. This was recorded in the PCG 1968 report.

The results of van den Broek's ministry were further described in the report as including the formation of the "Braintrust" in the Tamale Government Secondary School to reach the youth of the community. This body served as a think-tank and as such planned lectures with capable speakers. It was also responsible for publicity and the welfare of the participating students. The figures give credible evidence of the effect of the conference. For instance, twelve of the students were confirmed in August and fifty more were being prepared for baptism at the end of the year. The ministry to the students in which the van den Broeks participated when they first came to Ghana must have prepared them to appreciate the northern context well. However, the main problem with this ministry to the students lay in the lack of co-ordination between the local churches and the ministry. A situation therefore arose in which the students were identified as Christians at school but non-Christians outside the school, since there was no opportunity for them to attend church services.

As noted earlier, Mr. van den Broek was a determined man who had set out to leave an indelible Christian mark on the people of western Dagomba. He conceptualised and actualised the Mile 7 Programme. The then Synod Clerk of the PCG, the Reverend A. L. Kwansa, mentioned earlier, described van den Broek's work as "purely agricultural evangelistic." Kwansa acknowledged him in glowing terms in the PCG annual church report, "as a deeply honest, devoted and religious man and an evangelist" (PCG Annual Report, 1973).

Mr. van den Broek's ingenuity was evident in his vision for the Mile 7 Programme which was an innovation comprising the following components:

- A settlement cum extension agricultural work
- Evangelisation, preaching and teaching
- Agricultural mechanisation
- Direct marketing of farm products: crops and poultry and
- Direct contact with associated farmers in the area. (PCG Report 1973:66).

The aim of the Programme was to break away from institutionalism and reach people in their natural environment. Mr. van den Broek was a practical man and believed Christians must be connected to their neighbours and share in the aspirations of the community. With this philosophy as his guide he launched out to the rural Dagomba communities around Tamale. He was instrumental in the construction of dams, chapels and silos, as well as the organisation of church services. It was in the context of providing social services that the villages requested the Christian message. The then District

Minister of the Tamale Rural District, reported in a 2002 interview what the Reverend van den Broek had told him about the beginning of the ministry to the rural Dagomba:

> When we started the Mile 7 project to assist rural Dagomba farmers, we recruited the pioneer workers from diverse backgrounds. There was one of the workers thought to be mentally unstable. One day he was screaming for help and the other workers did not know what to do. So, they approached me to pray for this troubled man. The man became calm after the prayer to the amazement and joy of the other workers. They then requested that I teach them how to pray. I gave thought to their request and started to teach them the Lord's Prayer. The story of the healing of the man who was troubled mentally spread among the nearby villages where the model farm was sited. This story had a tremendous effect on the Dagomba in the villages surrounding the Mile 7 Farm and therefore created interest in the Dagomba for the Christian faith and hence the request to teach them how to pray. The initial villages that showed interest were Adublyili, Chanshegu, Fooshegu and Kotingli.

The "Lord's Prayer" in Dagbani thus became the beginning point in the rural evangelism. Van den Broek would painstakingly treat every concept on the Lord's Prayer over several weeks. Thus, prayer meetings were held, and converts were prepared for baptism. In 1973 he reported that four converted Muslim chiefs were baptised.

In addition to the preaching of the gospel, literacy, agricultural extension and primary health care services were being run for the villages. Another service that attracted people to the Christian faith was the provision of drinking water. The Reverend van den Broek embarked on constructing dams to mitigate the perennial water shortage that the rural Dagomba had been experiencing over the years. These services catapulted him into the limelight in rural Dagomba around Tamale. Sometime later he was enskinned as an honorary chief, *sulinboma na* 'goodwill chief' under the Adublyili chiefdom near Tamale.

The Mile 7 Programme is now under the Tamale Rural District of the PCG. This is a recent creation, with some changes. The Settlement Programme had five original visionary aims stated concisely as follows:

- To encourage young men with genuine interest in farming to engage in commercial farming
- To keep in contact with the subsistence farmers
- To introduce methods that can be copied by village farmers
- To encourage farmers to build up experience in village extension work and

5.4 Another phase of the Christian mission to the Dagomba

- To express the love, grace and blessing of God in their communal and farming activities. (PCG Report 1973:67)

According to the PCG Report of 1974, Mr. van den Broek's hard work and burden for the Dagomba earned him the title, Pastor for the Dagomba. He mobilised volunteers in addition to his staff to carry out the work in the rural areas and had his team of workers make use of literacy classes and lay preachers' courses as a viable strategy. Other activities were retreats for pastors and New Life for All Programmes, which contributed to the growth of the PCG in northern Ghana. Evangelism and social services in northern Ghana were always intricately bound together. Therefore, any attempt at separating them inevitably created needless difficulties because of the endemic poverty of the area.

For this reason, the evangelisation was linked with the boosting of agriculture and health services, and the Christian Service Committee was seen as a vital link between the people and the church as it acted as an arm to serve the people. This was necessitated by the fact that the area frequently faced crop failures resulting in perennial hunger and malnutrition. The Committee was engaged in the provision of food and clothes to the needy people. These laudable and necessary social services had their drawbacks: They created a dependency syndrome and led the parishioners to always look to the church to shoulder every responsibility. Thus, a "cargo-cult"[21] association with the church was created. Some of the Dagomba village churches died with the departure of the Reverend van den Broek. This is not unique to the Dagomba, for the Anufo churches of northern Ghana, which flourished at the time of the missionary, Reverend Krass, also collapsed after his departure (Kirby 1988:76). Thus, aid given to the poor can be a mixed blessing when it is not used advisedly. The dilemma is that aid can be abused but at the same time it is desperately needed in a deprived place like northern Ghana.

Jon Kirby (1988) explains that there was an urgent need to embark on the feeding of school children in northern Ghana, as well as the provision of incentives for self-help projects such as dams and wells. It was not only hunger that was the enemy, but equally worrying was disease; hence the church had to import drugs for the hospitals. To boost the nutritional status of the people, fertilisers and vegetable seeds were also imported for farmers. The chemical fertilisers that were imported, however, did more harm than good. First, the chemicals were not environmentally friendly as they destroyed micro-organisms that had enhanced the restoration of soil fertility. The second harm had to do with the farmers' inability to purchase the fertilisers because they had become very expensive.

The ministry of the Reverend van den Broek involved evangelism translated into deeds and agricultural activities, expressing God's love and

---

[21] Conrad Kottak (2002) defines the term, which tends to border on covetousness in his book.

concern for farmers. This holistic approach reconciles the "apostolate and diaconal activities," that is, proclamation and social service. The work in the villages had levels of activities and commitments. The levels of work included: regular church service, agricultural extension work, literacy work, health clinics, water development completed or in preparation and chapel building completed. Some villages had passed through all these levels. Where the response of a particular village was enthusiastic, the process of achieving the ultimate goal of having a completed chapel was short. Such a village would be perceived as having a viable Christian community (PCG Report 1975:78).

Although the Dagomba were often thought of as Muslims and therefore resistant to the Christian gospel, the Reverend van den Broek was ahead of his contemporaries in his perceptions. In his report to the PCG in 1975, he challenged the preconceived notion that the Dagomba were all Muslims. He conceded that although a large Muslim community existed in the towns, not all the Dagomba were Muslims. He also pointed out the fact that the Muslims were not and still are not, united. This had implications for Christian witness. In light of this fact, he urged Christians to reach out to the animist[22] rural population around Tamale. The fear that the Dagomba were disinterested in Christianity was to be proven otherwise.

Further, in the report of 1975, the Reverend van den Broek asserted that "there is interest in them [the Dagomba] to attach themselves to a new religion and the choice is between Islam and Christianity." For him the AG church, the Catholic church, the Baptist church and the Presbyterian church were spearheading the outreach among the Dagomba. In addition to being a trained agriculturalist, the Reverend van den Broek was unusually observant and developed his own ethnography of the Dagomba. From his observations the Dagomba society was stratified as shown below:

- Drummers – they were supposed to know the history of the Dagomba.
- Fiddlers – sang songs that praise the king and abuse the enemy.
- Blacksmith – traditionally made weapons and farm tools.
- Diviner – the traditional religious leader who was now under pressure from both Muslims and Christians.
- Barber – shaved heads, beards and circumcised male children.
- Butcher – slaughtered animals and sold the meat, a job that is now being monopolised by Muslims.
- Miller – operated the corn grinding machine and rice mills.
- Bicycle repairman – fixed peoples' bikes.
- Tailor – sewed peoples' clothes.
- *Mallam* – a Muslim cleric.

---

[22] Though Reverend van den Broek always tried to be different from other Europeans by identifying with the Dagomba, he inaccurately adopted the Western scholars' term for primal or traditional religions as "animist."

The contrast in attitudes between Christians and Muslims in regard to Dagomba festivals is revealing. Whereas Muslims pursue an agenda of making traditional Dagomba festivals assume an Islamic character, Christians in the past tended to have a negative attitude towards these festivals and consequently, did nothing about them in terms of giving them a Christian significance.

Initially, Dagomba Christians had shied away from taking the issues of gospel and culture seriously. However, from the Mile 7 Programme, the attempts at linking up the Christian feasts with agricultural events produced tremendous responses. For instance, at Easter, Christ's death and life are explained in connection with the cultural event of planting seed to get a new harvest. Here, prayers for the crops and for rains follow this concept. Similarly, at Christmas, the reaped harvest is presented to Jesus as the wise men presented their gifts to Jesus, as an act of worship.

The literacy level in Dagbon is still very low. The need for action was addressed by Reverend van den Broek with help from the Generale Diakonale Raad of the Reformed Church of the Netherlands. With this support a Mamprusi teacher was recruited to commence the women's work and literacy in the Mile 7 Programme. This was very strategic in that, at the subsequent production of the vernacular Scriptures, there were already functional literates in the communities.

5.4.6 The Scripture Union

Scripture Union (SU), an evangelical organisation, has been working in Ghana among the youth for over sixty years. The SU work is described by Peter Barker and Samuel Boadi-Siaw (2003). The fellowship the SU has provided in the schools since 1952 has enhanced ecumenism because Christians from various denominational backgrounds have been interacting in the forum they provide. This para-church youth group has been actively working in both first- and second-cycle institutions, including those in northern Ghana.

The SU committee for northern Ghana was formed in 1969 by Reverend Frits Rosingh and several others. Reverend Rosingh pioneered middle and secondary school conferences as early as 1965. By 1967, he had established such conferences as part of on-going youth ministry work in Tamale and other towns in the Northern Region and other upper regions of Ghana. Many northern Christian leaders are beneficiaries of the ministry of the SU, including Adam Haruna, a veterinary surgeon and a Presbyterian minister in the Tamale Rural District; the Reverend Isaac Issah Wuni, overseer of the Baptist churches in northern Ghana; Reverend Stephen Alando, a former Presbytery chairperson; and Reverend Manfred Wedam, Presbyterian minister in Yendi. Although SU did not directly evangelise the Dagomba and Konkomba, their role in the schools and through the Tamale Chaplaincy

Board contributed to the conversion and development of leaders to work among the northern peoples.

The English language was the medium of communication in the SU programmes. This factor excluded the non-literate Dagombas. As a consequence, SU is perceived as an elitist organisation which does not promote or use mother-tongue Scriptures. The organisation's strength, however, is in the area of the discipleship of young Christians.

5.5 Current challenges and opportunities in Christian mission to the Dagomba

5.5.1 The challenge of Islam

The greatest challenge posed to the Christian mission in Dagbon, according to a well-known historian and scholar, was Islam:

> There were problems for the early Christian missionaries in Dagbon and one of the major problems...was that of Islam. The Dagomba – though not everyone was a Muslim – have been influenced by Islam and this made it difficult for Christianity to make rapid headway...because they already had a religion in addition to their traditional religion. Islam is a foreign religion just like Christianity, but which had started very early in Dagbon as far back as the seventeenth and eighteenth centuries, especially when *Na* Zangina, one of the *Ya Nas* was converted into Islam at the beginning of 18th century. From then on Muslims went about freely in Dagbon. So, Christianity met Islam and it became an obstacle to conversions because people were already used to Islamic ways and Islamic teaching. So, although there were no conflicts between the missionaries and the Dagomba Muslims, it was difficult to convert them into Christianity.

It was difficult for Christianity to have effect among the Dagomba nominal Muslims because some Islamic teachings inoculated Muslims against accepting the Christian message. Mark Beaumont observes that though there are Qur'anic affirmations of Christian convictions about Christ, there are equally Qur'anic denials of Christian convictions about Christ. On the affirmations, he cites the birth of Christ by the Virgin Mary, Christ's endowment with God's power and the confirmation of the Torah given to Israel through Moses. The denials, on the other hand, include the following: that Christ did not seek faith in himself, Christ is not God's son and Christ did not die on the cross (Beaumont 2005:1–10).

Islam not only preceded Christianity and had taken deep root among the Dagomba but it had adapted to the Dagomba culture. For instance,

Islam embraced the traditional Dagomba marriage practice of polygamy and creatively transformed Dagomba traditional festivals and imbued them with Islamic meaning. In terms of solving crises that are traditional in nature, Islam had evolved adequate alternative solutions that Christianity had failed to do.

The challenge to Christianity is not so much that Islam preceded Christianity historically among the Dagomba but the current changing form of Islam; that is, the rise of an aggressive Islam in the latter part of the twentieth century. It is now common to hear Muslim religious leaders attacking Christians on the airwaves. In one instance, the Northern Regional Minister threatened to deport some Pakistani and Iranian radical Islamic elements. The history of Christian mission work in northern Ghana was generally peaceful. Currently, however, Muslim extremists are threatening the mutual respect that had existed between Muslims and Christians.

5.5.2 Initial perception of Christianity as alien

The initial European- or Western-type of Christianity that was introduced to the Dagomba failed to relate well to their culture. To be a Christian at that time implied withdrawing from the indigenous lifestyle of the Dagomba in order not to compromise one's new faith. Thus, taking part in the customary carrying out of funerals and marriages were some of the problems the pioneer northern Christians had not adequately addressed.

White missionaries and southern Ghanaians who introduced Christianity to the Dagomba from the 1930s to 1960s did not address their cultural issues, deepening the perception that Christianity was a foreign religion, as most new Christians shunned their own culture and traditions. Until recently, when they had the Scriptures in Dagbani, many Dagomba did not want to become Christians, for Christianity and the Dagomba culture were viewed as incompatible.

5.5.3 Poverty

Poverty has been a major challenge to the effective evangelisation of the Dagomba. It has been endemic in the Northern Territories because the economy depends on rain-fed agriculture. Since most Dagomba are peasant farmers they are at the mercy of rainfall to farm and to rear their animals. This situation has rendered the place vulnerable to economic hardship.

5.5.4 Ethnic conflicts

Another current challenge to Christian mission among the Dagomba is the issue of ethnic conflicts and polarisation of the chiefly and acephalous societies. The 1994 ethnic war between the Dagomba and Konkomba had religious undertones. Whereas the Dagomba accused Christian churches of supporting the Konkomba, the reverse accusation was made, that is, the Konkomba alleged the Arabic countries were supporting the Dagomba.

5.5.5 Church structures and the Christian mission to the northern peoples

The church structures among the Dagomba were the same as the denominational structures of the missionaries. Traditional leadership structures did not have a place in the churches thus established. This has added to the perception that Christianity is alien, for the church structures were not allowed to evolve using indigenous resources.

5.6 Good will towards Christianity

In spite of the challenges enumerated, Christianity still enjoys much good will; Christianity, by its practical mode of operation, carved a good image for itself among the Dagomba and Konkomba. From inception, the missions identified with the people and embarked on a holistic mission. This took the form of adult literacy, schools, health clinics, agricultural extension and relief services.

Role of Christian NGOs

Christian NGOs, like World Vision International, Catholic Relief Service, Adventist Relief Association, Assemblies of God Relief Services, Christian Council of Ghana, Christian hospitals, agricultural stations and other charitable organisations, have thrown a lifeline to many deprived northern Ghanaian communities, including those of the Dagomba.

5.7 Translation of Christianity among the Dagomba

From the account of Christian mission among the Dagomba, a number of issues came to the fore. First, Christianity, which was Western in character, came prior to the translation of the Bible into Dagbani. As a consequence, early Christianity was perceived as alien. Jon Kirby, a Catholic missionary and an anthropologist by training, identified European ethnocentrism as the cause. He pinpoints the missionaries' insensitivity to African culture.[23] The more challenging part of this is that they passed on this attitude to their converts. The foreign character of this kind of Christianity was to be challenged by African theologians like the Nigerian Methodist minister, Bolaji Idowu (Idowu 1965:1-8).

---

[23] Kirby's explanation of how Western Christian structures failed to address African problems, refers to the Anufo 'people of Anu' of northern Ghana, Benin, and Togo; also called Chakoso, mercenaries from Ano who assisted the chiefs of the Gonja and Mamprusi peoples (in Blakely et al. 1994:60).

Local Christians were accused of being alienated from their culture. For instance, early Western Christianity that was introduced did not help much with traditional problem solving (Kirby 1994:63). Christians who approached problems from a Western perspective were helpless when it came to dealing with traditional cultural issues like marriage, funerals, festivals and others. Interest in Christianity prior to the coming of vernacular Scriptures was at its lowest ebb. As indicated earlier, it will be shown that with the translation of the Scriptures into the mother tongue, serious engagement with traditional African culture and Islamic belief and practice would take place.

As Sanneh argued, Christianity, projected as the missionary culture, is an aberration of true Christianity rather than the norm. When the gospel is translated using the Dagomba culture and language as the basis of understanding, the local people would not only embrace the Christian faith as their own, they would find the true gospel that transforms them. For this reason, Sanneh advocated teaching translation principles as the central concept in mission studies (2001:174, 175).

This call to give translation the central role in understanding Christian mission work is justifiable. The motivation for Christian mission engagement has been to effectively communicate the gospel in a culturally relevant manner and the quest to achieve this has necessitated the translation enterprise. Though colonial influence has its place in mission studies, it was not the controlling force in effective Christian mission work.

The mission to the Dagomba revealed that if the people were to put behind them the perception of the Christian faith as foreign, then translation was called for. By TRANSLATION here, we mean the culturally sensitive communication of the Christian faith into Dagomba idiomatic speech and within their worldview. The Bible Society of Ghana, in the course of time, worked with the churches in northern Ghana to revise the New Testament and then to facilitate the translation of the Old Testament.

In conjunction with the churches working among the Dagomba, GILLBT established the Dagomba Literacy Project. This project promoted literacy among the Dagomba so that the translated Scriptures could be read with understanding with the goal of clear communication and resulting transformation of the Dagomba people as they grasped the truth of the message.

5.8 Early attempts at Dagbani Bible translation

The translation of the Bible into Dagbani began with the Basel Mission but was thwarted by the First World War when the British deported the Basel missionaries from the Gold Coast. German missionaries were thought to be supportive of the Axis cause (Prempeh 1977). The AG Mission resumed and completed the New Testament translation task, which was later revised by the Bible Society of Ghana, followed by a complete Bible translation.

5.8.1 The Basel Mission

The translation of the Scriptures into Dagbani was addressed from the outset by the Basel Mission, beginning at Yendi in 1913. Missionaries immediately began to study the language and developed an alphabet for Dagbani. Continued study and application of the written system culminated in the translation of portions of the Bible into Dagbani (Smith 1966).

Weiss reports that some of the translated Dagbani Scripture portions were lost in a fire at the Basel Mission house in Yendi on 9 March 1916 (Weiss 2005:185). Although the Basel missionaries' early translated portions of the Scriptures into Dagbani did not survive, they initiated an important missionary vocation that was to be taken up by another mission. In the process they demonstrated that cultural learning was fundamental to Christian mission work. As Legrand observes, "there can be no truly lived faith apart from its actualization in a culture" (Legrand 2000:174).

5.8.2 The Assemblies of God Mission

The AG Mission settled in Yendi in 1931 and completed the first New Testament translation in Dagbani, the *Naawuni Kundi Palli*. Pastor Daniel Wumbee, in an interview with this author, acknowledged Reverend Shirer as a pioneer of the AG Dagbani Bible translation. There is some speculation as to whether this translation was built on the early efforts of the Basel Mission. Pastor Wumbee recounts how Reverend Shirer and his wife wrote a number of Dagbani books, especially Christian stories. Shirer is credited with translating the Gospels and Acts in about 1952. Shirer later left the AG Mission and joined the government Mass Education Unit. Other translators and assistants continued with his translation project.

Pastor Wumbee describes the translation task as all-embracing. Activities included consultations with various professionals and institutions in the society. Thus, builders, weavers, carpenters, butchers, blacksmiths, herbalists, hunters, *lunsi* [24] and the general public have all had input into the Dagbani Scriptures. For instance, builders helped translators with the right terms for the materials and measurements used in constructing buildings. Weavers described the weaving process and gave vocabulary for clothing material. Carpenters helped with terms for measurements and the name of furniture used in the Scripture. Butchers helped with vocabulary describing parts of animals, especially those offered to God in sacrifice. Herbalists helped with the names of plants, whilst hunters helped with the names of wild animals. Blacksmiths and goldsmiths were of equal help, giving the names of utensils and minerals. Drummers and traditional orators helped with the composition of poetic texts and idiomatic expressions. Traditional Dagomba royal courts also provided an environment conducive to capturing the appropriate diction for meaningful translation. Thus, the translation

---

[24] *Lunsi* fulfil vital duties – that of counsellor to royalty, genealogist, cultural expert, etc.

process drew in both Christians and other community members from a variety of backgrounds and professions.

5.9 The translation and use of the Dagbani Old Testament

The Reverend van den Broek invited Pastor Wumbee to discuss the translation of the Old Testament into Dagbani. Pastor Wumbee and Joseph Neindow did the drafting. Later a pastor of the AG church joined the team, which included a Hebrew scholar from the Netherlands who served as exegetical coordinator. The work continued to enjoy support from van den Broek's successors, Reverend Minister Riley Edwards and Reverend Minister Arrie van Nierop.

The translators faced the challenge of the choice of terms acceptable to all segments of the recipients of the Dagomba Scriptures. One such challenge was the mysterious name for God, *Ndan be Wuni* (literally, 'eternal, sufficient God'), used sparingly by the traditional priests. The translators found it inappropriate to use that mysterious personal name for God for fear that the Dagomba Muslim community would consider it anathema. Since the Dagomba translators had a Muslim audience also in mind, they did not adopt it but instead used the common name for God, *Naawuni*.

There is also the challenge of the choice of an appropriate name for biblical characters. Moses' sister and Jesus' mother were both referred to as Mariyama by Muslims, which often created problems of identification. The translators found a way around this confusion by adopting Miriam for Moses' sister and then Mariyama for Jesus' mother. Other names that could cause confusion of identity are also referred to in the Qur'an. For example, the Qur'an refers to "John" as Yahaya and both "Jacob" and "James" as Yakubu.

In the event of difficulty in the translation of certain concepts, translators tended to use descriptive methods and adaptive words. Many animals and plants in the Old Testament are without a Dagomba equivalent, so the translators in this situation describe and adopt words. For example, to translate "oak tree," they used a tree in northern Ghana with similar characteristics. Other aids in communicating clear meaning are the retention of the original word plus an illustration or picture of that object.

5.9.1 The Bible Society of Ghana and Dagbani Bible translation

As mentioned in section 5.7, the became involved in the translation of the Christian Scriptures into Dagbani. The official opening of Bible House, Accra, the national headquarters of the Bible Society of Ghana, was on Saturday, 18 September 1965. A brochure commemorating that event explained that in 1962, the organisation had been registered as a non-denominational Christian organisation and as an affiliate member of the worldwide United Bible Societies, which operate in over two hundred countries. The organisations are autonomous but cooperate with each other.

The task of the Bible Societies is to oversee Bible translation, production and distribution. The international organisation is responsible for coordinating translation activities in numerous countries. This organisation has succeeded in facilitating co-operation between Catholics and Protestant churches to undertake Bible translation (Schaaf 1994). To ensure quality translation, this international body has established modern translation departments and staffed them with specially trained translation consultants who work alongside local language translators.

As an affiliate of this international organisation, the Bible Society of Ghana has as its goal, according to their 1965 brochure, "making the Holy Scriptures available in a language you can understand and at the price you can afford."[25] One wonders if this is just mere rhetoric or an achievable goal. The fact that there are many languages in Ghana coupled with an unstable national economy in the 1970s, made the realisation of this goal a daunting task. The international organisation was not unaware of these problems confronting the Ghanean national Bible Society. It co-ordinated all activities and shared resources. This measure helped to mitigate the challenges facing the Bible Society of Ghana. To avoid paternalism, the international body advocated the nationalisation of the Societies in Africa. This was achieved through the establishment of interdenominational advisory committees (Schaaf 1994).

The General Secretary of the Bible Society of Ghana and his advisory committee have the challenging task of promoting interest among Christian churches and mobilising them to support the national Society. In order to achieve its objective, financial support, personnel and other resources of the churches are tapped and the Bible Society of Ghana enlists the support of individual Christians by inviting them to subscribe as members of the organisation.

The membership drive is an ongoing exercise throughout the year in Ghana but assumes a high tempo in the annual Bible Week celebrated by the churches when the Bible Society's activities and projects are advertised to win support. The Bible Society of Ghana also partners with other Bible agencies to publish and broadcast the New Testament on audio-playing devices in local languages. These audio recordings form a centrepiece of church-based listening groups and also target the general public on local FM radio stations.

5.9.2 Faith Comes By Hearing and Scripture engagement

The Bible Society of Ghana, working among the Dagomba in partnership with the Faith Comes By Hearing (FCBH) audio Bible ministry, can be heard by thousands of Dagombas, Christians and the non-churched. Many listeners of Radio Savannah, an FM radio station of the Ghana Broadcasting

---

[25] Bible Society of Ghana 1965.

5.9 The translation and use of the Dagbani Old Testament

Corporation in Tamale, testify to the effectiveness of reading the Dagomba Scriptures. The coordinator, Evangelist Peter Tia of FCBH, unequivocally affirmed in an interview with this author, that the programme is having a strong effect on the Dagomba. In a personal communication in January 2004, he recalled that when funding for the playing of the Scripture recordings on Radio Savannah was exhausted and it was taken off the air, there were calls of protest from both the Christian and non-Christian Dagomba populace. It appears that they find common identity in the use of their mother tongue, the Dagbani language. What was astonishing to Tia was the willingness of some Dagomba Muslim philanthropists to contribute funds for the continuation of the Dagbani Scripture readings on the radio.

Inadequate funding proves to be one of the major obstacles to the Dagbani FCBH programme. Until recently the co-ordinator of the project was not paid a salary. Peter Tia recounts how many of the early group of Dagomba young men who served as supervisors withdrew from the programme because there was no remuneration for them. This should not be interpreted as lack of commitment on their part but rather, is more due to the local people's need to earn an income – their economic privation. Lack of job opportunities in northern Ghana has created endemic poverty amongst the people.

5.9.3 The role of GILLBT in the Dagbani Literacy Project

Though the Ghana Institute of Linguistics, Literacy and Bible Translation (GILLBT) did not translate the Dagbani Scriptures, it was instrumental in the organisation of the Dagbani literacy project (Quaye 1991:26). There were a number of reasons for initiating literacy: Literacy was one of the felt needs of the Dagomba, who had a high illiteracy rate. Though portions of the Scriptures in Dagbani were in print, they remained inaccessible to the majority of the Dagomba – who could not read them. Judging from the enrolment numbers in the Dagomba Literacy Project, the Dagomba were not sufficiently motivated to appreciate the literacy programme. Two reasons might account for the Dagomba lack of interest: first, the time gap between the literacy programme and the Bible translated into Dagbani, and secondly, influence of the Muslim Arabic schools. Possibly for fear of being converted into Christianity, many non-Christian Dagomba in the urban centres are wary of literacy programmes or education based on the Western model.

Paa Ekow Quaye, an accountant at GILLBT who wrote an historical record of the Institute's work, explains that the organisation has "developed functional literacy programmes wherever they operate." Quaye's perspective on the logic of GILLBT's literacy campaign is that the Scriptures would be of no use to the Dagomba if, when translated into their mother tongue, that message were hidden in a book that they could not read. For him, therefore, what is written must be read. Literacy could be viewed then as an "after-sale service" provided as a result of Dagbani Scripture translation. Quaye concludes that "literacy puts language into the hands of its speakers so that they may use it productively" (Quaye 1991:8, 9).

The literacy project for the Dagomba serves as another useful forum for cooperation between the Bible Society of Ghana and GILLBT on one hand, and the churches working among the Dagomba on the other. The cooperation is seen in the complementary roles being played by the various groups. The BSG produced the Dagbani Bible, and to make it accessible, GILLBT produced Dagbani literacy materials for the churches to use. The added advantage of this programme is the opportunity it affords Christians and non-Christians to work together. Thus, the literacy programme fosters unity among the Dagomba communities as well as ecumenism among Christians of different denominational backgrounds.

As noted earlier, literacy has played an important role in the Scripture engagement of the Dagomba. Reverend Imoro cites the case of a Dagomba man of the Kumasi *Yurilim* 'love' Church, who converted to Christianity through the AG literacy programme. As will be shown, literacy paves the way for the full utilisation of the Dagbani Bible, as it would produce many readers. Again, for him, the mother-tongue Scriptures in conjunction with the "Jesus Film" Project® have helped to galvanise rural Dagomba to the Christian faith (Whiteman 1990:131).

5.10 Conclusion

The initial mission outreach by the Basel Mission and Wesleyan Mission, among the Dagomba in 1913 suffered numerous setbacks. However, the AG church later continued with the translation of the Dagomba Scriptures. They were then followed by the Catholics, Presbyterians and Baptists prior to the translation of the Bible into Dagbani. The Basel missionaries, the AG and the Catholic Missions were fervent in the study of Dagomba culture and Dagbani as part of their missionary strategy. Literacy served as a catalyst in the evangelisation of the Dagomba. The indigenous leadership of the AG and the Baptists were products of the campaign of missionary bodies. Literacy and the translated Scriptures have paved the way for more Dagomba people to shed the notion that Christianity is a foreign religion.

This chapter sought to demonstrate that Dagomba perception of Christianity prior to the translation of the Bible into their mother tongue was that it was a foreign religion, specifically, *suliminga adiini* 'a white man's religion' and later *kambonga* or *ayigbe chichi* or *gingli* 'Akan or Ewe (southern) church'. Thus, the initial Dagomba perception of Christianity, coupled with the non-availability of the Dagbani Scriptures, subsequently affected the receptivity rate of the Christian message. Furthermore, the Dagomba perception of Christianity was influenced by their earlier contact with Western colonial authorities.

6

Christian Mission in Northern Ghana: The Konkomba Story

6.1 Introduction

To appreciate the influence of the vernacular Scriptures on the Konkomba people, we need to understand how the Christian message was introduced to them. The Basel Mission and the AG Mission, followed by the Catholic church, the EPC and the Worldwide Evangelisation Crusade (WEC) initially carried out the evangelisation of the Konkomba. Several factors affected the mission work among them, including the British colonial policy in the Northern Territories. As discussed in chapter five, the Basel missionaries did some work to analyse and describe the Konkomba language. However, they could not carry this to its logical conclusion because they were expelled by the British. Subsequent missionary entities did not learn or work with the Konkomba language. Consequently, the Bible translation into Likpakpaaln was delayed until recently; this affected the spread of the Christian faith and the educational and social development of the Konkomba region.

The attitude and policies of the British colonial government and the failure of the missionaries to present their teaching in the mother tongue, convinced the Konkomba that Christianity was a foreign religion.

6.2 Colonial policy and the evangelisation of the Konkomba

There were no restrictions from the British with respect to Christian missions among the Konkomba, because there was not enough competing Muslim influence to warrant such restriction. Since they were generally considered wild and quarrelsome, the Konkomba did not receive much attention from the colonial authorities in terms of development. The one major concern was to restrain the Konkomba from fomenting trouble against their neighbours, especially the Dagomba.[1] The colonial government authorities did not act favourably toward the Konkomba people.

The attitude of the British was a mixed blessing in that, on the one hand, missionaries had a free hand to carry out their activities, but on the other, the Konkomba area lacked the infrastructure needed for development. Missionaries, therefore, had the herculean task of providing health facilities and schools for the people.

6.2.1 Assemblies of God mission to the Konkomba

In an interview with a pastor of an AG church in Saboba, it was revealed that Christianity came to the Konkomba from the indigenous initiative of one Mr. Akonsi from Yarkansie, a Konkomba town sixteen miles from Saboba, their traditional capital. He first heard and accepted the Christian message at Yendi. He later brought the Christian message to his people, the Konkomba, prior to the coming of the AG missionaries to Konkombaland in the 1950s.

The AG church, which was the first Christian mission to be established in Saboba, built a clinic there in 1951. The mission tended not to involve the indigenes initially in the running of the clinic but relied on expatriates; it took a long time for them to engage Ghanaian nurses. The clinic had to be closed down, much to the anger of the indigenes, because the church could not provide staff for it. The clinic closed down the last week of October 1967 because the nurse in charge had cancer and the two other trained sisters who assisted until then, had left. The closure brought much suffering to the sick since they had to travel to more distant health facilities for treatment for about a year. However, in 1968, a maternity block was added to the clinic to address the health needs of the people who had agitated for the government to take over the running of the clinic. These initial challenges facing the AG in the Konkombaland could have been one of the contributory factors for a delay in translating the Bible into Likpakpaaln.

As they treated the sick, the missionaries also ministered the gospel, although they probably started the clinic simply because the health conditions of the people there were deplorable; the incidence of communicable

---

[1] PRAAD Tamale. NRG 8/2/88.

diseases like leprosy was high among the Konkomba.[2] With this medical work and proclamation of the gospel, the AG church took deep roots in the Saboba area and then spread out to other Konkomba areas. The fruitfulness of the AG church among the Konkomba is evidenced by the fact that a significant number of prominent Konkomba Christians who occupy leadership positions in the church and Konkomba community are her members. These include the Reverend Solomon King, Dean of the Assemblies of God Bible School, Kumasi, David Mankron, pastor of the biggest AG church in Tema and Mr. David Kutin of World Vision International.

6.2.2 The Evangelical Presbyterian Church

Hans Debrunner, commenting on the state of evangelisation of the ethnic groups in the former German colony of Togo, said it was similar to northern Ghana. He explained that the Konkomba in northern Togo frequently embarked on seasonal migration to southern Togo and Ghana. In his view, the Konkomba and their neighbours constituted a big mission field. Christian effect had been minimal, as the figures he gave demonstrate: The whole of the north was still predominantly "pagan", with less than 1% being Protestants and 5% Catholic. The Catholic Mission had a larger Christian community than the Protestants because the former preceded the latter in reaching out to the Konkomba.

Supporting his claims with figures, Debrunner acknowledged that the Catholics had the most extensive network of mission stations with 19 priests, 20 sisters, 2 brothers and 93 catechists in the mission service. The Protestants were late in beginning work in the north; they founded a few outstations in the 1930s but did not open a permanent mission station until 1940 (Debrunner 1967:261). Christian mission to the Konkomba in Ghana, including both Catholic and Protestant, began at this time.

The Basel Mission and Bremen Mission share a common Germanic-Dutch background that permitted a cordial relation between them in their missionary endeavours. Similar cooperation was demonstrated in northern Ghana between the PCG and the EPC. They agreed to train nine PCG students in the EPC seminary in Peki, in the Volta Region of Ghana. It is at this seminary that most Konkomba EPC catechists were trained. The PCG also trained catechists and teachers of the EPC at their centre in Abetifi and Training College at Akropong. The Bremen and Basel missionaries had a strategy to work in different parts of the Northern Territories to avoid duplication and competition. The Bremen Mission worked in the eastern part of the Northern Territories all the way down to the Volta Region. The Basel Mission was to direct its missionary efforts towards the west of the Volta. The Scottish and American Presbyterian Missions came in at the time the British drove out the Bremen and Basel Missions because of the First World

---

[2] PRAAD, Tamale, Colonial Annual Report, 1932.

War (Barker 1986:31). Through their work, the EPC was born and nurtured among the Konkomba.

The EPC worked among the Konkomba in the then Yendi District. In parts of the Volta Region, the church also evangelised the migrant Konkomba. The Reverend Klaus Winter from Lippe Church in Germany started the church in Saboba. He worked from 1968–1976 and did well by fostering a link between his home church and the Saboba one. The church also started the Saboba Agricultural Project in 1972 for the Konkomba people (Ansre 1997:219ff.).

The challenge that faced the EPC stemmed from their lack of translating the Bible into Likpakpaaln. Ewe hymns and liturgy had dominated the Konkomba church until the coming of their own mother-tongue Scriptures. Again, the perception of the Christian faith as an alien religion because it came to them in Ewe or in English impeded the growth of the church. It could be argued that if the Bremen Mission had not been deported as a result of World War I, the EPC among the Konkomba might have come earlier and the Bible would have been translated much earlier into Likpakpaaln. Samuel Prempeh enumerates the incalculable loss World War I brought on the areas where the Basel and Bremen missionaries worked. These losses were in the economic, social and religious spheres (Prempeh 1977).[3]

6.2.3 The Worldwide Evangelisation Crusade

Another mission agency that worked among the Konkomba was the Worldwide Evangelisation Crusade (WEC), which later gave birth to the Evangelical Church of Ghana.

On 26 July 1940 the Secretary of the WEC, Norman P. Grubb, wrote to the colonial authorities of the Gold Coast, expressing the desire of the organisation to extend its missionary work into the northwestern area of the Northern Territories of the Gold Coast. He went further to describe the nature and work of the organisation as follows: "The society is an interdenominational one with the objective of bringing the message of Christ to any peoples who are still unreached by Protestant missionary effort. The work was founded by C. T. Studd in the Belgian Congo in 1914" (Grubb 1940).

In West Africa, the WEC had a centre in Senegal and had a cordial working relationship with the government as well as with other missionary agencies there. The WEC also had centres in both Liberia and the Ivory Coast. The organisation's next objective was to open stations in northern Dahomey [Benin] and the Gold Coast [Ghana]. This objective was achieved when Mr. and Mrs. John Seaman, who had been working in the Ivory Coast, obtained permission to cross over to the Gold Coast. Upon arrival they interviewed

---

[3] The Reverend Doctor Samuel Prempeh was a past Moderator of the Presbyterian Church of Ghana.

6.2 Colonial policy and the evangelisation of the Konkomba

with the District Commissioner at Lawra, who proved very supportive. This collaboration between the mission and colonial authorities paved the way for the WEC to transition smoothly and begin work among the minority groups of northern Ghana.

In his letter of request to the colonial authorities, the Secretary of the WEC explained that, "the work they desire to do is evangelistic. They preferred to settle among a tribe or tribes which are still pagan." Could it be that the reference to some African ethnic groups as "still pagan" reflects a misguided arrogance on behalf of some Western missionaries at that time? Perhaps they were not sensitised to the fact that Africans were a staunchly religious people and worshipped God with the limited revelation they had of Him? Grubb, in his letter, throws still more light on the ethos of the WEC:

> Our missionaries are accustomed to living very plainly and simply and their method of work would be to rent some small, suitable house (until they were able to build), begin to acquire the language and concentrate upon visiting the villages...and holding meetings amongst the people.
>
> When there are converts, give such instruction in reading, writing etc. as would enable the converts to have and read the Bible in their own language and to train some of them to be teachers and evangelists to their own people. They would also be ready and willing to give simple medical attention, if required and allowed. But our central objective would be neither education, nor medical, but evangelistic.
>
> As a mission, we hold no doctrinal tenets of a less essential character which would hinder us from full fellowship with all other Protestant missions and we would only desire to enter the territory not being worked by existing missions. (Grubb 1940)

It is clear from the outset that the WEC valued incarnational ministry: language learning and the translation of the Scriptures into the languages of the people they work among as fundamental to their mission.

Mr. John Seaman on 30th August 1941 subsequently applied for and received a certificate of occupancy for three acres of land at Tuna near Bole in the Northern Region for a mission station. Another mission station was applied for at Kpandai in east Gonja on 28 November 1942 and was also granted. A mission station and a leprosy clinic were built there to serve the Konkomba, the Nawuri and the Gonja. The parent mission, WEC, later formed an indigenous church by the name "Evangelical Church of Ghana" which has been working among the Gonja, Vagla, Konkomba and recently among the Dagomba. The WEC was involved in the translation of the Gonja Bible and oversaw the Gonja literacy program. The WEC is also working on another Konkomba version of the Bible, for those at Kpasaah area in the northern part of the Volta Region of Ghana, because they do not fully understand the Saboba dialect. The Konkomba dialect, Limonkpeln, is spoken in the Kpasaah and Tatali areas.

The WEC has also been working among the Konkomba, the Basari and the Nawuri people around Kpandai providing health and other social services. However, as they stated in their vision, these other services are geared toward the proclamation of the gospel. The first leaders among the Konkomba were mainly the house help of the missionaries with no high academic education. However, over the past decade the academic standing of the Konkomba has changed very much.

6.3 An evaluation of the missionary enterprise among the Konkomba

As with the Dagomba, the kind of Christianity (Western) the church initially introduced to the Konkomba lacked the tools for these indigenous people to meaningfully solve the puzzles their worldviews posed to them (Kirby 2006). However, it has contributed significantly to the development of Konkombaland. The Christian church has provided many schools, relief services and other social amenities. Here we may need to qualify missionary philosophy by pointing out that not all the various missions had the same philosophy and attitude to the provision of social services to the communities in which they served. In chapter five, we describe these different approaches.

For some of the missions, the provision of spiritual needs of the people mattered. Not that they thought that the provision of social amenities was unimportant, they just did not want to lose their primary focus, conversion to Christianity. For a very long time, many Pentecostal and charismatic churches accused the mission-founded churches of socialising the people, but they (the Pentecostals) had come to evangelise them. With this as a focus, they sent the message that the soul mattered more than the body, a concept alien to the African understanding of religion, for the African there is no dichotomy between the spiritual and the physical. There were also different attitudes among several missions towards the cultures of the people to whom they were ministering. It was the opinion of Der that fundamentalist missionaries disdained African culture; and not only that, they encouraged their followers to do the same. Missionaries' attitude toward African culture has generally been negative and Christian converts under their teaching were warned not to tolerate anything "pagan." Consequently, traditional customs, rites and institutions were banned. It therefore appeared to the Konkomba that to become a Christian meant they denounce their own culture. Very committed followers had to reject even traditional cultural practices such as funeral rites and dancing.

The White Fathers became more tolerant of traditional culture after Vatican II, which called for more forbearance for people of other beliefs. Fundamentalist policy was antagonistic towards African culture because of their fear of syncretism (Der 1983:268). Since one cannot have one's cake and eat it too, the fear to get close to the Konkomba culture produced a counter effect; many Konkomba also avoided Christianity. As we noted earlier, if the missions succeeded in alienating their converts from their traditional roots, it would naturally prompt a hostile reaction towards them and Christianity from the wider society.

6.4 Konkomba preference for Christianity

Generally, one can observe a contrast in attitude toward Islam and Christianity between the Dagomba and the Konkomba. Whereas the Dagomba have the propensity to convert to Islam and increasingly adopt an Arabic culture, the Konkomba would more likely convert to Christianity (Boi-Nai and Kirby 1998). This has become more pronounced among the Konkomba since they received the Scriptures in their mother tongue in 1978; this has created in them a new awareness and appreciation of their indigenous culture.

The Dagomba associate Christianity with the Konkomba and, therefore consider it an inferior religion. The Konkomba on the other hand associate Islam with Dagomba, and hence view it as an oppressor's religion.

Some of the pioneer missionaries from the outset made the attempt to learn the languages of the indigenes and engaged in language development. The ultimate goal of these missionaries was to be able to communicate the gospel directly in the vernaculars of these recipient communities. When there were no vernacular Scriptures and preachers had to rely on instant translation, there were bound to be problems ministering accurately the word of God in the peoples' native language. This fact underscored the need for Bible translation.

The need for Christianity to reflect African culture more closely has been taken seriously by African theologians (Idowu 1965). Abraham Akrong has captured the dilemma the missionaries found themselves in as they sought to communicate the Christian message in Africa. He explains as follows:

> This unfortunate but understandable entanglement of the nineteenth-century missionary work with Western European nationalistic and imperialistic interests prevented the missionary movement from making the kind of effect it could otherwise have made on the African society. And to the extent that the missionary movement allowed itself to be drawn into the orbit of the colonial ideology of domination, its vision was somehow blurred. This flirtation with the colonial ideology of domination, based on the myth of

> so-called Western European 'civilizing mission' to the rest of the world lured the missionaries to succumb to the cultural imperialism of colonialism. The cultural imperialism is reflected in the strand of missionary perspective that saw the whole missionary work in Africa as the westernisation of Africa. And it was such an ethnocentric view of mission work that saw African culture as the very antithesis of Christianity. (Akrong 1998:59)

The missionaries were products of their day, and so had the Enlightenment mentality and could not have been anything else. They often found themselves torn between the demands of the message of the gospel and that of their cultural socialisation. For instance, their culture told them they were at the pinnacle of civilisation and therefore were superior to non-Westerners (Bediako 1997:39–45). The core message of the gospel, however, counteracts this notion, as it stressed the equality of all peoples.

As Sanneh argued in chapter five of his book, *Translating the Message*, Christianity, projected as the missionary culture, is not authentic Christian mission but an aberration (2001:174). However, when it assumes the phase of translation, with the Konkomba culture being the ultimate destination, then the people of the receptor culture would not only embrace the faith as their own, they would have found the true gospel that would transform them and their culture. Sanneh, therefore, advocated the objective study of translation in mission studies.

> The historian of religion may, therefore, attempt to retrieve the subject of translation from its isolation in colonial studies and bring it forward as a central category in the revitalization of indigenous societies, a step that does not bypass deserved criticism of mission. What it does do, however, is to review the ideological opposition to mission for such opposition is an obstacle to open-minded inquiry and to the advancement of the subject in its own right. If we proceed in this manner and overlook the ideological rhetoric in much of the literature, we should be able to restore a corrective perspective to the place of translation in both mission and the renewal of African societies. (2001:175)

In light of our discussion of Christian mission to the Dagomba and Konkomba, the motivation for Christian mission has been to effectively communicate the gospel in a culturally relevant manner. The quest to achieve this has necessitated translation. Though colonial influence cannot be ruled out completely from mission studies, it was not the controlling force in *authentic* Christian mission.

6.5 Mission as a translation movement: The Konkomba Christian Scriptures

Philip Noss's introduction to Aloo Majola's book, *God Speaks Our Languages*, makes it clear that Bible translation influences, and is influenced by, the context in which it is being done.

> Aloo Majola offers...the story of Bible translators and their translation.... The story is comprised of many elements: early mission and church policy, political, economic and social policies of colonial governments, world wars and independence movements, politics of new states and developing nationhood, and contemporary policies for language management, education and literacy. These factors, as well as the personal vision and vicissitudes of the translators themselves, are woven into the fabric of Scripture translation. (Noss 1999:vi)

Thus, the prevailing socio-cultural factors enhance or hinder its successful execution. The African context has been prepared for the translation of God's word, that is, the Bible and the living Word in the person of Jesus Christ. It is based on this conviction that Sanneh spoke of the TRANSLATABILITY OF THE CHRISTIAN GOSPEL. By translatability, he meant that every culture is capable of receiving the Christian gospel as if it had anticipated God's revelation, that is, translation from one culture to another, not just from one language to another.

The Kenyan theologian, John Mbiti, is convinced that African traditional religion was prepared to receive the gospel. For him, many Africans are becoming Christians mainly because of the role their indigenous religion has been playing, hence his argument that:

> African religion has prepared the religious and spiritual grounds for many of its adherents to listen carefully to the teachings of the Bible, to reflect seriously upon them, to discover meaningful parallels between their world and the world of the Bible, and in many cases to convert to the Christian faith without feeling a sense of spiritual loss but to the contrary thereby gaining a new outreach in their religious experience. (Mbiti 1986:11)

Thus, African Christians have found fulfilment in Christianity because their indigenous religions have nursed them in preparation for the gospel of Christ and with its coming Africans can now be weaned from their pre-Christian religion because the Christian faith when translated successfully fulfils their spiritual aspirations. To give rich nourishment to the young Christians, missionaries, aided by indigenous people, translated the Scriptures into the mother tongues of the converts. Modelling and teaching the fundamentals of Christian conduct and the rendering of the Scriptures into the mother tongues became the principal activities of the various mission bodies. Everything else was directed towards this goal.

Colonial archival records reveal that in northern Ghana, social services often preceded the literary translation of the Bible. The social services acted as the foundation and practical translation for the people prior to the textual translation of the Bible. For this reason, schools, literacy, health care, modern techniques in agriculture and other services were essential parts of the missionary strategy.

It is clear that translation of the Scriptures into Likpakpaaln is a natural outflow of Christian mission. In the Konkomba project there was sociolinguistic research done before the translation work began. This resulted in the production of a practical orthography and literacy primers so that a literacy programme preceded the Scriptural translation into the mother tongue. Literacy and translation complement each other.

The Konkomba have the whole Bible translated into Likpakpaaln, sponsored by GILLBT in partnership with the Summer Institute of Linguistics (SIL). There was no time gap between the literacy and translation work. The news that their language has a written form motivated and generated high interest among the Konkomba, and they received the vernacular Scriptures with great enthusiasm, apparently more so than had been the case with the Dagomba. The response of the Konkomba reflects Sanneh's prediction, that "there would follow a cultural revitalisation from translation" (Sanneh 1989). Certainly the Konkomba are discovering a new self-understanding and increasing self-confidence, which will likely help, and enable them to take their rightful place in the world. The literacy programmes of the Dagomba and Konkomba reveal that more people enrolled in the latter than in the former even though the Dagomba has a greater population.

Expatriates and local people worked together in the Konkomba translation team, which was non-denominational and para-church. The Konkomba Bible translation took a relatively short time to complete which may have been due to a healthy cooperation that prevailed between SIL and GILLBT. Also, the translators on the Konkomba project[4] had good support and worked within a strict time frame. In the case of the Dagomba translation, in contrast, some of the churches, according to Pastor Daniel Wumbee of Tamale, withdrew from the translation project because of insufficient resources needed for the project, which slowed down the work.

---

[4] A cooperative effort of Wycliffe Bible Translators and partner organisation, the Summer Institute of Linguistics.

6.5.1 Literacy among the Konkomba

From the discussion so far, we can surmise that missions, translation, education and literacy are indispensable allies. The missionaries and the churches they founded embarked upon massive literacy campaigns in the mother tongues because these were the languages being used in church services. The Christian gospel leads its adherents to a desire for deeper understanding and knowledge; literacy and education follow quickly upon conversion. It is no wonder that Muslims refer to Christians as "the people of the book."[5] Literacy no doubt acts as the umbilical cord of translation of the Christian Scriptures.

Vernacular literacy has been recognised throughout the ages as a key to Christian evangelism and church growth. GILLBT underscores the role of literacy in its work: "Literacy puts a language into the hands of its speakers so that they may use it productively. It is easiest for people to learn to read and write in their mother tongue. Once this is done, literacy skills can easily be applied to any other language which a person learns to speak" (Quaye 1991:8). One would have expected that all target groups for literacy campaigns would embrace the teaching efforts offered to them, but that is not the case. It takes great effort to persuade adults to embark on a literacy programme. Even when they do begin it is a constant challenge to keep the students coming.

6.5.2 SIL International and GILLBT

SIL International (SIL) is a linguistic organisation that focuses on ethnolinguistic research, language development and translation among minority ethnic groups. William Cameron Townsend founded SIL with the aim of serving the language groups and nations of the world in a facilitating role. In partnership with like-minded agencies, they have accomplished a great deal during their years in Ghana.

GILLBT traces its origins to an incident that occurred in the United Kingdom in 1960 involving a police officer who attended an SIL Council meeting. A native Ewe of the Volta Region, he invited SIL to come to Ghana to facilitate the translation of the vernacular Scriptures for his people. Although Ghana was not part of SIL's strategic plan at the time, the organisation soon responded to this urgent call and came to Ghana, establishing its headquarters in Tamale. GILLBT came into being as an organisation in relation to SIL's work in Ghana.

SIL's first director in Ghana, Dr John Bendor-Samuel, of the United Kingdom (UK), arrived in Ghana in 1962. Initially, he worked with the University of Ghana's Institute of African Studies, and later with the

---

[5] The Qur'an refers to Christians and Jews as people of the book (Surah 2:62; 5:69; 5:82; 9:29–31). Also, among the Muslim-influenced Kusasi of northern Ghana, Christians are referred to as *Karim bisi* 'learners'.

Department of Linguistics (Quaye 1991:5–6). This professional relationship helped Bendor-Samuel become familiar with the Ghanaian academic and linguistic context so that language and ethnographic surveys could be carried out to enable language development work to begin smoothly. Facilitating Bible translation work with local people was a natural outgrowth of the linguistic research and acculturation. This professional partnership as a backdrop explains the strong bond that continues to exist today between GILLBT and the University of Ghana in the areas of research, training and publication.

An SIL expatriate team initially managed the language development work, gradually integrating Ghanaians as staff members. By 1980 the cooperative effort became legally incorporated and adopted its current name, GILLBT. It is now led by Ghanaians, with the consultant involvement of expatriate colleagues. Though the overall aim of GILLBT is Bible translation, other related functions can be identified in their aims and objectives, as captured in their mission statement: "GILLBT, in partnership with other stakeholders, facilitates access to God's word in the mother tongue in Ghana and beyond through linguistic research, Bible translation, Scripture Use, literacy and community development."

The following GILLBT mission statement is found in all the organisation's strategic offices:

> **G** That is, **Ghana**, is the heart of the organisation, hence it seeks to preserve the linguistic resources of Ghana's language communities and thus strengthen their contributions to Ghana as a nation.
>
> **I** As an **Institute**, it promotes training and learning, thus enabling Ghanaians to creatively use their languages to gain new insights and information in a fast-changing world.
>
> **L** The organisation uses **Linguistics** as a tool necessary to open the door of literacy for hitherto unwritten languages. Their sounds are studied, and the orthography undertaken, and consequently, books written.
>
> **L Literacy** is a by-product of linguistic work. If the literatures produced are to be useful, then the target audience must be literates. Thus, literacy is a natural consequence of the work of linguistics.
>
> **B** Being a Christian organisation, the **Bible** is central to all the work of the organisation. Thus, the central goal of the organisation is to disseminate the truths of the Bible through its members and literature.
>
> **T** The organisation embarks on the Modern Science of **Translation** with the goal of reducing the Bible into the mother tongues of Ghanaians particularly the minority groups. (Quaye 1991:7–8)

As has been the trend of GILLBT's work in northern Ghana, the New Testament was translated into Likpakpaaln as a first step, then the Old Testament. The New Testament was completed in 1978 and then the Old Testament started by the same team. The stories of the Old Testament strike familiar chords among many Africans; so much so that, as soon as the people receive the New Testament in their mother tongue, they yearn for the Old Testament as well.

Prior to the translation project two SIL linguists, Mary Steele from Ireland and Gretchen Weed from the USA, undertook a sociolinguistic and ethnographic survey of the Konkomba. They initially settled among the people at Yankazia in 1962, identifying with them and learning their language and culture. The Yankazia people speak the Nafeba dialect of Konkomba. However, these linguists learned that Nafeba was not intelligible to many of the Konkomba. Further research revealed that the Saboba dialect was the most intelligible to the majority of Konkomba. Thus, the field workers moved to Saboba, the capital of the Konkomba, to carry out continued language development, literature development and the translation. Though expatriates initiated the project, they worked closely with indigenous assistants and accomplished the task together.

The language project was eventually assumed by GILLBT administrative oversight. Orthography decisions were made, literacy materials were developed, with the holistic educational development of the Konkomba in mind and eventually, the translation of the Christian Scriptures were produced. The translation of the Scriptures was not a terminus but rather has become the watershed of Christian mission among the Konkomba. SCRIPTURE ENGAGEMENT is the follow-up to a successful translation of the Scriptures in the mother tongue of a people group. The stated goal of Scripture engagement is to actively promote the use of the translated Scriptures. Audio-visual aids are being employed in communities to facilitate individual and corporate listening of the vernacular Scriptures by audio recording and by viewing films that have been dubbed into the Likpakpaaln language.

6.6 The role of the indigenous Konkomba in Bible translation

In the translation of the Scriptures into Likpakpaaln, Konkomba indigenous resources were employed. These resources included native translation assistants, the perspective that traditional religion and indigenous worldview gave to the wording of the translation, the indigenous language itself, and the checking feedback provided about the translation by members of the indigenous community.

Bible translation has always involved teamwork even in situations where a prominent figure is championing the task. This is what informs Sanneh's standpoint when he declared the role of the indigenous personnel to be most crucial (1989:159); the success or failure of the translation task depends largely on the role of the indigenous people. Alan S. Duthie explains that a typical translation involves four stages, namely: (1) drafting the translation, (2) a review by a panel of consultants, (3) a review by a larger number of church and other community representatives and (4) polishing by the original translators (Duthie 1985:17). In all four stages, the indigenous personnel make significant input.

Mr. Justin Frempong, past Director of GILLBT, in an interview in 2002, explains further how this team works together:

> Bible translation involves a team. To start with, it cannot be the work of just one or two people. We work with members of the language community and...study the meaning in the original language. We discuss it together and then they, too, help us get the best way of expressing that same meaning in the language that we are working on. And then after we have somehow written it down, they take it out and read it to the old men. They read it to their wives, and they read it in church services to see whether it really communicates well, and to see if it really is the language of the people.

Marge Crouch, an SIL member who has served in northern Ghana for over forty years, had this to say in an interview about the crucial place indigenous people occupy in the translation enterprise:

> We [expatriates] work with members of the language communities through experts in their own language and together we take the Scriptures and try to put [translate] them into whichever language we are working on in a way that is accurate, meaningful and natural – the normal language of the people. So, it takes time, because you need to understand the meaning of the original and then think of the best way to express it in the language that you are working in so that the full meaning comes across. Doing that is what translation is – transferring the meaning that we find in the original [source language] and re-expressing it in the grammar structure of the language we are working on.

Thus, the indigenous people, as the day-to-day speakers of the receptor language, are the experts of that language; and the translators look to them to suggest equivalent wording to the way the source message was expressed, and to express it in the appropriate grammatical structure of the receptor language, for quality translations that will stand the test of time.

Apart from personnel, another important factor which comes into play in the translation effort is the traditional religion of the receptor society, sometimes called primal religion. The term *primal* suggesting its ancient roots with non-industrialised societies, is preferred by Gillian Bediako in her

6.6 The role of the indigenous Konkomba in Bible translation

writing because of the sometimes-pejorative perceptions associated with "primitive" or "animistic" (Bediako 1997).

Bediako asserts that PRIMAL RELIGIONS have an affinity in their worldviews and concepts with Christian biblical views (1997:13). Other scholars perceive of traditional religion as an important resource for Bible translation as well as Christian faith in general. Sanneh pointed out that "Africans had heard of God, described God most eloquently and maintained toward God proper attitudes of reverence, worship and sacrifice" before the missionaries appeared on the scene (2003:32). Thus, primal religion laid a foundation for the receptor society for understanding the eventual translation of the Bible.

The African context engenders the knowledge and worship of God. The African is socialised in an environment where knowledge of God is so pervasive that the Akans of Ghana have a maxim: *obi enkyere abofra Nyame*, that is, 'nobody teaches a child about God'. It is perhaps due to Sanneh's knowledge of the African religious context that he claims that the situation in Africa might be *too much* religion, not too little (1989:159). Following Sanneh's premise, we can expect that the traditional religious worldview of the Konkomba helped them to make great contributions in the translation of the Bible, and a comprehension of the message, once translated.

Another important role played by indigenous Africans to Bible translation is the feedback they provide for translators. The indigenous people are, of course, the best judges of the translation efforts of the translators, both those who are native speakers as well as those involved who are not native speakers. They can ascertain if the translation is comprehensible and natural to the receptor language. Thus, the indigenous people in this sense play the quality control function in translation, a point appropriately observed by William Smalley, an authority on Bible translation (1991:15). Smalley notes that the role of the native speakers is as the primary source of information for translators. Natives have further weighty advantages over the expatriate translator-linguist (1995:61–70). This is clear in the case of the Konkomba language development and Bible translation, roles which have depended substantially on the indigenous people and their resources. The expatriate must absorb as much as he or she can in their contribution to the translation effort. Sanneh was very helpful here in explaining the necessary and rigorous preparations, which serve as the foundation for translation. He noted that,

> The distinguishing mark of scriptural translation has been the effort to come as close as possible to the speech of the common people. Translators have, consequently, first devoted much time, effort and resources to building the basis, with investigations into culture, history, language and physical environment of the people concerned, before tackling their

concrete task. This background work was often indispensable to the task of authentic translation. (1989:192)

Thus, many aspects of the original context of Scripture must be studied because the Bible itself is a book reflecting living people and the society of the source situation. In like manner, a translator must be intimately familiar with the receptor culture, the people whose whole life, worldview and environment are involved. This deep knowledge of the people in the receptor culture aids the translation process and determines the consequent acceptance of the Scriptures in order that the gospel find a natural home among the people, accepted as their own and not a foreign message.

Smalley further explains the importance of the context of the receptor culture:

> Ever since the Christian message was expressed in tongues other than its original ones in the first half of the first century, the gospel has been clothed in multiple languages and has also been coloured by those languages and by the cultures of which they are a part. We cannot translate into Thai without Buddhist terminology, which then gives the Christian message a Buddhist cast, different from the Jewish and Greco-Roman cast of the original, or the cast given by Muslim or Hindu or Confucian terminology, or the cast of the mediating North Atlantic culture. Even the word for "God" is weak in Thai because the deity is not strong in Buddhism. But although the Bible is coloured by the Buddhist medium, it also challenges the medium because the Bible reverberates with the story of a strong God, and if that story is translated powerfully, it partially changes the colouring for those who hear [it]. (1995:62)

In translation, the receptor culture both gives and receives from the translation process, because concepts are modified, reinforced and amplified as they are measured against the source language, the mediating language and the receptor language. So, for the Konkomba translation, the biblical languages, English and the respective Ghanaian language have all interrelated. The process, therefore, calls for deep knowledge of the receptor language and culture to facilitate the translation task, as the translator and team discover together cultural keys that can be utilised in the communication of the Christian message.

The Konkomba traditional religion in the translation process

The indigenous religion of the Konkomba has played a vital role in the process of Bible translation. The Konkomba indigenous religion is an integral part of their worldview, has provided their religious vocabulary and shaped the

6.6 The role of the indigenous Konkomba in Bible translation

attitudes and appropriate posture towards the divine. Sanneh explained that receptor indigenous languages supply vital concepts and generate aspirations but because of the vast linguistic, societal and environmental differences from the source context, include nearly insurmountable challenges to the translation of biblical concepts and the message of Christianity as a whole (1989:158–159). We will examine each of these more closely in relation to the Konkomba.

One of the most important resources that the indigenous religion of the Konkomba has contributed to Bible translation is their worldview, reflected in their religion, because religion is at the heart of their culture (Busia 1955:1). Charles Kraft, writing on culture, communication and Christianity in 2001 defines WORLDVIEW as "a social structuring of a people's perception of REALITY (where the big "R," reality, is God's view)" (Kraft 2001:130). This definition implies that worldview is not individual but is a societal construct which has been informed by existential realities. Kraft explains: "Humans are affected by such factors as limitedness, culture, experience and psychological idiosyncrasies and sin. All of these combine to form a lens through which we view REALITY" (2001:131).

Closely related to worldview is the vocabulary that Konkomba indigenous religion has contributed to Bible translation. These have supplied the vocabulary required for translating the Bible into the receptor languages (Sanneh 2003:31, 32), in this case, Likpakpaaln. A case in point is the adoption of *Uwumbor* for 'God' by linguists working amongst the Konkomba. For Sanneh, this choice is as appropriate as it is revolutionary. In commenting on the effect of using the indigenous term for God in Bible translation, Sanneh pointed out the ripple effect that it has on the recipient culture and its institutions. He noted, for instance, that

> missionary transmitters, having stooped to conquer the native idiom, set off ripples in African societies and commenced a transformation process in culture by drawing on mother tongues and giving them documentary backing. There was change involved in this, for while it might be possible in the pre-Christian period for Africans to think of God in highly refracted tribal and clan terms, terms that were inclined to be uncritical and inward looking, now a new scale of identity was introduced that included a critical, outward looking view of God as the God of all tribes and races, of God, in fact as the clue to all history. (2001:25)

Since God is fundamental to the African religious setting, which in turn undergirds all of life, the indigenous name of God is bound to affect the worldview of the recipients of the translations and then trickle down to their economic, social, political and interpersonal relationships. The use of the indigenous term for God in the Konkomba translation implies that

God is not a stranger but is now also known from the biblical perspective. Sanneh was fascinated by the adoption of the indigenous term for God by missionaries because of the far-reaching consequences of that decision. The adoption of the indigenous name for God would carry corresponding implications for Konkomba social and cultural renewal, leading to their ethnic and historical consciousness. This is bound to have a deep effect on indigenous African societies.

> The name of God contained ideas of personhood, economic life and social/cultural identity, the name of God represented the indigenous theological advantage vis-a-vis missionary initiative. In that respect, African religions as conveyers of the name of God were in relevant aspects anticipations of Christianity, in the relevant cases. Christian expansion and revival were limited to those societies that preserved the indigenous name for God. It suggests that theologically, God had preceded the missionary in Africa, a fact that Bible translation clinched with decisive authority. (Sanneh 2003:31, 32)

In saying this, Sanneh echoed an earlier African theologian, John Mbiti who asserted that God had always been with Africans; missionaries had to bear in mind that God was calling them to make his Son Jesus the Christ known. The Bible in the mother tongue powerfully affected all aspects of the indigenous institutions and society. Indigenous perceptions and attitudes were challenged, particularly the negative ones which were not life-enhancing. Sanneh's appreciation for the use of the indigenous name of God in Bible translation finds resonance in Mbiti's argument:

> African religion has prepared the religious and spiritual ground for many of its adherents to listen carefully to the teachings of the Bible, to reflect seriously upon them, to find a high degree of credibility in them, to discover, meaningfully, parallels between their world and the world of the Bible, and in many cases, to convert to the Christian faith without feeling a sense of Spiritual loss but, to the contrary, thereby, gaining a new outreach in their religious experience. The chief new element brought to African religiosity by biblical teaching is the Lord Jesus Christ and His gospel. Western missionaries did not introduce God to Africa – rather, it was God who brought them to Africa as carriers of news about Jesus Christ. African religion had already done the groundwork of making people receptive to the gospel of Jesus Christ. They already knew God through this traditional religion. (Mbiti 1986:11, 12)

6.6 The role of the indigenous Konkomba in Bible translation

Both Sanneh and Mbiti articulated the enormous contribution of African indigenous religion, yet the missionaries and most of the early Christian converts failed to recognise this fact. Many traditional priests and adherents showed hospitality to missionaries, even at times hosting them in their homes, as did a traditional priest when a missionary first moved to Abetifi. Basel missionary from the 1830s, Andreas Riis, fell ill and was given a medication by a native herbalist that cured him of fever (A. Opoku 1978:9, 14).

Sadly, most early missionaries did not reciprocate the amicable gestures of African traditionalists; rather, they often derided and belittled traditional religion as "animistic" and lacking in religious content. Dutch anthropologist Birgit Meyer cites an encounter between a missionary and a traditional religion priest in which the traditional priest alluded to the fact that he worshipped the same God as the missionary, whereupon the missionary countered arrogantly that he, the priest, worshipped the devil (Meyer 1999:54, 55). Another disquieting account reports that a missionary in Akropong flogged and humiliated a traditional priest. Amongst the Konkomba, however, there have been no such disagreeable confrontations. The incidence of missionary accommodation of non-Christians in northern Ghana might have been due to lessons learnt from earlier conflicts in southern Ghana.

This problem of negative perception of African traditional religion still persists, however, because most practitioners of the present-day Deliverance Ministry, in Meyer's words, perceive African traditional religion as "demonic" (Meyers 1999:xxi). Sanneh and Mbiti admonish Christians to have a more gracious perspective. In view of the immense contribution of African indigenous religion to African spirituality, Christians must change their prejudiced and negative attitude toward the African worldview and rather, appreciate the African indigenous religion. The African ethos has, in Sanneh's submission, supplied Bible translators with the vocabulary, nurture and appropriate attitudes towards God. It has also provided African Christians with religious concepts that have affinities with those of the Bible. As Mbiti and Sanneh also pointed out, Africans have embraced the Christian faith because it meets their indigenous aspirations. Indeed, African indigenous religion has both challenged and strengthened Christianity on the continent. One is expecting more Africans to translate this openness to God into more "godlikeness" so that the Christian faith can lead Africa out of her numerous problems and challenges.

As we have discussed, the worldview of the recipients of the Bible translation is informed by their pre-Christian religions. Not only does a previous religion affect worldview, it also predisposes people to respond in a certain way to Christianity. Pre-Christian religions of the Konkomba have influenced the process of the translation of the Bible into their mother tongue. Aware of this, Sanneh highlighted the role of African traditional religion in the Bible translation process and the transmission of the Christian faith:

Many missionaries assumed that Africans had not heard of God and that it was the task of mission to remedy this defect. In practical terms, however, missionaries started by inquiring among the people what names and concepts for God existed, and having established such fundamental points of contact, they proceeded to adopt local vocabulary to preach the gospel. This field method of adopting the vernacular came to diverge sharply from the ideology of mission. After all, it turns out, Africa had heard of God, described God most eloquently, and maintained toward God proper attitudes and reverence, worship and sacrifice. (1989:158, 159)

6.7 Some aspects of the translation process

6.7.1 Anthropological research

Translators must, as a matter of necessity, know the people for whom they are translating the Bible. For the expatriate this knowledge comes about through anthropological research which explores history, culture, religion, institutions and worldview. Thus, through the pioneering work of missionary translators, local histories, politics, economics, culture, religion and lives have been documented. The Konkomba now have, in their mother tongue, literature on their traditional stories, proverbs and cultural practices as well as articles on modern techniques of agriculture, health and politics.

Even though some anthropologists are hostile to Christian missions among non-Western people, their discipline was born out of the sweat and fruit of Christian missions. This has been substantiated by the accounts of Bible translation projects among various linguistic groups. As trailblazers of Bible translation (Sanneh 1989:193), missionaries opened up hitherto unknown ethnic groups for anthropological research. As Sanneh noted elsewhere, modern historiography in Africa had its foundation in Christian exploration of indigenous societies (1995:398).

Missionary contact with the Konkomba is very recent, that is since the 1950s, hence the transformative effect has been rather minimal. Very little is known of Konkomba ethnography as compared to the Dagomba because Muslim scholars saw the former as an appendage of the Dagomba and therefore wrote very little about them. Another reason for the Muslims' lack of interest in documenting the history of the Konkomba might be because of the Konkomba disinterest in converting to Islam.

6.7.2 Sociolinguistic survey

For any successful translation work, there is a need for linguistic survey at the outset, to know the language and its dialects and levels of intelligibility. Also, translators must explore the language and culture to survive and communicate with the people prior to working on the translation (Smalley 1995:62).

We mentioned earlier that the Konkomba language variant spoken by the Saboba people was chosen for development and translation. Several factors might have contributed to that decision: Saboba is the largest Konkomba town and it is also perceived as the traditional seat of government. Therefore, it is the rallying point of the Konkomba. The linguistic survey also revealed that of the twenty-three variants of Likpakpaaln, it was the one most commonly intelligible to the majority of the Konkomba.

In contrast, Ben Fulford discloses that when the Igbo Bible in eastern Nigeria was about to be translated several variants of the language were explored as well. However, in their case, they ended up with a union language, which belonged to no particular group of Igbo (Fulford 2002:457–501). The fact that it was not owned by any particular group of Igbo spelt its own doom and in Fulford's view, why the Scripture translation was subsequently rejected. With the Hausa Bible translation, however, the Kano variant of the language was adopted (Gaiya 1993:59). The Kano variant had become a trade language in the region; therefore, that translation of the Bible could be used by the minority non-Hausa people of northern Nigeria.[6]

Though the Konkomba translation is not perfect, all the linguistic groups of the Konkomba have embraced it because of the unifying effect of their mother-tongue Scriptures. Where the people have a strong sense of solidarity, the selection of a widely used version of the language unites them. However, where there is a strong competitiveness among the various groups, the selection of one may lead to its rejection by the others – as Fulford recognised in his analysis of the failure of the Igbo Union Bible. The intense rivalry among the various factions of the Igbo ethnic groups accounted for the final rejection of the Union Bible (Fulford 2002:457). Various factors, therefore, have to be considered before selecting an appropriate language variety that all the people will be ready to embrace.

Another important preparation that linguists must consider is the development of the orthography – that is, assigning written symbols to the sounds of the language. Sanneh noted that most languages owe their orthography or alphabet to missionary translators. He explains:

> Christians became pioneers of linguistic development with the creation of alphabets, orthographies, dictionaries and grammars. The resulting literacy, however limited, produced

---

[6] Bible translation use in the trade language, however, led eventually to the marginalisation of the mother tongues of these minority groups.

social and cultural transformation. A culture that for the first time possessed a dictionary and a grammar was a culture endowed for renewal and empowerment, whether or not it adopted Christianity. (2003:99)

Sanneh's observation is true in the case of the Konkomba. SIL, along with GILLBT, pioneered the development of the Konkomba language and followed up with the Konkomba literacy campaign.

6.7.3 Literacy

The vital role of literacy was underscored by Justin Frempong in the previously mentioned interview (section 6.6). It is the key that opens up vernacular Scriptures and other relevant literature in the language. The Konkomba response to the literacy programme was with high interest compared to other northern Ghanaian language groups. They found that learning to read their own mother-tongue by means of the literacy programme lifted them to a level of self-respect – and respect by others. Many of those who took advantage of the Konkomba literacy programme benefitted from reading and writing enough to catch up with their neighbours who were relatively advanced academically and socially.

6.7.4 Securing funding

The Bible Society of Ghana and GILLBT depend on both internal and external funding. The former relies on Ghanaian churches for annual funding through the Bible Week Celebration. The latter was mainly funded from abroad until autonomy was granted to the Ghanaian leadership. Both organisations indicate in their annual reports that they promote membership drives through programmes whereby they encourage people to become members and supporters of their work. The World Vision director for the northern Ghana sector, in a 2004 interview with this author, explained that World Vision International (WVI) has also been helpful in enabling these two organisations achieve their literacy campaign goals by sponsoring development programmes in communities. It is obvious from the large number of Christian missions and Non-governmental organisations (NGOs) involved in language development and translation, that people of diverse backgrounds and skills can cooperate to achieve success.

6.7.5 Personnel

Many volunteer workers are needed in the process of Bible translation because of the immense scale of the translation task. Often only a few full-time personnel are recruited; most other personnel are volunteers. In northern Ghana the Bible Society of Ghana and GILLBT are two examples of organisations who utilise many volunteer workers. The personnel include experts with specific skills, such as Bible exegetes, linguists, publishers, consultants, mother-tongue language experts and others. In order to meet the personnel requirements of the two organisations, local churches are co-opted into their translation projects. Sometimes the need for these projects arises from requests to them by local churches. To show their commitment, the churches may second personnel or agree to pay salaries for experts to undertake the work.

6.7.6 Involvement of the churches

As part of the exploratory work towards Bible translation, denominational and local churches' support is solicited by translation organisations. For example, the Christian churches were brought together for a joint effort to work amongst the Konkomba. GILLBT thus promotes ecumenism and often organises programmes in which the various churches participate.

6.8 Conclusion

Translation of the Christian message has been the dominant feature of mission bodies that have worked amongst the Konkomba. Socio-cultural factors also determine the course of the translation enterprise. The process is an all-embracing task which involved Christian and non-Christian people. Translation and literacy play complementary roles in Christian mission amongst the Konkomba.

Though Western missionaries pioneered the development of most African languages, they rely on indigenous Africans to achieve that language development – and eventual translation of the Scriptures. An appreciation of, and teamwork with, the indigenous agency is therefore key to understanding and appreciating Christian mission efforts in Africa. The translation of the Bible into Likpakpaaln was a simultaneous effort with mother-tongue literacy with all its ramifications. Vernacular Scriptures, along with mother-tongue literacy, became the catalyst for the realisation of socio-cultural development among the Konkomba, something we shall examine more closely in the next chapter. In this light, Christian mission via translation is a cooperative effort, and precludes Western cultural hegemony.

7

Sanneh's Hermeneutic of Mission as Translation and Anti-hegemony: Test Case of the Dagomba and the Konkomba

7.1 Introduction

In this chapter, we analyse interviews, testimonies, reports and observations to ascertain if the Dagomba and Konkomba experience of their mother-tongue Scriptures substantiates Sanneh's paradigm of mission as a dynamic translation movement and anti-hegemony. For the purpose of illustration of the general effect of Bible translation, a brief mention of some other ethnic groups is made. Those interviewed in this work include translators, pastors, community leaders, Dagomba and Konkomba Christians, as well as scholars, and include a personal interaction with Lamin Sanneh. Reports on the Hosanna/FCBH and the "Jesus Film" Project® and literacy, are then analysed. The assessment draws mainly on the testimonies of the persons involved. In a similar vein, we examine the testimonies of beneficiaries of the vernacular Scriptures and the results are summarised in the conclusion.

Chapters five and six reveal that in northern Ghana colonialism delayed missionary work especially among the Dagomba and Konkomba and was an obstacle to the growth of Christianity. However, when colonialism ended, and mother-tongue Scriptures were produced about twenty years later, in the 1970s, Christianity began to expand. Sanneh noted that Bible translation into African languages is accompanied by cultural renewal, and subsequently encourages Africans to re-evaluate Christianity in a favourable light and to embrace it. Could it be that a society with its traditional culture intact, and those translations which adopt the indigenous name for God, experience Christian expansion more than those that do not? Sanneh observed that the inverse seemed true for Islam: "Muslim expansion and growth which occurred were most impressive in the areas where the indigenous religions, particularly as organised cults, had been vanquished or else subjugated" (1989:187). He also notes that, whereas colonialism was a stumbling block to Christian expansion, it acted "as a secularizing force and helped to advance Muslim gains in Africa" (2003:19.) Both Muslim scholars and colonial administrators had a low regard for African traditional religions and took active steps to suppress local belief systems in favour of advancing their own platform.

Bible translation and use of the Bible occupied a central place in the work of missionaries in northern Ghana although with varying degrees of success, according to the missionary organisation. For instance, as described in chapter five, as soon as the Basel Mission settled in Yendi in 1913, the missionaries began studying Dagbani. Soon after that, they started translating the Bible into Dagbani – but had to abandon the work because the British deported them during the First World War.

The next missionary agency to take up the translation cause was the AG Mission from the United States of America. They also began studying Dagbani and began the translation of the New Testament. The Catholic church, working through the Society for the Propagation of the Divine Word, subsequently began work in Dagbon. Though Bible translation was not a priority, they did translate the catechism and some liturgy.[1] Protestant mission agencies gave a focal role to translation of the Bible in their work because of the centrality of the word of God in their doctrine and practices. Mary Steele, key facilitator/translator in the Konkomba Scripture translation project, explained that SIL, in partnership with GILLBT, undertook primary responsibility for facilitating the Konkomba Bible translation. Once the complete Bible was translated into their language, many Dagomba and Konkomba Christians, both Catholics and Protestants, are using these mother-tongue Scriptures actively.

Useful as is the role of missionaries in communicating the Christian message, Lamin Sanneh nonetheless argued that the missionary focus should be directed towards the indigenous recipients of the gospel and what they do with it. After all, the success of mission enterprises is judged by how the

---

[1] Though the Catholic church translated some portions of the Bible into Likpakpaaln after Vatican II for the Catholic daily lectionary, their emphasis was more focused on sacramental liturgy. To their credit, the Catholic church has held the view that the Christian message ought to reflect the culture in which mission is being carried out.

receptor audience responds to the message, and mother-tongue Scriptures are an unquestionable aid to indigenous people embracing and becoming successfully rooted in the Christian faith. For this reason, Bible translation justifiably occupies a central place in missionary work.

For the Dagomba and Konkomba Christians, the Bible, as it is for all Christians who follow the gospel message, is the word of God and, for that reason, is read for private edification as well as in public worship. Southwell, cited in Franklin's study, articulates the fact that the early church fathers also had great reverence for the Bible as God's word and advocated that it must be read and listened to; as a result, many Christians became literate. The Bible is central to the life of both the church and individual Christians because it is a means of deepening the spirituality of Christians (Franklin 2008:5). This, therefore, is where the compelling need for mother-tongue Scriptures lies.

Although expatriate missionaries initiated the translation of the Bible into Dagbani and Likpakpaaln, they relied on the indigenous people for expert knowledge of the languages. The latter were experts in the language, helping generate an accurate translation and able to check and revise drafts of the translation. Various drafts were generated until both the expatriate exegete and speaker who controlled the vocabulary and syntax of the receptor language were satisfied that their joint effort communicated the accurate source message fluently in the receptor language. The results of the translation teamwork were what was widely accepted and sought after as we saw in the case of the Dagomba in chapter five and that of the Konkomba in chapter six.

The translators of the Dagbani Scriptures used *Naawuni*, the name for God in Dagbani. Similarly, the Konkomba name for God, *Uwumbor*, was used in the Likpakpaaln translation. Furthermore, Dagomba and Konkomba religious and cultural vocabulary, expressions, images and attitudes were incorporated into the translation. For Sanneh, the use of the indigenous resources in the translation of the Bible into the mother tongue carries theological import. The use of the indigenous name for God communicates to the people of the receptor culture that their worldview and society have value; and the appellation for God is a fundamental underpinning that adds truth to the message since the social and religious life of the people depends upon this same God. Making his case for the redemptive role of the mother-tongue Bible, Sanneh argues that, rather than stifling indigenous initiative, Bible translation has created favourable conditions for indigenous innovation and motivation in the religious life of the recipients (2003:10).

7.2 The effect of mother-tongue Scriptures in light of Sanneh's paradigm

The Konkomba and Dagomba Christian leaders claim that their mother-tongue Scriptures have helped them improve their grasp of their respective languages. Solomon Bagmae, a Konkomba graduate of the University of Cape Coast, testifies that his grasp of Likpakpaaln had been weak and adulterated with other languages, but improved when he started using the Likpakpaaln Scriptures. Mr. Winston Binabiba, director of a Konkomba NGO, Rural Integrated Literacy and Development Programme (RILADEP), also affirmed the redemptive role of mother-tongue Scriptures with respect to establishing a standard and putting a halt to the corruption of the mother tongue by other, more dominant, languages.

These testimonies make clear that the vernacular translation of the Bible has had a lasting effect on Dagbani and Likpakpaaln, just as Christopher Lensch contends that the translations of the Latin Vulgate into Middle English by John Wycliffe had a major effect on the shape of the modern English language. It armed English lay preachers with copied portions of the Scripture that enabled them to embark upon preaching tours of villages and the countryside. It was for this reason, he points out, that in certain circles, Wycliffe was called the "father of English prose" (2003:27–30). In this regard, it can be seen that Bible translation elevates a people and their language. This was demonstrated by the launching of the Konkomba Bible.

The launching of the whole Bible in Likpakpaaln in the Konkomba capital, Saboba, in 1998, resonates with the initial experience of the Germans at the reception of Luther's translation. The entire Konkomba community comprising Christians, Muslims and traditionalists were there.[2] Expressing the dynamic transformative effect of mother-tongue Scriptures on their speakers, Lensch points out that "Luther's translation had a universal appeal and formed the rallying point for modern German literature and performing arts" (Lensch 2003). Similar experiences have been reported in connection with the mother-tongue Scriptures of the Dagomba and Konkomba.

7.3 The Dagomba and Konkomba use of the Bible since publication

Prior to the translation of the mother-tongue Scriptures, some translation in oral form was already in progress among the Dagomba and Konkomba. Since the complete translation has become available in printed form, these mother-tongue Scriptures are now widely used by Christians from the various denominations both for personal and corporate worship. A pastor who is considered an authority on Dagomba customs and practices, underscored in an interview the indispensability of the Dagbani Scriptures in the church's evangelistic outreach: "We have been using the Dagbani Bible for our evangelistic work. I can say that about 98% of Dagomba

---

[2] The Dedication of the Konkomba Bible in 1998 drew people of diverse backgrounds to the ceremony. This event was covered in different media forms. People from all walks of life attended the launching ceremony.

preachers use the Dagbani Bible. Only about 2% of Dagomba may be using the English Bible to preach. So, the Dagbani Bible has been very beneficial."

In rural Dagbon where most of the churches are located, the Dagbani Bible is widely used by pastors as well as congregants. The centrality of the vernacular Scriptures in the life of the Konkomba was also articulated by A. N., a member of the literacy and development organisation, RILADEP: "The Bible is now central in our lives and determines how we should live. At first, it was, 'they say,' but now it is, 'the Bible says.' Christians are now more committed, which has led to an increase in the number of Christians and churches. Prior to the translation of the Likpakpaaln Bible, Christianity was seen as a religion for whites or literates."

7.4 The effect of Bible translation on the Dagomba

7.4.1 Testimonies from Faith Comes By Hearing

In spite of the fact that the Dagomba are largely Muslim with a cultural life heavily influenced by Islam, Bible translation has made a significant effect on them. Indeed, for the former Director of GILLBT, Justin Frempong, "the effect of the mother-tongue Scriptures and literacy on the Dagomba has been phenomenal." He asserted in an interview that "before the New Testament was translated many of the Dagomba did not understand what Christianity was about, but now that the Dagbani New Testament is available and many of the populace can read it and hear it being read and explained on the radio, they are more able to understand it."

Our study of the rural and non-literate Dagomba, who, hitherto, had been cheated and looked down upon by the urban elite, supports Sanneh's claim that mother-tongue Scriptures strengthen indigenous cultures.

As a result of this language development, Frempong concludes that there is a significant shift in the attitude of the Dagomba towards the Christian gospel. The evidence is obvious because there are churches being planted in the villages; villagers are becoming Christians and enrolling in literacy classes and there are even some Dagomba communities which are inviting Christians to come and start literacy programmes and schools. The Dagomba tend to associate Christianity with modernisation and the provision of modern amenities such as schools, good drinking water, clinics and hospitals. For this reason, it is understandable that they invite Christian churches and NGOs into their communities. The availability of the Dagbani Scriptures and the accompanying literacy work are opening the way for the Dagomba to see that they have something valuable if they follow Christ and believe in his Word.

In order to promote the use of the mother-tongue Scriptures, the Bible Society of Ghana, Hosanna/Faith Comes By Hearing and GILLBT initiated the FCBH Audio Bible Ministry in 2004. The programme involves listening circles that play recorded vernacular Scriptures on audio playing devices.[3]

Working with churches and Christian organisations, listening groups are formed and audio recordings are played to them. Another aspect of FCBH is reaching out to Dagbani speakers through the audio Scripture broadcasts on Radio Savannah in Tamale. The radio programmes are a source of spiritual information for both Christians and Muslims living in the Dagbon area of northern Ghana. The reading of the Scriptures in Dagbani has helped the new Dagomba literates improve upon their reading skills. Many Dagomba who do not go to church can access the Dagbani Scriptures through these FCBH programmes.

Another dimension of FCBH is the opportunity it offers for relevant Christian themes, such as Christian marriage and Christian giving, to be taught on occasions such as at community gatherings. Apart from rallies, workshops are also organised for supervisors and group leaders of the Christian communities. The training workshops[4] offer participants new knowledge and through the roles of the FCBH coordinator and supervisors, now filled by local people, communities are educated in the Christian faith and its existential impulse in northern Ghana.

Initially, audio programmes were given out to individuals to use, depending on their religious and traditional circumstances. The coordinator explained the rationale in an interview as follows: "People of other faiths would prefer not to be seen listening to the Dagbani New Testament on audio in public places." The privacy of individuals was therefore protected, then, in a very strong Muslim context where listening to Christian messages could be problematic. FCBH has achieved a measure of success in contrast to the common mode of evangelism in the form of open-air preaching, which does not ensure privacy.

A man who was deeply involved in *juju*[5] claimed that he became a Christian as a result of his participation in the FCBH programme. *Juju* is cherished in societies like Dagbon where one is conscious of both physical and spiritual enemies. This knowledge naturally calls for adequate protection against one's enemies. When a person finds a more dependable source of protection, however, the person discards the *juju*; this is why some embrace Jesus Christ. For them, becoming a Christian implies they are coming under Jesus' protection.

---

[3] Information in this section about the FCBH program, goals, and results was taken from the FCBH Report on their trip to northern Ghana: Tamale and Gushiegu, 9–13 March 2004. Initially audio cassettes were used. Currently a dedicated audio chip replaces audio cassettes.

[4] The workshops are usually restricted to certain people and locations. For example, the FCBH's March 2004 workshop, was attended by 12 supervisors drawn from the Gushiegu-Karaga area.

[5] *Juju* is traditional medicine for protection, as well as for harming, other people.

7.4 The effect of Bible translation on the Dagomba

Others come to Jesus for reasons other than protection. Life crises such as burdens of poverty and sickness can draw people to Christ as one listener testified upon hearing Jesus' words in Matthew 11:28, "Come to me, all of you who are tired from carrying heavy loads and I will give you rest" in the Dagbani Bible. When this listener heard Jesus' exhortation, he realised he had reached the crossroads of his life and so he had to make a choice. He said the words of Jesus shook him to the very core of his being and he felt restless. In that state, he found his *juju* to be a burden rather than a relief. He experienced freedom from the fear of death and the unknown as he discarded it and placed his trust in Jesus.

After listening to the FCBH audio programmes, Yussif also decided to give his life to Jesus whom he found to be the answer to his search for a satisfying life. As an act of his total commitment to Jesus he resolved to jettison all the charms in his house. He was very confident that Jesus would give him rest and protection. Passionately, Yussif declares, "I have become free ever since." For him, God has not only forgiven him his sins; He has, in addition, given him the spiritual gift of healing. According to the FCBH report, "Yussif prays for people bitten by snakes and other ailments and they have been made well, by the grace of God."

Yussif's conversion assumed a dynamic dimension because through his testimony many in his community came to believe in the Christian faith as Good News for them too. As an evangelist who is non-literate, playing the FCBH audio programming is his access to the mother-tongue Scriptures, not only for his personal use but also for the entire community. In his own words: "Since I cannot read, I use the [audio] cassettes to preach." Apart from listening to the audio programming, this determined young man has been able to memorise a large portion of the New Testament Scriptures. Though the written text of the vernacular Scriptures seems to benefit only the literate, Yussif adopts the strategy of oral people, who often memorise the vernacular Scriptures.

The altering effect of the mother-tongue Scriptures on the Dagomba can be inferred from the story of a villager who is referred to as "doctor" because he is a seller of pharmaceuticals and provides health services to surrounding villages in the Northern Region of Ghana. In addition to his profession this man is also a FCBH supervisor. This responsibility permits him to offer healing on a spiritual level as he promotes listening to the vernacular Scriptures in all the villages he visits with his medicines. For him, the FCBH programme is the "best drug for the soul." He is able to say this because of the positive responses that he receives as he shares the vernacular Scriptures. Thus, he has a dual role as an evangelist and a pharmaceutical seller, which is increasingly appreciated because the people do not make any distinction between spiritual and physical illness. However, he thinks his spiritual role is overtaking his original profession. The people find in God's word healing and eternal life that no drug can give.

To maximise the FCBH ministry, rallies are organised to address people's concerns. In a report on a trip to northern Ghana, Tamale and Gushiegu, it was explained that topical issues are generated through the question and answer time in the FCBH listening sessions. These topics are subsequently collated from the FCBH groups from several villages. The various groups are then brought together to a rally where an invited pastor addresses the issues. The topics discussed include the gospel and culture, tithing and Christian marriage.

The evidence suggests that FCBH's audio recordings are bringing about a transformative effect on ordinary listeners among the Dagomba people, and their receptive audience crosses religious affiliation. The FCBH programmes prompted Muslims to purchase copies of the audio Scriptures for personal use. The coordinator of FCBH listening groups reports of a Muslim cleric who has made it a regular practice to listen to the radio broadcasts. For him, Sunday to Wednesday, the four days allotted to FCBH on Radio Savannah per week, were not enough. Another Muslim man recently decided to join the church after listening to the FCBH radio broadcasts for four months and "believes the 'good path' is the way to church."

Apart from the positive response of some Muslims to the reading of the Dagbani Scriptures on the FCBH audio programmes, others, including traditional rulers, have experienced transformation. An elderly man revealed, that "the reading of the Dagbani Scriptures is softening the hearts of chiefs and this is helping handle issues that could have led to divisions and conflicts." Thus, some traditional authorities see the Dagbani Bible as a tool for promoting peace and unity. At the beginning of the chieftaincy dispute between the two royal gates that led to the murder of the *ya na* in March 2002, many Dagomba this author interviewed said, "If only we were all Christians this crisis would have been over by now, for Christians easily forgive and reconcile."

The FCBH report on the Dagbani of 2003 refers to testimonies at Gbulahingu, near Nyankpala in northern Ghana, of God's miraculous healings through listening to FCBH audio programmes. This is possible because those who gather to listen also pray for each other's needs. The listening groups also have the belief that God is speaking directly to them and so they expect His answers to their requests. The group meetings are occasions for teaching themes relevant to the Christian life.

However, in urban centres where about half of the residents claim to be Muslim, the fear of ostracism is a valid concern for the Dagomba who may wish to convert to Christianity. For instance, a Muslim at Diare, thirty-three miles north of Tamale, wanted to become a Christian as a result of listening to the FCBH audio programmes but did not because he was afraid of his father's reaction. Similarly, other residents of that town who consider converting to Christianity worry about the reaction of their families against them. Fear of ostracism by family and Muslim neighbors results in a lower rate of conversion to Christianity in urban areas.

7.4 The effect of Bible translation on the Dagomba

A generally held perception is that to be a Dagomba is to be a Muslim, but reception of the Christian message in many rural areas illustrates that the Dagomba people are not closed to Christianity. A chief in the Northern Region found FCBH audio programmes so beneficial that he and the village elders asked the supervisor to organise a gathering to hear Christian preaching in his courtyard. The success of the open-air preaching and his desire to continue to listen to the audio programmes prompted him to request that a church be established in his village. The chief and his elders recognised that the vernacular Scriptures were meeting the needs of their village.

The coordinator of the FCBH programme also cites examples in which using the Dagbani Scripture audio recordings have transformed people's lives. For example, the chief of a village sixty-nine kilometres from Tamale is a member of a listening group. This chief attests that, until the age of sixty-five, he had never heard of a religion that teaches forgiveness, apart from Christianity. Although he does not call himself an active Christian, he has benefited greatly from listening to the audio recordings. He recounts his response to opposition he had had from some of the inhabitants of the village when he was to be enskinned as their chief: "Once I became the chief, initially I planned to punish my opponents in the village but changed my mind after the pastor played the [audio] cassette on forgiveness to me.[6] When I requested the cassettes from the pastor he gave them to me to listen to again."

The church members at Nafaring near Nyankpala went beyond merely listening to their Dagbani mother-tongue Scriptures, to memorising them. With a repeated listening of the FCBH audio programmes they have increased their comprehension of Scripture passages, which also helps them improve their reading skills based on those passages. With more confidence and an improved grasp of the Scriptures, Dagomba Christians have now begun to share those Scripture passages with other village residents.

As mentioned earlier, Christians are not the only beneficiaries of the Dagbani Scriptures; some Muslims have grown in their appreciation of them, too. For example, a Muslim cleric is reported to have regularly requested the audio programmes to listen to with people in his shop. He confessed he never believed the Bible was the word of God until he started listening to the Scriptures broadcast by radio. However, though he now realises that Christianity is a good religion, he is too deeply immersed in Islam to leave it. It seems there are many secret Dagomba believers in Christ who, for fear of the unpredictable consequences of openly identifying themselves with Christianity, maintain the outer appearance of Islam.

Though many Muslims listen to the Dagbani Scriptures, there is suspicion among some Muslims of their authenticity, that the mother-tongue readers have replaced the words of the Christian Bible with their own words in order to convince people to accept. The allegation that these Scriptures

---

[6] In that type of situation forgiveness is regarded as a desirable virtue.

are corrupted cannot be supported; nevertheless, it has become a justification for some to not embrace Christianity.

During a hiatus when FCBH was forced, because of inadequate funding, to be off the air for ten months, the organisers took the opportunity to assess the broadcast programmes. A questionnaire sent out to listeners indicated that a great number of them wanted the re-introduction of the programmes on Radio Savannah. This was indication that the Dagomba audience was listening and benefiting from the reading of the Dagbani Scripture. For this reason, the radio broadcasts were restarted on 4 May 2003, this time from Sunday to Wednesday. The response of many listeners was that "life had suddenly returned." They were happy they could listen again to "the most important and educative programme on radio." Dagbani speakers and speakers of related languages like the Mamprusi and the Nanumba, patronise Radio Savannah's FCBH programme, and twenty-six new listening groups were started in the Langbinsi area within Mamprugu in the Northern Region. The use of the Dagomba and Konkomba FCBH audio programming has boosted Bible knowledge and sharing of Scripture with others. This has had a positive result; the Tamale Prison officers and inmates have started listening sessions using the audio programmes. Following a good response, a preparatory baptismal class was started on Saturday, 7 June 2003 for the prisoners. There is a wide range of people who are becoming Christians, especially in the rural areas, as a result of the FCBH vernacular ministry.

The elderly as well as the young people are responding to the message of the Dagbani Scriptures. For instance, at Tunayili, near Tamale, an elderly man decided to become a Christian. The traditional spiritual powers he consulted had failed to heal him, but he was eventually healed as a result of listening to the FCBH audio programmes. Another elderly man from Gbandu near Nyankpala became Christian after listening to Radio Savannah's broadcast of FCBH on the theme: "How elderly men came to Christ." Previously, he thought Christianity was for young people, but listening to the broadcasts changed his perception. A Muslim listener who appreciated the programme exhorted Christians to continue on their righteous way and not to copy the wrong ways of some Muslims.

Another Muslim from a village near Tamale has testified to the truth of the gospel of Christ as he listened to the radio programmes. According to him, the Qur'an does not express the acts of Christ as the Bible does. The clarity of the Dagbani Scriptures has helped him to have a good understanding of the gospel. Similarly, a group of five Muslims in another village also attested to the effect of the mother-tongue Scriptures manifested through the audio recordings. They were happy because the radio broadcasts afforded them the opportunity to listen to God's word, which otherwise they could not do openly for fear of their fellow Muslims.

The reading of the Dagbani Scriptures is having an effect on marriages as well. In the village of Bagiyili, near Tamale, this is manifested in improved gender relations. For instance, some husbands testify that "their wives are now humble and lovely since they started coming to the listening sessions." A man who had previously driven his wife away brought her back after listening to the audio programmes. Since then he has been encouraging her and his children to listen regularly to them, because he had found them helpful. He is also convinced that God is in the Bible and so it is not "an empty book."

The FCBH programmes have further strengthened the faith of Christians. A Christian in Gbungbum near Tamale confessed that his Christian background notwithstanding, it is only now that he feels he has become a true follower of Christ as a result of listening to the audio programmes of Dagbani Scriptures.

Several people have reported their conversion through listening to the audio programmes. Others have expressed their confidence in the truth of the Christian faith. Though once in a while one can find somebody disputing with Christians, many more seem to be receptive to the Dagbani Scriptures. From these testimonies, we can deduce that the FCBH programmes have been beneficial not only to Christians but to some Muslims such as one who wished the authorities of Radio Savannah could withdraw some other programmes to give more time for the FCBH programmes because of how beneficial and remarkable they are. In his view, if the FCBH programme had come earlier to the north, especially Dagbon, it would have had more of an effect than it has now because many more would have known the truth about God.

In the village of Kukuo, a witch camp and suburb of Bimbilla, eleven people became Christians through the FCBH programme on Radio Savannah. According to the coordinator,

> many more people in Tamale town and its surrounding villages are listening to the radio programme. We received verbal reports from people that the [audio] cassettes are not here for us Christians alone but for all. One man from a village called Kpukpaligu requested a Bible from his supervisor. He told him that whenever the cassettes were played on air he usually writes down some chapters and verses which some people want to know. He added, 'we have to teach them.'

He concluded by acknowledging the support of the Bible Society of Ghana and raised the issue of donating Bibles to enquirers. From testimonies and FCBH reports already mentioned, it is evident that the Dagbani Scriptures have had an effect on all aspects of the lives of Dagbani speakers.

7.4.2 Dagbani Scriptures and social change

The Library of Congress Country Studies identifies colonial rule, Christianity, money-driven economies and Western-style education as key factors contributing to social change in Ghana. For instance, contact with Europeans had a significant effect on traditional societies and their institutions.[7] Though social change was no stranger to traditional society, the studies observe that Kwame Nkrumah's Accelerated Development Plan for Education intensified the rate.[8] This development brought in its wake new social institutions formed outside the traditional lineage system which profoundly challenged existing patterns of interaction. More strain was put on traditional relationships and interrelationships as a formal market economy was adopted. Nkrumah's ambitious programme helped mitigate the disparity in development between the north and south of Ghana introduced earlier by the colonial governments and NGOs. Rural-urban migration was set in motion, thus paving the way for the clash of values between traditional communality and Western individualism.

Social change is inevitable in every human society, with or without the mother-tongue Scriptures. Change is bound to occur because societies are made up of human beings who interact with one another as well as with other societies in other parts of the world. A significant area where this change occurred was in the relationship between the ruler and his subjects. Western-style education and Christianity curtailed the chief's powers whilst enabling some of his subjects to gain power, thus challenging the customary notion of the exercise of power.[9] Also, the abolition of the slave trade meant that domestic slavery as well as commercial slavery had to be halted and traditional rulers and African slaveholders who benefited from slavery had their fortunes overturned. The positive side of this social change was the freedom and empowerment of people who had been marginalised.

Benedict Der demonstrates that Christian missions have played a vital role in the social change of the people of northern Ghana. By social change, he means "any action that triggers off the people's response to do things in a new way, which leads to the transformation of the cultural life of a people" (Der 1983:306). Though the changes he mentions are not the direct result of mother-tongue Scriptures, indirectly they are. Since translation is a process, the Christian message was becoming encoded in indigenous cultural forms before culminating in the vernacular Scriptures.

The first phase of Christian missionary enterprise involved the establishment of schools, which produced the first elites who took up the fight

---

[7] These observations were downloaded from the Library of Congress Country Studies on 17 October 2003. The article explains how money re-assigned roles in traditional society. People with money and education assumed leadership roles that had been the preserve of chiefs and elders of families.

[8] The Library of Congress country study can be viewed on the website, https://www.loc.gov/resource/frdcstdy.ghanacountrystud00berr_0/?st=gallery. Accessed 26 July 2019.

[9] The Library of Congress Country Studies, https://www.loc.gov/resource/frdcstdy.ghanacountrystud00berr_0/?st=gallery. Accessed 26 July 2019.

7.4 The effect of Bible translation on the Dagomba

for independence from the colonial authorities. Most mission bodies not only built Western-style model schools, but they also developed the mother tongues of Ghanaians. The development of the mother tongues invariably enhanced the identity of indigenous people who hitherto were not recognised by the colonialists. As we have already seen, the Basel Mission, the Bremen Mission and the White Fathers were at the forefront in the development of most of the languages in Ghana (Hall 1983:9). The attitude towards the development of the mother tongue became a divisive issue between the missionaries and the colonial administrators. The colonial authorities resisted the development of the mother tongues because they wanted their subjects to learn European languages (Howell 1997).

Christianity, particularly through Bible translation, has allowed the Dagomba to appreciate their indigenous names and has therefore provided an alternative to the Islamicised naming ceremonies in most Dagomba communities. A Dagomba pastor from Nyankpala related how his choice of indigenous Dagomba names in Christian naming ceremonies is very much appreciated by a Muslim neighbour who complained that Islam had been gradually supplanting indigenous Dagomba names. Another *mallam* lamented that Dagomba Muslims most often do not know the meaning of some of the Arabic names they adopt. As a result, it has happened that animal names have been unknowingly given to their children. This point, noted in an earlier chapter, places Dagomba Muslims in a dilemma. How are they to maintain their identity as Dagomba as well as remain committed Muslims? From their perspective, choosing Arabic names for their children is a mark of orthodoxy. On the other hand, the naming of babies, called *sunna*, demonstrates the fact that most Dagomba Christians are increasingly adopting indigenous Dagomba names, sometimes in addition to biblical names, thus affirming their ethnic as well as Christian identities.

The Dagomba Scriptures have further enabled the Dagomba to modify their first pregnancy ritual, known as *presigu* (see section 3.11.2). For the Dagomba, the celebration of a woman's first pregnancy is a significant event and offers opportunity for the young woman to be educated in healthy prenatal care. Dagomba Christians have developed a liturgy to give the practice a Christian touch. It is in the form of a church service where the pregnant woman is advised on safe practices, exhorted from the Scriptures and then prayed for. It had hitherto been an occasion for providing spiritual protection for the unborn child and mother in the form of a talisman with Arabic writings. Now, instead of the talisman, the Dagomba Christians donate a copy of the Bible to the pregnant woman, urging her to study it daily and "to trust in the Lord Jesus Christ" for the protection He offers. All those present are urged to put their faith in Jesus Christ and to become his disciples.

According to Sanneh, Bible translation has triggered a much broader process of ethnographic field research and historical documentation, to produce a ripple effect on politics, economics, culture and society, as well as on religion (1989:167). Indeed, embarking on Bible translation into the mother tongues has made it possible for histories, ethnographies and daily issues to be documented. This is true for both the Dagomba and the Konkomba.

7.5 The effect of the Likpakpaaln Scriptures on the Konkomba

The complete Konkomba Bible has had a greater effect on the spread of the gospel among the Konkomba than the Dagbani New Testament alone had done for the Dagomba. It has influenced more people to identify with Jesus Christ and accept him as Saviour. Churches have grown and believers have been nurtured because Konkomba Christians have been able to share with understanding to their own cultural group as a result of having a translation of the Bible in Likpakpaaln. Though the Dagaaba, of the Upper West Region of Ghana, do not have the complete Bible, they have some portions of Old Testament translation based on their lectionary readings. This has been used for church services and also as the means whereby the people learn the demands of the gospel to continue to follow Christ. For Frempong, therefore, "Bible translation is very important to evangelism and to church growth, church planting and anything that has to do with the life of the Christian in a community" (interview 2003).

Bible translation and literacy have the potential to empower persons and communities, and the Konkomba communities are no exception. In the 2003 interview, Frempong commented on the empowering role of mother-tongue Scriptures:

> Jesus has already given us the mandate and the promise that anyone who believes in him would have the power of the Holy Spirit, so the power of the Holy Spirit empowers the Christian to live the Christian life and to witness for Christ. But we know there is a question which Paul asked in Romans 10... 'How can they hear without a preacher, and how can he go when he is not being sent, and how can he preach if he has no mandate'. Therefore, the mandate is given in the word of God and that empowers the community of believers to stand firm and to be able to communicate the Gospel to all those in that community who need it.

Thus, for Frempong, empowerment is an integral part of the Christian mission and made possible by God's word being available in the native tongue. He stresses the mother tongue because it ensures people's understanding in a way that a foreign language is unable to do. Prior to the translation of the Likpakpaaln Bible, sermons were translated spontaneously, and many things went wrong with such "on-the-spot interpretations." The

7.5 The effect of the Likpakpaaln Scriptures on the Konkomba

mother-tongue Scriptures have been able to empower the rank and file of the Konkomba to preach confidently and to minimise a misunderstanding of the Scriptures. In this sense, Bible translation first provides the power for Christians to strengthen their faith. Secondly, it empowers the whole church for church planting and sharing the Good News with others.

The development of indigenous music and hymns has been made possible as an outgrowth of understanding the Likpakpaaln Bible. Some Konkomba Christians shared their experience on the use of their native language in worship: "When we use the Bible in the language we know best, our worship, with music based on the Scriptures in our own language, becomes meaningful." Traditional song composers who are Konkomba, are using their Likpakpaaln Bible to compose songs for Christian worship.[10] Thus, the use of their own language gives impetus to indigenous creativity in the realm of liturgical development. It elicits spontaneous response to God's word under the inspiration of the Holy Spirit. SIL team members, as facilitators of the Bible translation, also encourage the Konkomba to adopt indigenous lyrics and music forms, i.e. ethnomusicology, using the translated Scriptures.[11] Hymn creation allows indigenous lyricists and native community instrumentalists to experience Christian music from their own cultural, natural-sounding perspective rather than from another.

The work of GILLBT has had a tremendous effect in that, before the Konkomba people had access to the Likpakpaaln Bible, very few Konkomba were interested in the church. As mentioned in chapter six, although there were few churches, and they did not attract the Konkomba. However, with the successful translation of the Bible, many more Christians and churches have emerged in the Konkomba homeland and other places to where they had migrated, such as Kintampo in the Brong-Ahafo and Kpassa in the Volta Regions. Only the Catholic church and the AG churches could be found in Saboba prior to the commencement of the translation of the Bible into Likpakpaaln. Today there are over twenty churches in Saboba alone. According to W. B. of Harvest Covenant headquarters in Accra, churches are now being planted, not only in Konkombaland but wherever the Konkomba have settled elsewhere. Undoubtedly, a better understanding of the Bible, now in the language they speak best, has contributed significantly to the growth of Christians among the Konkomba as well as in the transformation of their communities.

Concurrent with Scripture translation, literacy has had an effect on Konkomba identity. Frempong notes that, before the literacy programme was initiated and the Bible was translated, the Konkomba, who are known

---

[10] Toma Assemblies of God Church, Saboba. The Dicheem community, behind the Saboba Secondary Technical, and Trinity Foundation Church, is a case in point.

[11] SIL organises ethnomusicology workshops to sensitise and incentivise leaders in the use of native worship style and traditional music form, to encourage the development of indigenous hymnody and choruses.

to be hardworking farmers, took pride in themselves mainly as being the best yam producers in Ghana. Likewise, taking advantage of the mother-tongue literacy programme, which they embraced enthusiastically, some determined individuals learned English, some even going on to technical school and university. This love for education, triggered by mother-tongue literacy, has paid off. This gateway to academic development was only possible through literacy and Bible translation, according to Justin Frempong. Thus, school is increasingly becoming a way for the Konkomba to establish an identity.

Making a case for the effect of Bible translation and literacy, Frempong, in the 2003 interview, cited other ethnic groups, such as the Frafra of northern Ghana, and reveals that they are also becoming Christians because they can now read God's word in their mother tongue for themselves. People who are oral users of their language and not yet literate are also becoming Christians. But the emphasis on literacy is a strategy to arouse interest in learning to read and write in Likpakpaaln. Thus, it is becoming more and more evident that the availability of the Bible, plus literacy, is affecting the people positively. He illustrated this point further in the interview by describing his own experience as a translator working among the Sissala of the Upper West Region, in this testimony:

> Before we went and [translated] the New Testament, there were one or two churches [established] by the Baptists and Catholics, which were struggling. Since the New Testament has been available the last ten years, the Lord has really used it, and now there is a church in almost every village among the Sissala; the churches are growing, and people are beginning to understand what Christianity is all about. It is not a foreign religion, it is [the message that] God [who] loves us, sent Jesus Christ, and they are beginning to accept that message and make it their own.

Thus, Bible translation gives impetus to church planting and growth. In addition, Scripture in the mother tongue nullifies the erroneous impression that Christianity is a foreign religion. The greatest legacy of the translation of Scripture is the testimony of mother-tongue speakers who now understand the Christian message fully.

The agency, Rural Integrated Literacy and Development Programme (RILADEP),[12] has as its focus the development of the total person in Konkomba society. It involves churches, works with women's groups in income-generating activities, and has members who are key participants in the translation project. Some of these serve as reviewers of the Scriptures that have been translated, while others contribute actively to the translation of portions of the Scriptures.

---

[12] RILADEP grew out of GILLBT.

7.5 The effect of the Likpakpaaln Scriptures on the Konkomba

Community members have always been involved in the work of the Konkomba Bible translation. Because the people are participants, it is not outsiders who impose on the Konkomba, rather the receptor audience contributes to framing the right words for the translation. M. M., a longstanding member and leader in RILADEP, testified to the beneficial nature of using his native language, as follows:

> The translation has made me a better Konkomba. Before I came into contact with the translated materials, I was not interested in reading [my] local language. There are a lot of friends who cannot read the Bible, so I have an advantage by [in the ability to] read the Likpakpaaln Bible. The translation of the Scripture has not come to destroy the [our] tradition in any way, but rather has come to preserve the culture of the Konkomba. Even in the Bible, the Lord said he has not come to destroy, but to save. If you look at the practices we have here, they are all in the Bible, be it marriage, leadership, festivals or others. Translation has rather come to strengthen the culture and to take away its negative aspects. Since culture is dynamic we [can] throw the negative away to enhance its good aspect. For example, during Christmas people come together to talk about development, family issues etc., so it has rather come to better the lives of the people.

The Likpakpaaln Bible has deeply affected the KOYA, which brings together many Konkomba from various places to Saboba during Christmas and Easter conventions, to talk about how to improve their lives, among other things. The Likpakpaaln Bible has also helped the Konkomba discard some practices that often cause conflicts, such as plural- and forced-marriages; as a result, even most non-Christians now marry only one wife, avoiding the many problems plural marriages pose. On criticism from some traditionalists that the Bible undermines their culture, M. M. responds that when some older Konkomba say the mother-tongue Scriptures have negative effects, it may be because they have misapplied the message. Their concern is that the Bible condemns some of their traditional worship practices, plural marriage and drunkenness. For M. M., the Likpakpaaln Bible has no negative aspect but rather, has come to change people's lives for the better.

The Konkomba now have, not only the full Bible translated into their language, but also the "Jesus Film" in Konkomba and oral Scripture portions produced by the FCBH Audio Bible Ministry. Though M. M. laments that many of his brothers have not had formal education, the trend is heartening because some have learnt to read in their local language, and by means of that ability, many have been able to continue with formal education – some have even become pastors. Apart from the educational benefits of the Bible and other materials available in their language, M. M. submits that vernacular translation and literacy skills have also helped others get employment, as if they had gone to formal schools. To substantiate this claim, he cites the work of the staff of RILADEP who help youth groups and churches write hymns in Likpakpaaln. This project is creating jobs for the youth as they receive money from the sale of recorded songs. Under the auspices of GILLBT, the youth also dramatise Scripture, which apart from generating income, also provides entertainment and a deeper appreciation of Likpakpaaln.

Though many Konkomba find the mother-tongue Bible a valuable asset, deeply traditional Konkombas may be uncomfortable with use of the vernacular translation and not want to accept use of it, claiming the translated Bible is foreign. They may claim that Konkomba Christians are changing their culture. During interview sessions some of the Konkombas with whom this author spoke were adamant that those who accept the message of the Scriptures improve their way of life which does, consequently, influence others to change – but for the better.

For those who cannot read, alternative audio and video methods promote the gospel in the language they understand best. For example, the professionally produced "Jesus Film," based on the Gospel of St. Luke and dubbed into Konkomba, is shown in public events to which people attend for entertainment; but proves also to be a means of transforming their lives.

M. M. gave additional examples of the consequence of Bible translation and literacy among the Konkomba. Churches have been established, women's groups have been formed to engage in income-generating activities. The most beneficial aspect of this development is the formation of fellowships which are uniting women of varying social circles. Communities that are making use of the translated Scriptures are more aware of issues related to their welfare than those who do not.

The Likpakpaaln Bible and the literacy programme have played positive roles both in communities and in the churches. They serve as the rallying point for people who hitherto did not practice coming together to discuss issues concerning their welfare. Furthermore, the mother-tongue Scriptures serve as a peace-making instrument by bringing people together as a herald of peace. That other people can live together peacefully is appealing to the Konkomba, so they seek to find a key to experiencing the same themselves. With more exposure to the Likpakpaaln Bible, gifted Konkomba musicians have composed songs in their language, centred on the theme of peace.

The positive roles that the Bible and literacy play in ethnic cohesion is more evident now, as group meetings are easier to organise. These include occasions when the community decides to honour facilitators and supervisors. These functions, to which Christians and non-Christians are invited, serve as a forum for people to share ideas, learn and cooperate with one another wherever they meet. In the churches also, people can now read the

7.5 The effect of the Likpakpaaln Scriptures on the Konkomba

Scriptures for themselves, with or without pastors, and are therefore motivated to grow into spiritual maturity, weaned from spiritual dependency. An area where the effect is felt is that of the family. According to the Konkomba, the Likpakpaaln Bible has been able to bring families together through its central teaching on love, and this has led to improvements in the relationship between husbands and wives, which in turn, has brought domestic peace.

Two RILADEP workers in the Konkomba region met with the author for an interview in 2003. The information and observations in the next few pages, except where otherwise noted, are taken from that interview. One, Mr. Binabiba, expresses his appreciation for the mother-tongue Scriptures as follows:

> For me in particular, I benefitted greatly from the translated materials because it is my dialect and I don't need any interpretation, as compared to English where certain words are strange. With the Likpakpaaln there is no problem at all. With the wider communities it has helped a lot of people. We started with the literacy work and all people, traditional worshippers, priests and priestesses, among others, joined and eventually became Christians. So, to me it has helped in the community.

Apart from promoting literacy, Bible translation has affected the Konkomba way of life in a positive way. First, many people are now Christians and so they no longer purchase animals to sacrifice to divinities. This has helped to minimise witchcraft accusations and help struggling families financially. Bible translation and literacy programmes have also boosted numbers and strengthened the church community. Consequently, many people, especially the youth, have been helped. Many young people, who are now Christians, no longer become involved in activities involving alcoholic drinking and the marriage of many wives. In other words, the mother-tongue Scriptures have transformed the lives of the Konkomba people of all ages.

As was pointed out earlier, some elderly Konkomba feel the Likpakpaaln Bible has affected them negatively because their perspective is that the Christian religion is not theirs, but foreign. One practice the elderly Konkomba hold onto strongly is divination, for spiritual guidance. According to the Konkomba, no death occurs without a cause; once somebody dies, a soothsayer is consulted to find the cause of the person's death.

Some Konkomba also continue the observance of sacrifices to divinities. In addition, the traditional Konkomba look for powers such as *juju* to protect themselves against cutlass wounds and gunshots. The elderly Konkomba observed these practices because of the hostile environment in which they live and work. They felt they needed protection for their daily occupation and in times of fighting. It is also understandable, therefore, that non-Christian elders such as these hold such a negative view of the Likpakpaaln Bible, because the teachings of the Bible are not compatible with their strongly-held traditional practices.

Another thorny issue is that Konkomba traditionalists object to the perspective on monogamy in the New Testament. The Bible translation has enhanced awareness of human rights among the Konkomba, specifically in the area of women's rights and marriage. Some girls now claim the right to choose their own husband. This development is therefore helping to stem the tide of forced or exchange marriages. Often those marriages do not include the consent of the young women involved. If a young woman resisted a prescribed marriage, she would have been forced into it. In addition, the practice of betrothal of young girls to elderly men is becoming less frequent as a result of this awareness. As more Konkomba become Christians, they tend to embrace monogamy. The Bible is understood to espouse marriage as a willing participation by both man and woman in a monogamous relationship. It is thus most favourable to the young Konkomba women.

Another redemptive role of the mother-tongue Bible which we shall consider concerns the events surrounding death. According to those interviewed, some Konkomba widowhood rites can be dehumanising, as they are in other Ghanaian ethnic groups, such as the Fante and Akan (Aidoo-Dadzie 2001 and Senavoe 2001:39–46). They claim that when a Konkomba man dies, his wife is expected to fulfil certain rituals like "walking around naked." Another practice involves a woman who has had an affair with another man in her husband's house. When her husband dies, she is made to walk backwards out of the house during the funeral rites. This is done to humiliate her and to reveal that she committed adultery. Thus, in addition to her grief, the widow undergoes a degrading humiliation before a crowd of mourners. From an outsider's perspective this practice appears unfairly biased since men who commit adultery against their wives do not undergo similar rituals.

Although the Likpakpaaln Bible sets a standard for marital chastity, at the same time it calls for punishment to be correctional, not humiliating. It offers opportunity for confession and fortification and compassion towards all people caught in activities that are unethical. A case can be made therefore that Bible translation and literacy have contributed to a respect for human rights among the Konkomba.

Before the coming of the mother-tongue Scriptures, the northern Ghanaian woman had endless tasks including cooking, fetching water and wood, farming, childbearing and childcare, with little or no help from her husband. It has been observed that now the message of the Scriptures has encouraged men to share the domestic burdens with their wives. Since the Bible challenges men to love and care for their wives, many Christian men are now doing their best to minimise their wives' suffering by helping with some of these activities previously considered to be women's work. In many

7.5 The effect of the Likpakpaaln Scriptures on the Konkomba

Christian homes, love and tenderness are replacing aggressiveness and quarrels. Thus, the Likpakpaaln Scriptures are credited with introducing civility and peace to homes which had hitherto embraced domestic violence as part of their tradition.

Interviewees were unanimous in their response that the Bible in the mother tongue has helped to preserve Konkomba traditions and culture rather than destroy them. Mr. Binabiba, a RILADEP worker, sums up the responses indicating that the Likpakpaaln translation generally preserves Konkomba culture, as follows:

> On the preservation of culture among the Konkomba, it is generally a custom that the young should respect the elderly. You are not supposed to insult your mother, father or elder brother or sister - and this is supported in the Bible. So, those who became Christians have seen that it is a good thing for them, and it is being preserved in the culture. I don't know, but in the negative aspect, it is some elders who think the culture or some aspects of it have been captured by Christians; I feel everything is good. But for the elderly, because of ritual performance and polygamy and faith in other powers, they think that their culture has been destroyed.

The Likpakpaaln Bible affirms some relational values in Konkomba culture, though the prescription on forgiving and being kind to one's enemy sounds rather strange and at variance with traditional Konkomba culture. Overcoming and humiliating one's enemy is more in consonance with their traditional culture than Jesus' prescription of turning the other cheek. The traditional Konkomba will view that as a weakness. For those who have become Christians, cultural values which are compatible with the Likpakpaaln Bible are welcomed and seen to be affirming Konkomba identity.

Another helpful area in which the influence of Bible translation on the Konkomba can be assessed is the preservation of the Konkomba language. One pastor testified in a 2003 interview to the way the Likpakpaaln Scriptures have helped them in the area of preserving the purity of the language:

> It has now made the sermons very short and lovely. Besides composing the songs in the local language, I personally enjoy this translation because initially my parents were not Christians so when I learnt the Bible in school I could say things in English but when it came to my local language, things were usually hard. But now with the translation I can read in my own language sharing with them and this motivates them to also read and when they get the word it helps to practice their faith very well. It has also improved my Likpakpaaln

> very much. I used to adulterate it with other words like Twi, English, etc., but now my vocabulary has improved.

According to some interviewees, prior to the Bible translation, many of the youth brought some foreign words into the Konkomba language, but now, because of the Likpakpaaln Scriptures, they have realised that many of the words they were using were borrowed from other languages. In addition, a Konkomba dictionary was produced, though it is now out of print owing to lack of funds to reprint more.

The interviewees further explained that to fully empower the Konkomba, GILLBT embarked upon a literacy strategy that ensures the total development of the people. The Rural Integrated Literacy and Development Office, which is an offspring of the translation project, has over the years embarked upon developmental programmes with the sole aim of alleviating poverty among the people. These are in the form of literacy programmes. Initially these were poorly patronised by the women, according to a RILADEP report. To arouse more interest among them, development activities, such as soap-making, pomade-making and cloth-dying were included in the agenda for women's meetings so that the literacy programmes would be introduced. The strategy worked and many of them now appreciate a growing depth of knowledge and therefore have accepted literacy as important due to its functional role.

Many children under normal circumstances would not have been allowed to go to school because parents expect their work participation on the farm. Now, however, children attend school whether their parents agree enthusiastically to it or not. This is the outcome of a successful literacy campaign that has enabled children to master Likpakpaaln primers. Literacy has created awareness of the wider world and established a platform to higher education. Mr. Binabiba of RILADEP voiced his personal observations, as follows:

> In the year 2001, we had about 145 or so people going from the literacy school to formal schools at 15 or 16 years of age, even though this is above the formal age for basic schooling. Many of them have managed to advance subsequently and entered technical schools, Bible schools, and some even [have been accepted] to universities. So, it has really helped a great deal.

In addition to functional literacy, the RILADEP introduced credit facilities. The organisation gives women loans for trading and farming. This has been effective because many women are now engaged in various businesses including soap making, pomade, batik, dyeing of cloth, as well as baking and providing booths where bread and cakes are sold. The result is that they can now better maintain their children and husband financially. According to one source, "they were unable to do this initially because they did not

7.5 The effect of the Likpakpaaln Scriptures on the Konkomba

have the means to start with, but now they have their own funds and can pay their own hospital bills and other expenses."

In addition to informing and empowering the Konkomba, Bible translation and literacy have also helped in the Konkomba people's relationships with other ethnic groups. The interviewee asserts:

> [Literacy] has helped in the people's relationship with other tribes in that through literacy people now know their rights. They have got new ideas about civil rights. There are different books in the language; for example, there is the abridged version of the constitution translated into Likpakpaaln. People read it and now know their rights. Other ethnic groups have similar [publications] and so people know others' basic rights and how to live peacefully with them.

Thus, the knowledge acquired through literacy, coupled with the mother-tongue Bible with its message of love and forgiveness, contribute to peaceful co-existence at various levels of Konkomba society.

The information from here to the end of this section has been gleaned from an interview with a pastor of the EPC and members of his congregation. The interview took place in Saboba in January 2003.

In order to properly translate the Scriptures into a vernacular language, translators must immerse themselves in the culture and the language, gaining considerable scholarly knowledge in the process. The Konkomba, with the production of Likpakpaaln literature through Bible translation, then breached the frontiers of indigenous knowledge. Thus, the newly literate Konkomba have been helped to broaden their horizons as they share in the intellectual, experiential and cultural world of the non-Konkomba.

Another result of the Likpakpaaln Bible and literacy is that these tools have raised Konkomba morality by reawakening their "indigenous narrative impulse,"[13] in other words, inciting the Konkomba to rediscover their tradition of passing on moral values to their young people through storytelling. The Konkomba Bible translators collected the indigenous stories that were told by the fireside at night to teach Christian morals and wrote down the stories in the Konkomba language to encourage literacy. In doing this, the Konkomba language has been enhanced and mother-tongue literature has already been produced for the new Konkomba literates. Thus, the literacy level has improved because both those who go to church and those who do not can read the Bible and other mother-tongue literature at home. Interviewees were elated that in many Konkomba villages today it is possible to find people who can read and write in English. Even more community members can read and write in their own language, which seems to be a catalyst to the additional propagation of the gospel and literacy.

---

[13] Lamin Sanneh saw this as a natural outcome of mother-tongue translation.

The Konkomba appreciate the role of Bible translation and literacy in helping preserve their cultural tradition of storytelling. Church members say that many of their cultural narratives have been recorded and written in their language. Furthermore, those interviewed claim that

> These stories have helped us to learn the moral values of our people. And not stories alone; our poems, rhymes, riddles and others have been recorded. A Konkomba child of about five years can tell a story in Likpakpaaln but the brothers and sisters who have left Konkombaland cannot do that.... The literature [written in Likpakpaaln has] addressed health issues, hygiene and cleanliness.... And the Bible translated into our language has relieved us of fear in connection with death. We now know from the Bible that if somebody dies we...do not have to fear the dead person, for we know where the person has gone.

Another effect of the Likpakpaaln Scriptures is seen in the area of burial and the performance of funerals. Rather than destroy culture, Christian influence has enhanced Konkomba culture. For example, people have now seen that the way Christians bury their dead is more attractive and less costly than what they were used to doing. Another attraction for the Konkomba is the honour given the dead, by the laying of the body in repose in the church for people to pay their last respects. This is perceived to be more dignified than the Konkomba tradition in which the body of the deceased is buried naked. According to one pastor, "many Konkomba confess that they like the way Christians handle funerals, and will become Christians so that when they die, they will also be treated with such dignity."

Naming ceremonies take place after the birth of babies among the Konkomba, and include times when prayers are said for the safety of baby and mother. The Likpakpaaln translated Bible is helping the Konkomba Christians in these ceremonies. Traditionally, the Konkomba set aside a particular day for shaving the child's hair and requesting spiritual protection, as well as for performing purification rituals. Nowadays, Christians usually offer prayers for the baby's father and mother, the baby, and then the whole family before the child is named. The Konkomba are increasingly opting for the Christian practice rather than the traditional one. For many young Konkomba, therefore, Christianity is seen as a modernising influence, not a way to destroy it.

Bible translation coupled with literacy are locomotives for transforming as well as preserving Konkomba identity. In other words, the group identity is more enhanced than diminished. This supports Sanneh's claim that translation excites the indigenous impulse of vernacular narrative, thereby preserving a people's cultural identity.

7.5 The effect of the Likpakpaaln Scriptures on the Konkomba

From the scenario just painted, we can see the difference translation has made in Konkomba communities. The interviewees explained that, prior to Bible translation and literacy, it was often difficult for them to travel to big towns like Accra and Kumasi because they were handicapped by not knowing how to read. The situation has changed, however, because, according to these interviewees, "they can now travel alone, identify traffic lights and buy things in stores without anybody guiding them. Initially, we got people to assist us who we thought were educated or 'better' in certain areas whenever we found ourselves in the big cities." Frequently some of the so-called friends or guides exploited them.

Another significant effect has to do with the improvement in intra-ethnic and inter-tribal relationships. Those EPC members interviewed explained that

> most of our people were afraid of strangers because there were a lot of quarrels among people, especially marriage-related issues. But since this translated Bible came to be part of us, we have become used to strangers. We now mingle with them and they are part of us. They have learnt from us, but at the same time they educated us and so our people started getting used to some of their modernised way of life. Of course, the fear in our people was still fresh on our minds, because of the colonial masters' treatment, slave raiding and the slave trade. This created xenophobia so whenever we saw strangers, we felt that they were agents of such people and so we tried to keep our distance. However, after this translation, our parents now accept other people and have positive views of them. Now also they see other occupations apart from farming as useful. In previous days, if you were a Konkomba man and not a farmer, you were seen as a lost person for it was not your forefathers' occupation. Our people now allow their children to go to school and hence we can speak English just like others and so the translation has brought a lot of positive changes to us.

Bible translation makes an effect on the community for whom the task is undertaken, whether in southern or in northern Ghana. Justin Frempong emphasised that the Likpakpaaln Scriptures have made a socio-cultural effect in the Konkomba context in ways similar to the effect of vernacular Bible translation on other ethnic groups of southern Ghana. The mother-tongue Bible has proved to be a powerful and an indispensable tool, which is enabling people to be grounded in the Christian faith and stronger in their own culture. We see the same phenomenon among other language groups which have had the mother-tongue Bible. Mr. Frempong affirms that the best way to test the definite effect that has been made on the life of the

Konkomba is to compare their lives before and after they had their own Bible.

7.6 The effect of Bible translation on the Bimoba people – a comparison

In order to assess the full effect of mother-tongue Scriptures on recipient communities, I interviewed two Bimoba pastors of AG churches in Naati and Tamale, in 2003 near Gambaga in the Northern Region of Ghana to determine whether the experiences in the Dagomba and Konkomba reports apply to the Bimoba as well. This section reflects the pastors' responses during the interview. The Bimoba are neighbours of the Konkomba in the Mamprusi Traditional Area. They are an acephalous society like the Konkomba. The pastors explained that when the translators started the translation work among the Bimoba and were not able to find the correct translation to bring out the meaning for a word in the Bible, they went round to enquire from the old people. They noted that at times one word could have several meanings, so if they came across such a word they would have to leave it until the appropriate translation was agreed upon by those consulted. This contributed considerably to reviving the language.

The Bimoba Bible has helped the pastors greatly within their community. They recalled how the translators organised workshops with church leaders and pastors and considered some topics from the mother-tongue Bible to find answers to some disturbing happenings in the community, such as rampant suicides and forced marriages. An additional benefit of the mother-tongue Scriptures is the opportunity it offers the Bimoba Christians to compose songs, which are then recorded on audio recording devices for sale to the Bimoba in Togo as well as those in the United Kingdom and elsewhere, thus spreading the effect of the Bimoba Scriptures beyond their traditional borders.

It was revealed further that Bimoba women who were non-literate can now read and write because they enrolled for the literacy programme and have subsequently been using the Bible as their guide. Through this they have gained confidence, knowing that they are of equal worth with the men. Conscious of their enhanced status, they now go to church with their Bimoba Bibles and participate actively in church worship by reading and answering questions.

The Bible for the Bimoba is not merely a book to answer their questions; it is also seen to be helping to preserve their culture. The pastors explained the centrality of the mother-tongue Scriptures to the Bimoba as follows:

> If something is happening in the community that is bringing harm to the people, we refer to the Bible in our mother tongue. We quote some of the Scriptures to the people so that it can help them to stop certain unhelpful practices. So,

> the people are interested to read their own mother tongue so that they can profess their faith in Christ intelligently. So, the Bimoba Bible has helped us a lot.

These Bimoba pastors say they are able to know and to uphold the moral standards given in the Bible, and this makes them respected Bimoba and faithful Christians. They argue that translating the Bible into their own mother tongue has helped them a great deal by encouraging them to improve upon their lifestyle. They explain that when they compare their culture to the Bible it helps to strengthen their faith and provides them with solutions to their problems. Two problems that confront the Bimoba society are rampant suicides and conflicts. These problems were mitigated by resorting to the mother-tongue Bible. They testify below how they went about tackling their problems:

> So, we searched from the mother-tongue Bible and saw that suicide was not good. So, we organised a workshop and invited chiefs, Assemblymen, opinion leaders, pastors and *magaziers* or women leaders within the area. When they came, we treated these particular two topics – suicide and conflicts – using the Bimoba Bible translation. We read through some passages and there were many questions. We came to the conclusion that, yes, the Bible is actually a guide and answers every problem. So, we found answers to all these things in our own mother tongue and it was a great help to us. People stopped these social evils and even formed committees to look into all the causes. Therefore, we can say the mother-tongue Bible has actually helped our area and we are so pleased and feel so blessed that we have the Bible in our own mother tongue.

For the two pastors, it was a relief to have the Bimoba Bible because it solved the problem of using interpreters who sometimes were not helpful because they distorted the message. Now these pastors say they are able to speak directly to the people unhindered during the church service.

With the literacy rate now raised, about a quarter to half of the Bimoba population carries their mother-tongue Bibles to church. This has made a remarkable difference in church services because when a verse is announced from the Bible everyone, not just a small elite, is eager to open to it. Apart from promoting reading their mother tongue for clearer understanding, their Bible has given birth to messengers of the gospel. It follows as a natural consequence that the mother-tongue Bible has boosted evangelism among the Bimoba because they no longer see Christianity as an alien religion. For this reason, the Bimoba have taken the responsibility to go out and witness to people and many are now getting converted to the Christian faith.

The pastors explained that when the Bible was not yet translated into their own language it was very difficult for one to become a Christian. If parents were not Christians, they would prevent their children from going to church, and if they disobeyed and went to church on Sunday instead of to work, they were told they could not eat at home. The situation has changed since the Bible was translated; many parents now allow their family members to become followers of Christ without any cultural hindrance.

The Bible translation among the Bimoba has contributed to literacy and formal education, according to our interviewees. The adults who did not go to school have resolved to give their children the chance of doing so. Some of the students in these mother-tongue literacy classes have gone on to formal school. Among these are students who have continued their education in Bible colleges and become pastors.

The pastors revealed that many Bimoba now have access to God through their mother tongue and this has engendered change. In their words,

> The Bimoba are now leaving their "colonial" or past ways of worship and becoming Christians with the result that there is more respect and happiness now in their communities. Even some old men are now leaving what they were doing and becoming Christians and so one soothsayer who was an elder in a clan stopped all he was doing and has become a Christian. So, God is doing miraculous things at our place.

It is not the case, however, that Christians are being weaned from their culture; rather, they are rediscovering their identity through the Bimoba Bible. Peace and unity are being enjoyed in the process of the continuous engagement of the mother-tongue Scriptures and the indigenous people. Much has been achieved through the Bimoba Bible in the communities as the interviewees concluded:

> If we are going to count what God is doing one by one we will need to talk until daybreak. God is doing marvellous things. Some gifted people who composed songs to sing in praise of wealthy people are now Christians and compose songs to praise God through our local way of drumming in the traditional style. Now we sing, drum and dance in the traditional way. When our old people come to hear some of the songs they say, "aah, we will give our lives to Jesus." That was exactly what happened in the case involving the soothsayer. He gave his life to Jesus and we went and burnt all the *juju* and everything and prayed for him. He is now a changed person. In fact, in our area we have been blessed for knowing the Scriptures and practicing what is required.

The testimonies of the Bimoba are eloquent statements supporting the transforming power to which the Dagomba and Konkomba had earlier testified. The Dagomba, Konkomba and the Bimoba all agree that mother-tongue Scriptures have made them better indigenous Christians who live in a well-integrated world. There is a recognised affinity between the world of the Bible and that of the peoples of northern Ghana; the concepts and practices of the Bible resonate with the local people.

7.7 The mother-tongue Scriptures and conversion

Sanneh explained why Africans embrace Christianity so enthusiastically. For him, "people receive new ideas only in terms of the ideas they already have." Therefore, he argued that "Africans embraced Christianity because it resonated so well with the values of old religions" (1989:171). Further, Sanneh observed that though the African traditional religion "provided the rules, rewarding good conduct and punishing wrong, they had only a limited ethical range" (2003:43). In other words, they were tentative, awaiting full realisation by Christ the Incarnate Word. Other scholars like John Mbiti hold a similar view, that the African traditional religion anticipated the fulfilment of this need, which the mother-tongue Scriptures achieved. The testimonies of the Dagomba and Konkomba indeed confirm that their mother-tongue Scriptures have been answering the questions and longings posed by their traditional religion. As succinctly put by Mbiti, the Christian gospel had come to fulfil and not to destroy African traditional religion (1969:12).

Missionary interventions, in the form of social services alongside the translation, aided the receptivity to the vernacular Scriptures. The literacy programmes and social services that went hand in hand with the translation laid the ground for many Dagomba and Konkomba to embrace the Christian faith. It is illuminating from an interview in 2004 with the coordinator of the Dagomba Literacy Programme to hear of some of the avenues that facilitated the encounter between the Dagomba and Christianity. He explains:

> A lot of people have testified that they got to know Christ through reading Dagbani. It is a fact, and this has encouraged many. Not only have people become Christians, they have had their faith strengthened more through the reading of the Bible in Dagbani for themselves without someone instructing them. They have read it, understood it and have become better Christians. It has made us better Dagomba and better Christians. For instance, it has made us better Dagomba for the first time, because it has preserved our culture. It has made us better Dagomba Christians because we can hear Jesus speak in our language. The translated version

of the "Jesus Film" in Dagbani has encouraged the Dagomba because Jesus can speak Dagbani, and this has strengthened their faith.

Certain contextual factors such as the formation of the KOYA have been used by God to draw the Konkomba to the Christian faith. That the launching of the New Testament coincided with the inauguration of KOYA, created Konkomba national awareness and their determination to chart a new path into a brighter future. Apart from converting to Christianity, the Konkomba saw the occasion to "catch up" with other ethnic groups that have advanced in terms of physical development. The quest for education was inspired by this occasion.

In Sanneh's perspective, Christianity, where it has been true to its emphasis on Bible translation, has been "behind the creation of more dictionaries and grammars of the world's languages than any other force in history" (1989:167). From the experiences of the Dagomba and Konkomba, Sanneh is justified in his call upon the Western academic community to look beyond their "default Christianity," that is, the Western one, to World Christianity, which is something much greater and much fresher (2003:69). Mother-tongue Scriptures have contributed to Christian diversity and yet the Scriptures also retain the universal stamp.

7.8 The effect of the Scriptures on theological understanding

Access to the mother-tongue Scriptures has given the Dagomba and Konkomba Christians the opportunity to do grassroots theology. They now apply the Bible to their daily cultural issues, and the mother-tongue Bible has now become the means of dealing with issues of existential import. Christ is given more and more space in their cosmology thereby indigenising the Christian faith. For the Dagomba and Konkomba, the mother-tongue Scriptures are not ancient documents but are current and relevant in their lives. They identify deeply with the biblical characters because of the similarities of their worlds.

Bible translation has helped to bring about a historical shift in Christian theology in Africa, which was in the past dominated by Western ideas. Bible translation now considers local realities so that what Sanneh called "indigenous theological domestication" could be achieved and is expressed even in their songs. Thus, Bible translation has contributed not only to the expansion of Christianity but also to its deepening. Mother-tongue Scriptures enable new communities to have indigenous insights into embracing Christianity and in so doing bring about a fresh understanding of the Christian faith (2003:14). As a consequence, mother-tongue Scriptures have given the Dagomba and Konkomba the impetus to contextualise their theological orientation. A testimony to this development is found in the Dagbani songs and Likpakpaaln songs in the Appendix.

One other contribution of the Dagomba and Konkomba Scriptures is the promotion of Christian diversity or pluralism. Bible translation dispels the notion that Christianity is a transplant from Europe and North America because it has taken indigenous roots and therefore minimises or eliminates the accusation against it that it is alien (Sanneh 2003:40 and Mbiti 1986:12). Sanneh also looked at the unifying role of Bible translation in that mother-tongue Scriptures foster links among denominations rather than creating barriers (2003:41).[14] This point has been demonstrated by the joint weddings, naming ceremonies and other social functions attended by Christians from diverse backgrounds among the Dagomba and Konkomba. Traditional values have been rediscovered and reinforced by Bible translation, which is why Sanneh explained that, "mother tongue development and Bible translation have led to indigenous cultural renewal, empowerment of local agency and the theological stimulation of the Christian adoption of African names for God" (2003:41).

7.9 Socio-cultural effect

This present study shows how Bible translation into the mother tongue, with its attendant literacy programmes, has effected Dagomba and Konkomba languages, cultures, traditional religion, identity, physical infrastructure, health, education and economic ventures. The mother-tongue Scriptures have played crucial roles in the empowerment, advocacy and peace initiatives amongst the Dagomba and Konkomba. The outcome of Bible translation has been the new unity and a sense of destiny among the Konkomba. For the Dagomba, it is in the villages that the Dagbani Scriptures are having a tremendous effect on marriages, giving them a new appreciation of education and a greater spirit of cooperation. Case studies, below, authenticate this effect on the Konkomba and Dagomba.

From the African religious context, Sanneh observed that Bible translation has led to the renewal of local languages, old customs, traditions and ethics. According to the Dagomba and Konkomba interviewed, the indigenous morality taught them by their ancestors has found resonance in the translated Scriptures. In interviews with this author, Dagomba and Konkomba Christian leaders asserted that the mother-tongue Scriptures have reinforced their traditional values. Perceiving the universal nature of the Christian faith, Sanneh confidently claimed that Bible translation has given birth to World Christianity in that it induces indigenous responses; mother-tongue Scriptures have caused a shift from the understanding of Christianity

---

[14] Sanneh's view was corroborated in interviews with Dagomba and Konkomba Christians who confirm how the Bible translation has brought them together despite their different denominations.

as a Western religion to an indigenous one thus ensuring the indigenisation of the faith and decolonising Christian theology (2003:23–24).

The Dagbani Scriptures have brought about a perceptual shift. The Dagomba now see God and hear Him speak to them in their own language and not in Arabic, Twi or English. Elderly Dagomba have expressed that they are particularly happy that, for once, they can hear God talk to them in the depth of their being before they die (FCBH Report, September 2002).

The Konkomba and Dagomba are re-interpreting their worldview as a result of acting on the teaching of their mother-tongue Scriptures. The two groups desire to shift their allegiance: converts to the Christian faith burn occult charms as well as destroy other objects of traditional worship. This re-interpretation of worldview due to the influence of the mother-tongue Scriptures is not unique to the Dagomba and Konkomba.

7.10 Mother-tongue Scriptures and modern challenges

The mother-tongue Bible is a source of guidance for the numerous challenges posed by modernity on the Dagomba and Konkomba. These modern challenges include environmental degradation, migration, urbanisation, politics, international trade, secularisation, education and moral relativism. Through the constant cultivation of farmlands of the Dagomba and Konkomba, the soil is leached and losing fertility, which induces migration to southern Ghana. This trend has contributed to urbanisation and change in lifestyle. In order to derive full benefit from the modern state, both the Dagomba and Konkomba take a keen interest in national politics. The Konkomba in particular have seized the opportunity to assert their rights to independence from the Dagomba, Nanumba and Gonja. As we noted earlier, the vernacular Scriptures and literacy have created awareness among the acephalous societies that they are not inferior to the Dagomba or other ethnic groups with whom they neighbour. The Ghanaian constitution has been translated into Likpakpaaln. As the Konkomba become aware of their rights and responsibilities as Ghanaian citizens, they are able to participate more meaningfully in governance.

The Bible translation and literacy programmes have brought a new awareness of the world around them to the Konkomba. According to Mr. Binabiba, Director of RILADEP, this has helped them to look beyond their traditional occupation as farmers to other professions. When the Konkomba harvest their farm produce, traders, usually Dagomba and Asante women, come to buy the produce directly from the farmers, and then they sell them to market women who in turn sell them finally to the consumer. Now, rather than leaving the marketing of their farm produce to these middlemen who buy their farm produce cheaply and then sell it expensively, a good number of Konkomba have taken to marketing their own produce. In this connection, it is worth mentioning how international trade has served to boost the yam market, as yams are now an exportable commodity. The Konkomba who are the key producers of yams stand to benefit when they acquire more efficient marketing skills.

Western education is introducing secularism into Konkomba and Dagomba societies, questioning traditional assumptions that do not have any scientific basis. The once religious societies are now imbibing some secular attitudes by basing their analysis of issues on scientific principles. These are more evident in the moral liberalism of society. Old religious morals are not fully enforced because of increasing freedoms given to people by the constitution of the modern state. However, traditional cultural beliefs are still intact even with the outward secular advances. The antidote for these modern challenges is the mother-tongue Bible, which, because of its status as the word of God, provides light, life and guidance, which are keys to the realisation of abundant life (Lensch 2003:27–30).

7.11 Mother-tongue Scriptures and primal religious aspirations

In Sanneh's scheme of things, Christianity shaped by vernacular Scriptures was bound, not only to fulfil expectations of the traditional religion, but also to bring about a "reorientation of the worldview so that the old moral framework was reconfigured without being overthrown" (2003:42). African culture has the approval of Jesus and therefore can convey God's eternal truth, hence his argument that "Jesus did not mock their [Africans'] respect for the sacred or their clamour for an invincible Saviour, and so they beat their sacred drums for him until the stars skipped and danced in the skies (1983:166).

As a result of the mitigating influence of Bible translation, the Dagomba and Konkomba now use their traditional instruments, music forms and dances to worship God in their churches. This has made it possible for "Africans to become renewed Africans, not remade Europeans" (Sanneh 2003:44). Being African Christians rather than remade Europeans was the import of J. H. Nketia's article, "The Church and Culture: The Contribution of African Culture to Christian Worship." Nketia states, "If churches in Africa are to grow as African churches and not as extensions of Western parishes and bishoprics they must be allowed to take root in the soil of African culture so that they may grow in stature as indigenous institutions" (1958:60).

Another effect of Bible translation is that it sets in motion "the process whereby the Christian message is appropriated into existing local frameworks but still remains recognizably Christian" (Sanneh 1983:244). Bible translation makes Christianity more attractive and therefore people embrace it of their own volition. Sanneh made a distinction between

Christian discovery of indigenous societies and "indigenous discovery of Christianity," as follows:

> The Christian discovery of indigenous societies describes the process of missionaries from the West coming to Africa or Asia and converting people, often with political incentives and material inducements. Indigenous discovery of Christianity, by contrast, describes how local people are encountering the religion through mother tongue discernment and in the light of the people's own needs and experiences. (2003:56)

One of the effects of Bible translation is that it turns Christianity into a "multicolored fabric [like the Ghanaian *kente*] where each new thread chosen and refined at the designer's hand, adds lustre and strength to the whole" (2003:58).[15] The innovations that are emerging from the Dagomba and Konkomba churches because of Bible translation undergirds this assertion: "the gospel is not the monopoly of the West, as African Christianity has demonstrated" (2003:59).[16] For him it is absurd to call Christianity a Western religion because today's "Christianity is the religion of over two thousand different language groups in the world." Furthermore, he argues, "[m]ore people pray and worship in more languages in Christianity than in any other religion in the world" (2003:68).

7.12 Bible translation and renewal of Dagomba and Konkomba cultures

Sanneh argued that languages and their purity have been preserved by the work of Bible translation. Mother-tongue Scriptures not only preserve indigenous languages from dying, they also help preserve them from being absorbed by or into other languages. In 1991 the Director-General of UNESCO chaired a special session to award the Nessim Habif prize to GILLBT for just such an effort to preserve and develop the languages of Ghana. The award, under the auspices of the Regional Programme for the Eradication of Illiteracy in Africa, recognised GILLBT's efforts to produce school textbooks, other teaching materials and literature.[17] We now examine the effect the Bible in Dagbani and Likpakpaaln has had on these two indigenous languages and cultures, and how both their language and cultures have

---

[15] The Ghanaian *kente* is a highly valued multicoloured woven cloth worn on festive occasions by traditional rulers and those who can afford it.

[16] The Konkomba and Dagomba Christians interviewed in 2003 in the Dagomba city of Tamale, as well as in the Konkomba capital town, Saboba, no longer see the Christian faith as alien but as their own religion.

[17] See http://www.unesco.org/education/pdf/11_105.pdf. (Accessed 4 June 2019).

been fortified through Bible translation. Much of the information in this section is taken from interviews with Dagomba and Konkomba Christians.

Just as one's worldview influences Bible translation, so does Bible translation influence worldview (Lensch 2003:27). The religious beliefs and practices of the Dagomba and the Konkomba have been challenged and modified. For instance, beliefs and rituals related to the creator God, divinities, and ancestors are being modified through reading the Bible in the vernacular language. The most important factor introduced into their worldviews is the historical person and current active role of Jesus, which are new concepts introduced into the Konkomba and Dagomba cosmology. Their traditional understanding of who God is becomes expanded. Though the divine Being is not a new God being introduced by means of the translation, the mother-tongue Scriptures nevertheless give systematic teaching on God's nature and reinforce an understanding that was partial in their traditional religion.

If Lensch is right, that Bible translation influenced Western beliefs about cosmology, anthropology and justice, which, consequently, affected Western institutions and traditions, then we would expect the same to happen in the case of the Dagomba and Konkomba. Though Bible translation is relatively recent among these people groups, the effect of the person of God and His nature are rapidly being felt in the areas of their cosmology, institutions, interrelationships and languages. For example, primal divinities and ancestor worship now have little or no place in the beliefs and practices of the Dagomba and Konkomba Christian. As noted earlier, the place of women has also been altered as a result of the influence of the Dagbani and Likpakpaaln Scriptures. Dagomba and Konkomba Christians now honour and respect women. Consequently, boys and girls are treated on a more equal basis, offering the same opportunity with respect to formal education. Peaceful coexistence is evident in Christian homes as Christians attempt to follow biblical injunctions on themes such as love, forgiveness, self-control, and mutual respect. Thus, Bible translation has had a stabilizing effect on their language, and a nurturing and healing influence on the Dagomba and Konkomba cultures, and consequently, in all other aspects of their lives including their beliefs, practices, and self-identity.

7.12.1 The vernacular Scriptures and festivals

Realising the import of festivals as cultural assets of the people, GILLBT has been organizing annual workshops on gospel and culture issues. Participants in the workshops include Bible translators, pastors, community leaders and the general public.[18] The Dagomba and Konkomba are regular participants

---

[18] Kwame Bediako, a key theologian of African Christianity, has been running these workshops. Some of the themes he covered include: Ancestors, Festivals, Epistle to the Hebrews, and Gospel and Culture.

in these workshops. The vernacular Scriptures challenge the Dagomba and Konkomba to have a sympathetic understanding of their culture and to reinterpret their festivals, which had been ignored by Christians because they were deemed "pagan." A reassessment of traditional festivals is now possible because the Scriptures have imbued persons with the knowledge to appreciate their history and to locate God within it in order to reach a new and positive self-understanding. In this area, Konkomba Christians have taken the lead in the cultural transformation. The KOYA executives who are Christians have transformed some of the local festivals and made God and development the focus of their celebrations. Ross Gaskin also mentions how Konkomba leaders are using Easter for uniting Konkomba people and initiating developments projects (Gaskin 1986).

7.12.2 The mother tongue and guidance

The Bible is increasingly acknowledged by the Dagomba and Konkomba not only because they hold it as God's book of light and life but because it is also perceived as providing guidance to the individual as well as to the community. Among the traditional religious practitioners are the soothsayers, otherwise known as diviners, who have lost their clients as a result of people gaining new insight from reading the mother-tongue Scriptures. In an interview, a RILADEP leader reported that the translated Scriptures help the Christians in their prayers and seeking God's will. The Dagomba and Konkomba Christians now find guidance and resources from their Bible to deal with their future instead of resorting to the soothsayers. They do this not because the Scriptures act as a divinatory object, but they show them how to pray and find the will of God for their lives. Allison Howell observed in a 1992 seminar at Nima Presbyterian Church that a similar experience occurred when the Kasena of northern Ghana received the Scriptures in their mother tongue. The Christians ceased going to the soothsayers and, instead, formed Bible study and prayer groups to give them guidance and security. Through Bible studies and prayers, Christians, including the Dagomba and Konkomba, are able to handle their daily life issues.

7.12.3 Mother-tongue Scriptures as the moral frame of reference

For Dagomba and Konkomba Christians, the Bible is the decisive authority in matters of morality and conduct. The teachings of the Bible, rather than denominational doctrines, are the deciding factors on ethical issues. For this reason, the Dagomba and Konkomba Christians mix and fellowship freely, thereby surmounting doctrinal barriers that divide churches. The evidence that the Dagbani and Likpakpaaln Scriptures are shaping the Christian communities can be found in the composition of their songs, integrating their culture with their liturgies and then giving serious attention and significance to their spiritual worlds.

7.12.4 Mother-tongue Scriptures and subversion of hegemony

As was noted in chapters three and four, historical and cultural factors led to the Dagomba and Konkomba having a hierarchal society with unequal relations between the two groups. The Dagomba claimed the Konkomba were their subjects. Gender inequalities also existed in both Dagomba and Konkomba societies. The exercise of dominion is sanctioned by traditional cultures. The liberating gospel of Christ in its teachings challenges the domination of one group of people by another. The import of this came out forcefully during a Bible study on Luke 4:18–19 with both the Dagomba and Konkomba. They agreed that domination was not compatible with Christ's vision and mission.[19]

Another effect of Bible translation among the Dagomba and Konkomba is the fact that it levels the ground for all the different categories of people in their communities. The Bible teaches equality of all human persons (Genesis 1–3 and Galatians 3:28). It also affirms the concept that all persons are created in the image of God. Thus, the affirmation of the dignity of all human persons is the seed of anti-hegemony. The Christian story is one of liberation so the message questions oppression or domination. To be faithful to the task of communicating the message of liberation, translators seek to convey the meaning from the source language to the receptor language for all to understand, irrespective of their social standing.

In Sanneh's view, the vernacular Scriptures allowed a naturalised Christianity to take root, and in so doing, fomented local subversion against colonial rule. For him, mother-tongue Scriptures motivate their recipients to seek independence and oppose any forms of hegemony. When we examine the evidence from the documents on the Dagomba and Konkomba we can see merit in Sanneh's claims. The mother-tongue Scriptures influenced the Konkomba to rise up against Dagomba domination. When we base our assessment on the redemptive and empowering role of Bible translation, we can question the notion maintained by some, of "Christian mission as cultural imperialism and religious bigotry" (2003:20–22). As we shall demonstrate, Sanneh's assertion can be sustained because when Christianity was first introduced to the Dagomba and Konkomba, it may have been Western in character, but that reality is in the process of giving way to a Christianity shaped by local cultures.

---

[19] The author had separate interviews with both Konkomba and Dagomba on their understanding of Christ's so-called Manifesto.

7.12.5 The Dagbani and Likpakpaaln Scriptures and holistic development

Sanneh traced the source of social and cultural transformation generally to literacy, which was initiated alongside Bible translation (2001:166). Missionaries among the Dagomba and Konkomba are credited with pioneering roles in linguistic development. Mother-tongue literature in Dagbani and Likpakpaaln has been produced in various fields, such as health, agriculture, history, ethnography, politics, economics and religion. These have had a tremendous effect on the Dagomba and Konkomba because of the attendant transformation this has accomplished. Modern techniques in the management of health, improvement in agriculture and social developments have resulted through vernacular Scriptures and literacy. The meeting of the felt needs of the Dagomba and Konkomba certainly paved the way for acceptance of scriptural translation.

From a historical and theological perspective, Sanneh concluded that Christian mission is best described as a "dynamic translation movement." If Christian mission is Bible translation, then as far as the Dagomba and Konkomba are concerned, one would anticipate nothing less than a palpable effect of the mother-tongue Scriptures on the whole spectrum of Dagomba and Konkomba life (1989:175). Indeed, other studies have shown that vernacular Scriptures with literacy have contributed to the holistic development of communities including those of the Dagomba and Konkomba. A study by Darrell Whiteman of the Melanesian people amply demonstrates the efficacy of Bible translation and literacy (1990:120–141). Commenting on the effect of Bible translation on the subjects of his study, Whiteman notes how the vernacular Scriptures had transformed them spiritually, culturally, socially, economically and politically. That the mother-tongue Scriptures have transformed and empowered the Konkomba is a fact that was not lost on the Dagomba. For instance, in the 1994 Dagomba-Konkomba war, the Dagomba threatened to burn down the offices of GILLBT because they accused the organisation of "opening the eyes" of the Konkomba who had hitherto been regarded as wild and backward people.

Benedict Der in his study on the "Missionary Enterprise in Northern Ghana" also highlights the positive and negative Christian missionary effect on the socio-cultural and economic life of the people of northern Ghana (Der 1983). On the positive side, Der notes how missionary activities in northern Ghana promoted Western education, which in turn produced literates. This had an indirect link with the later production of the vernacular Scriptures. Another missionary influence he observed was a shift in the early twentieth century from wearing leaves and animal skins to wearing modern clothing, which enhanced health. Missionary agents also promoted healthcare and agriculture.

Other areas of missionary effect were in the introduction of architectural changes, a marriage system that encouraged monogamy and changes in some funeral and burial practices. The architectural adjustment improved ventilation in living spaces and thus contributed to better health. The new marriage system was welcomed by Christians but resisted in other quarters because traditional authorities perceived it as undermining their traditional marriage. Nevertheless, among the non-Christian Dagomba, monogamy has also become more common. It is not unusual to hear testimonies of how considerate Christian men are with their wives. Some people even accuse such men of pampering them. For example, one man told how he helps his wife by fetching water for her domestic chores. They also spend time together to discuss matters, have joint savings and pray together. Hitherto, men and women rarely spent time together. It is his understanding of what the Dagbani Scriptures teach about the relationship between wives and husbands that has influenced his attitude towards his wife. This man explained in an interview:

> The change of my attitude towards my wife came about when I read Ephesians 5:21–33. As a Dagomba husband, I am expected to act as a lord and command my wife as I like. Dagomba culture also expects me to act as a strong man and not to yield to my wife's demands. However, when I read this passage, it challenged me to also submit to my wife and to love her as how Christ loved the Church.

In the area of funerals in northern Ghana, the missionaries introduced coffins and uniform graves, replacing the traditional custom of wrapping the body with mats and burying it near the homes. This further perpetuated the perception of Christianity as an alien religion. Though some traditional authorities were not always sure of the missionaries' motives in what they did, Der suggests that they pursued a policy of improvement of the lives of the people in northern Ghana.

One of the greatest contributions to their well-being, however, was the development of their languages, thus paving the way for literacy and Bible translation. Since translation was not done in a vacuum, these missionary activities contributed directly or indirectly to the whole translation process. The activities created certain perceptions in the minds of the northern people about the Christian faith. The persistent perception of the alien-ness of Christianity could only be erased with the introduction of the mother-tongue Scriptures.

Bible translation has served to enrich the Dagbani language which is one of the six official languages used on national radio and television in Ghana. Before then, any Dagomba who desired to be literate other than in the Western style, that is English, was obliged to attend Arabic or Qur'anic schools. According to a Dagomba evangelist, Dagomba elders have noticed that many young Dagomba whose use of the language had previously been rather superficial now have a richer and more full knowledge of Dagbani, which could only have been brought about through their exposure to the Dagbani Scriptures.[20] Thus, the mother-tongue Scriptures have equipped users with a firmer grasp of their own language.

The Dagbani literacy programme took a major step forward when the Summer Institute of Linguistics was invited into the country. SIL developed and printed Dagbani primers and other reading materials. The primary goal of the primers was to impart reading skills to learners. The post-primers, on the other hand, provided the new literates with literature to broaden their horizon, with the ultimate objective of solving problems. As noted earlier, the themes covered in these supplementary publications included health, traditional stories, agriculture and an abridged Ghanaian constitution.

The mother-tongue Scriptures have also fostered a new bond of unity among the Dagomba Christians. It is now a common occurrence at funerals, weddings and naming ceremonies to find Dagomba Christians from different denominations, political parties and the traditional royal divide of the Abudu and Andani gates mingling together. There is a strong bond of fellowship among them. This is not the case among other sections of the Dagomba, especially since the chieftaincy crisis in which their king, the *ya na*, was killed in Yendi.

At the height of the crisis, when animosity was rife and married couples divorced each other because they belonged to different royal gates, the Christians were able to transcend the hatred, meeting to fast for three days and to pray for Dagbon. In fact, Muslims and traditionalists were often heard commenting that the Dagbon crisis could have been easily resolved if the majority of the Dagomba had been Christians. They that are Christians not only preach, but also practice, love and forgiveness. A well-respected Dagomba Christian articulated the general sentiment prevailing then when I asked him in 2003 what he thought the prospect of reconciliation was. He replied, "Only God knows. Most Dagomba think that if they had more Dagomba Christians, there would have been peace and reconciliation by now. Their claim is based on the fact that Christians preach forgiveness and reconciliation, whereas Islam does not urge them to forgive, but rather prompts them to retaliate."

The recognition of the virtues of Christians in northern Ghana is well noted here. *Naa* Mogri, a prominent Mamprusi and former Paramount Chief of Janga, often rebuked Muslim *mallams* (clerics):

> You are always impeding our progress. See the love and developments the Christians bring to our communities. As for the *Fathers* when anybody is sick they will quickly assist by treating the person or transport the one to hospital. This is what you *mallams* will never do. Wherever these

---

[20] This Dagomba evangelist oversees the showing of the "Jesus Film" in Dagbani at Tamale and Gushiegu in the Northern Region.

Christians are there is light. Any town or village without a church is in darkness.[21]

It is significant that as a Muslim himself, the ruler was not afraid to say this, but rebuked the *mallams* publicly for their extortions and deceit. His support for Christian mission was demonstrated when he gave a prime piece of land opposite his palace to a Christian NGO which built a beautiful chapel at Janga in West Mamprusi District of the Northern Region. The appeal of Christianity has been boosted recently with the translation of the Scriptures into the languages of the people of northern Ghana.

7.12.6 Bible translation as holistic mission

Where Bible translation is carried out in the context of holistic mission, the survival strategy is adopted to serve people's needs in the area of "agricultural, medical, religious, educational, commercial and household activities that contribute to human welfare" (Bradshaw 2000:966). Bible translation and holistic mission are bound together by the same vision and consequently, in the service of and for the glory of God. Some, however, see the two as one and the same thing. For instance, Dickerson, like Sanneh, conceived of Bible translation as mission.[22] For them, it is all encompassing and therefore embraces literacy [teaching the writing system of a language], sociolinguistics [how people use language in their social situation], ethnomusicology [understanding and valuing the music of a people group], anthropology [appreciating the cultural factors of a people group] and linguistics [language learning/analysis and use in communication] (Dickerson 2000:580).

Bible translation proceeds on the understanding that every culture anticipates the gospel and therefore can accommodate it. This special adaptability of the gospel, which enables it to find a natural home in every culture, is what Sanneh referred to as translatability (1994:38) and is at the heart of Bible translation. The translator has the onerous task of ensuring that God's word for a people group is "couched in their own language and culture" and in this way God's power comes to them directly in their culture (Shaw 2000:966). It is God's power through persons and communities that brings about transformation.

The power of God realised through Bible translation acts like a double-edged sword, a point that Sanneh made to refute those who claim that translators are cultural spies, translating for personal gain (2003:187). Shaw agrees with Sanneh when he asserts, that "the Bible empowers the powerless and forces the powerful to recognise their own weakness before

---

[21] Spoken by the former Mamprusi Paramount Chief, *Soo Naa* Mogri, at a development durbar (inaugural celebration), 10 January 1992, Janga, Northern Region, Ghana.

[22] Sanneh saw translation as mission in most of his works on the significance of mother-tongue Scriptures in Christian mission.

God" (2000:125). The responses of the Konkomba and Dagomba interviewed seem to suggest that vernacular Scriptures encourage harmony within emerging Christian communities. They also raise awareness of God and how to relate to Him in daily life. This role of mother-tongue Scriptures seems to suggest that the downtrodden such as the Konkomba, through their study of the Scriptures have found dignity and have now drawn on God's resources to rise up to the plane where God wants to place them, that is, a life of dignity and fulfilment. In the case of the powerful, such as the Dagomba, they seem to be coming to terms with the ultimate power of God and their own finiteness. Thus, the powerful are also being helped by the translated Scriptures to serve under God's redemptive power in humility. Like a double-edged sword, the Scriptures challenge ethnic hegemonic tendencies but at the same time promote ethnic integrity.

Christian mission in general, but especially among the Dagomba and Konkomba, brought health, education and income-generating projects. This was motivated by love and also was a corrective of the situation created during the colonial times. Whereas the colonial authorities imposed English on the Dagomba and Konkomba, the development of the indigenous languages came about because of missionary activities. Perhaps Sanneh's knowledge of this enabled him to argue that translation proceeded on a different understanding from that of colonialism. His reasoning is based on the fact that, whereas colonial powers subjugated African people, Christian mission through translation had the opposite effect of freeing and affirming African people (2001:17).

It is remarkable that the Bible translators came as servants and not as masters with authority, with the aim of translating in order to control the Dagomba and Konkomba. This questions the Comaroffs' assertion that Bible translators translated in order to colonise the Tswana people of South Africa (Comaroff 1989:267). Chapters five and six show that the translators identified with the Dagomba and Konkomba, learned their languages, then undertook the task of translation of the Scriptures. By their nature, the translated Scriptures have been imbued with power by God and therefore are able to effect the transformation of those who read them. Testimonies from Konkomba and Dagomba users of the mother-tongue Scriptures confirm this. For example, the earlier testimony of the chief of a Dagomba village demonstrates how the Dagbani Scriptures challenged him to forgive his subject who opposed his enskinment as a chief. For this Dagomba chief, the message of forgiveness was what transformed him.

Another testimony from a Konkomba side would be appropriate. A Konkomba woman's prayer life was changed when she heard the Scriptures read on the audio device. In her own words she stated, "I never understood the pastor when he preached, on 'ask, seek and knock' until I heard it loud and clear from the audio cassette on Matthew 7:7 in my mother tongue.

This made Christianity meaningful to me. I can now talk to God just as I am talking to a physical person before me."[23]

The mother-tongue Scriptures are able to speak clearly to people even when human preachers fail. Thus, they act as a direct bridge between persons and God. Such testimonies show that Christianity is a practical religion, providing the vital resources needed for a fulfilling daily life. Genuine spirituality correlates with one's ability to live a fulfilling life.

Important as literacy is, it is not conceived by the translators as an end in itself but as a handmaid of mother-tongue Scriptures. The mother tongue is perceived as "the language of the heart and is believed to communicate deep spiritual and personal matters of people" (Sheldon 1999:7). Thus, for most people, their mother tongue and their heart language coincide.

The Konkomba are proud of their literacy programme and "knock their chests," that is, they boast that when it comes to literature, they have more than all other languages in which GILLBT is working. Likewise, the Konkomba response in terms of enrolment on literacy programmes has been unsurpassed, as shown by statistics on enrolment of learners and teachers of the various northern language groups.[24] A prominent Konkomba leader, Mr. Kenneth Wujangi, attributes this impressive response from the Konkomba to the knowledge they acquire through literacy. In his assessment, this has bolstered the self-esteem of the Konkomba and raised the prestige of their language. In light of the Konkomba response we might agree that literates are assets to their communities in that they support various social and economic activities of the community and also the reading of God's word.[25] Stressing the relevance of Christian nurturing through literacy, Wayne Dye argues, that "literate converts are stronger and less likely to backslide than non-literate converts" (1985:221–232). His assessment presupposes that literates will read and meditate on God's word regularly.

Some caution, however, needs to be exercised in accepting Dye's assertion in its entirety because some non-literates have very good memories and are very loyal Christians. Thus, literacy on its own does not guarantee commitment to the Christian faith. Literates, in Dye's view, are less likely to be cheated than non-literates. For him, a person's ability to read increases his/her "ability for personal and economic achievement and self-esteem because using the vernacular builds personal and community esteem, respect and achievement" (Dye 1985:2). Literacy, no doubt, is a

---

[23] Testimony from Konkomba Faith Comes By Hearing and "Jesus Film" Project® report for 2005.

[24] Whereas up to 10% of the Konkomba are literate, only 3% of the Dagomba are literate. *Ethnologue: Languages of the World: Ghana.* 2017. https://www.ethnologue.com/countryGH/languages/. Accessed 19 October 2017.

[25] John Watters' "SIL's Service in the World," Intercom, (January–March 2003, pp. 2–3) in Franklin, sustains that a growing literate society leads to rapid transformation or development of their communities, p. 8.

potent force for personal and communal development. However, an unjust environment could undermine it, and it cannot be effective without other factors, like religion, culture, economics and politics. For this reason, developmental theorists, Like Samuel Voorhies, now insist on a multi-dimensional approach to developmental issues. Voorhies proposes a holistic approach to development that should be informed by the following ten principles of holistic Christian transformational development:

1. People and their culture have intrinsic value;
2. The local culture needs to be understood and respected;
3. People's needs and self-respect must be considered, to ensure ownership and self-dignity;
4. People rather than technology should be the focal point;
5. The whole person – mind, body and spirit must be involved in the development effort;
6. Development needs to communicate Christ through word (the gospel of Christ), deed (serving as Christ would) and sign (demonstrating Christ kingdom life);
7. All interventions into a group of people... carry a message that must be understood and interpreted from the recipients' worldview;
8. God is already at work in the community so this must be understood and supported;
9. Transformation in a person comes through a relationship with Christ; and
10. Churches are foundational for sustained and abundant transformation.

(Voorhies 1999:590–591)

The use of the mother-tongue Scriptures has challenged the social, cultural and intellectual lives of its beneficiaries, thus making holistic development possible in both Dagomba and Konkomba communities in the light of Voorhies' criteria. In this regard, Franklin comments: "Without Bible translation, the Word is not going to be available to people who are usually culturally and linguistically marginalised. If they are denied the Word of God in their heart language, then there is less likelihood of complete holistic transformational development occurring" (Franklin 2008:10).

Quoting Ghanaian theologian Kwame Bediako, Franklin continues: "African Christianity today is inconceivable apart from the existence of the Bible in African indigenous languages.... Africans had the means to make their own responses to the Christian message, in terms of their own needs and according to their own categories of thought and meaning" (Franklin 2008:10).

The mother-tongue Scriptures among the Dagomba and Konkomba has had this effect and effect in that they have paved the way for their holistic development in literacy, education, health, agriculture, political awareness, peace and vibrant indigenous churches.[26]

7.13 Summary

Sanneh's hermeneutic of Christian mission as "a dynamic translation movement," and the effect of Bible translation, has been confirmed with respect to the Dagomba and Konkomba of northern Ghana. Among some of the effects of mother-tongue Scriptures for them are: the enhancement of their identity, ethnic empowerment, opportunity for inter-religious dialogue, transformation of marriage, promotion of education and literacy, promotion of human rights, help in problem-solving, guidance, social harmony, evangelism, Christian nurture, development of their language, preservation of their cultural values and promotion of social change. In conclusion, Bible translation has had a redemptive effect on the northern Ghana peoples in our study.

The effects of vernacular Bible translation and literacy have had an effect on both the Konkomba and the Dagomba of rural areas. Rural Dagomba experience a new confidence in their ability to read the Scriptures and share their faith with Muslim neighbours, something they could not do previously. The urban Dagomba can no longer easily deceive and disparage the rural Dagomba as in the past, because the rural Dagomba have a new awareness of education and their own worth. From the experiences of the Konkomba, the rural Dagomba and the Bimoba, we can conclude that the translation of the Christian gospel affirms cultural identity and gives confidence and freedom from exploitation. The redemptive role of mother-tongue Scriptures in the lives of the Dagomba and Konkomba resonates with Sanneh's own conclusion of the efficacy and potency of Bible translation into the mother tongue: "…Africans began earnestly to inquire into the Christian Scripture, which missionaries had placed in their hands, to see where they had misunderstood the gospel. What they learned convinced them that mission as European cultural hegemony was a catastrophic departure from the Bible" (1989:162).

---

[26] Sanneh's views on translation as addressing the needs of African holistically have been amply addressed in his books, *Translating the Message* and *Whose Religion is Christianity?*

8

A Revitalised Indigenous Consciousness: The Fruit of Translation

Lamin Sanneh argued that Christian mission can best be described as a dynamic translation movement and that in this enterprise missionaries were committed to the task of transformation; this was the greatest legacy they left the church in Africa. The translation of the Bible has played a central role and it is now the lifeline of the church. Though the initiatives to translate were taken by Western missionaries, it has been clearly established that they could not have done it without the support of the local community, in this case the Konkomba and Dagomba. This book has sought to demonstrate that translation must take centre stage in mission outreach to people.

It is appropriate here to quote Geraldine E. Coldham, the granddaughter of the famous German linguist, Dietrich Westermann, who first translated the Bible into Ewe, a language of the Volta Region of Ghana. She appreciates the pioneering role of missionaries in relation to translation and writes:

> Many died, many of them lost wives and children and health, but those who survived taught and healed and preached, laying the foundations of the African churches of today. It is frequently forgotten how much is owed to these pioneers. Many of them went to people who had no written language and therefore no literature, and they laboured to give a written form to an astonishing variety of languages. Some of

them became skilled linguists, writing grammars and dictionaries, as well as translating. Their consuming desire was for the translation of the Scriptures. To build churches the Bible must be available in the language of the people and must speak in their idiom in order to speak to their hearts. No other language, however high the literary quality of its Scriptures, could speak with the compelling voice of their own language. It is recorded that when the Zulu Bible was published one old man asked if the English people had such a Bible. When told they had a Bible, but in their own language, not in Zulu, the old man commiserated with them, that they should lack such a treasure. What better verdict on his labours could the translator desire? (Coldham 1966:i)

8.1 The troubled beginnings of Christian mission in northern Ghana

The story of Christian mission in northern Ghana has been fraught with complex tensions, conflicts, misunderstandings and sometimes, complete lack of understanding, in spite of good intentions on the part of the missionaries. The tensions have been between religions, political entities and a complex array of cultures: Africans cultures versus European cultures, European cultures in dispute against other Europeans, Christian denominations competing for territory and influence, traditional ethnic rivalries, Islam versus Christianity versus African traditional religion. Adding confusion to all these issues was the lack of linguistic comprehension – the fact that missionaries did not learn the local languages, or even understand that there were a variety of mutually unintelligible languages in the region. Going through several levels of translation inevitably led to miscommunication and misinformation.

Islam was introduced in the region of northern Ghana many years before the first Christian missionaries made their way there, and therefore became established as a Muslim overlay in the life and culture of the local ethnic groups. Of the two groups featured in this book, the influence of Islam was more firmly entrenched among the Dagomba than among the Konkomba.

British colonial rule also played a part in the struggle to introduce the gospel of Christ to the people of Ghana. Sometimes sympathetic to fellow British countrymen and with an affinity of cultural values to Italians, Germans or Americans, the colonial authorities encouraged evangelisation. On the other hand, certain mission groups were barred from some areas for political reasons, to keep the peace with Islamic groups and in order to maintain absolute control over the region.

Western missionaries who rigidly promoted their cultural values made little headway with African indigenes who had no desire to become Westernised. Acceptance of this new religion seemed to require not only giving up their long religious traditions, but also their culture and their language. God, it seemed, belonged to the foreigners – even if the foreigners were from as close as southern Ghana.

Two world wars also interrupted the evangelisation of northern Ghana, when the British authorities expelled German and Italian mission groups simply on the basis of their connection with enemies of the homeland.

8.2 Lamin Sanneh's new look at Christian mission

Lamin Sanneh, Gambian born, by virtue of his upbringing and scholarship, has considered mission from the angle of translation. He champions the idea that Christian mission essentially is translation. Once a Muslim and educated in Africa, the United States, Europe and in the Middle East, Sanneh has deep knowledge of the nature of Christian mission from diverse contexts. Furthermore, his deep understanding of Islam enables him to compare and contrast the nature of mission in Christianity and in Islam.

The voluminous literature Sanneh produced on Christian mission attests to his immense knowledge of the subject. Fascinated by Sanneh's interpretation of mission, we have used his paradigm of mission as the key to investigate Christian mission carried out amongst the Dagomba and Konkomba of northern Ghana. A deeply religious man, Sanneh examined Christian mission from both historical and theological standpoints.

Christian mission is essentially a cross-cultural activity, which has produced multilingual and multicultural churches. Through translation of the Christian gospel, the Christian faith has been able to flourish in diverse indigenous cultural milieus. This is given credence by the production of mother-tongue Scriptures, which have tremendously propelled the growth of the Christian church worldwide, especially in Africa. God's mission has also touched the Dagomba and Konkomba people because the gospel has been translated for them. Interpreting Christian mission from the point of view of translation has given fresh impetus to the study of mission.

8.3 Christian mission against cultural hegemony

Some scholars, such as the Comaroffs and those of Marxist orientation, erroneously or intentionally depict Christian mission as a project of Western cultural hegemony (Comaroff 1989:267 and Comaroff 1997). They argue that Christian mission paved the way for colonialism. They further accuse Christian mission of subjugating the cultures of the non-Western world in order to project Western culture. Though this cannot be totally denied, for it happened in some contexts, it would be wrong to generalise it. The facts point rather in the opposite direction, that is, to the fact that Christian mission liberated indigenous societies from Western cultural hegemony through the translation enterprise.

Through the central task of translation in Christian mission, many indigenous societies find their souls. An unprecedented cultural awareness ensues from Bible translation. The result is that dominated peoples begin to agitate for freedom as their identity is boosted by this activity of Christian mission. In fact, the first people to be challenged were Western missionaries who exercised hegemonic tendencies. When the rural Dagomba had their mother-tongue Scriptures, their horizon was broadened, and this enabled them to assert themselves against their urban counterparts who had been looking down on them. Also, Konkomba pride was aroused to seek political freedom from their traditional overlords, the Dagomba.

8.4 A new approach to evangelisation: learning the languages of the people

In contrast to colonialists who promoted their colonial language and diminished the indigenous languages of their subjects, many second-wave missionaries showed respect for these indigenous languages. This was particularly seen in their Bible translation endeavour, a key task of this second wave. Missionaries engaged indigenous agents to assist them in language and cultural learning. Subsequent Bible translations ensured effective communication of the Christian message. The production of Christian Scriptures effected personal edification, the task of discipleship, indigenous leadership training and the general building up of an indigenous church.

8.5 Translation of culture along with translation of Scriptures

8.5.1 The Dagomba response to vernacular Bible translation

The Dagomba of northern Ghana have a centralised, traditional political system and this may be at the foundation of their high sense of security and confidence. There is a clear Islamic divide between the rural and urban Dagomba. The former, to a large extent, follow their traditional religious and cultural practices whilst the latter are increasingly being Islamicised. The rural Dagomba population is increasingly receptive to the Christian gospel because it is now presented in their mother tongue.

The Dagomba who live in urban areas, where Christians are a minority, seem resistant to the Christian message due to their adherence to Islam.

Though a minority in Dagomba society, Christian conversions are increasing among the Dagomba in recent years with the publication of the Dagbani Scriptures. These mother-tongue Scriptures and vernacular language development have enhanced their identity in several ways, by giving them an awareness of and an appreciation for their own linguistic heritage and education, which permits them to benefit from the global economy and wider worldview. Further, the Dagbani traditionally oral language, history and customs are now being preserved in the form of Dagbani literature.

Upon embracing the Christian gospel, Christian Dagombas now appreciate other ethnic groups to a greater extent, including their traditional subjects, the Konkomba. A Dagomba Christian song conveys this new perspective:

> If different ethnic groups are in communion, it is because of Jesus.
> If Dagomba are in communion, it is because of Jesus.
> If Konkomba are in communion, it is because of Jesus.
> If Akan people are in communion, it is because of Jesus.
> If White people are in communion, it is because of Jesus.
> We are all in communion with one another because of Jesus.[1]

A Dagomba prince observed that Islam has been in Dagbon for the past three hundred years. However, according to the prince, it has not helped to unite them but rather it has reinforced a power struggle in the royal families. Having seen how Christian organisations offered relief services to refugees during the Northern Conflict in 1994, the prince said he thinks Christian ministry with integrity can win the Dagomba over.

An influential Dagomba Christian leader enumerates what the Dagbani Scriptures have done for the Dagomba. This includes the conversion of some to the Christian faith, the development of indigenous leaders and the socio-cultural development of Dagbon. The message of Christianity offers an alternative way of being a Dagomba. Previously, the perception was that to be a true Dagomba was to be a Muslim. However, the vernacular Dagbani Christian Scriptures is helping change this perception. In addition to a positive change of self-identity, it contributes to the preservation of the collective ethnic Dagomba identity. For example, some Dagomba are beginning to adopt Dagbani names instead of Arabic ones and are using Dagbani instead of Arabic in the worship of God. The use of the indigenous name of God, *Naawuni*, instead of the Arabic name *Allah*, highlights the fact that God is not alien to the Dagomba.

8.5.2 The Konkomba response to vernacular Bible translation

Based on interviews with Konkomba leaders the number of Konkomba who are embracing the Christian gospel is rising steadily. This is due, in

---

[1] Author unknown.

part, to the fact that the Scriptures are now used in their mother tongue. They previously had an advantage over the Dagomba because the whole Bible has been translated in Likpakpaaln for a longer time.

The Konkomba historical experience has been one of marginalisation leading to a negative image. Other ethnic groups in northern Ghana perceive of them as a violent and primitive people. This has bred mutual distrust. Consequently, the Konkomba are suspicious of other ethnic groups and the reverse is also true. However, with the coming of the Konkomba Scriptures, together with mother-tongue literature, the situation is changing for the better.

For instance, Likpakpaaln literature is now in print,[2] which has raised the status of their language. This has also helped to preserve the language and to save it from extinction and has served to increase esteem for their mother tongue among the younger generation of the Konkomba. In addition to the development of a Likpakpaaln dictionary[3] and pedagogical grammar,[4] Konkomba traditional life and culture have been preserved in the literature. The mother-tongue Scriptures have contributed to an unprecedented awareness of the communicative attributes of their own language amongst the Konkomba. Thus, the Scriptures and the literature together have enlarged the world of the Konkomba and enhanced their self-image.

One of the greatest effects of the mother-tongue Scriptures on the Konkomba is a new confidence they have gained. Their identity having been enhanced, they can now claim recognition for their language and socio-political rights. Hitherto, other ethnic groups had regarded the Konkomba as a backward people to be exploited. However, having found an ally in the church, they have striven to gain all that is legitimately theirs so that they can participate fully in national life or church interaction as all other citizens, on an equal basis. Mr. Kenneth Wujangi, a prominent Konkomba leader, articulated this view as follows:

> Formerly, this is what used to happen: When we had Sunday School lessons…it was in a foreign language, it was either in Twi or Dagbani…they read and interpreted it in Likpakpaaln. So, when we finished I asked the pastor, "what are you people doing?" Why not teach the people to read Likpakpaaln itself? Or get the leaders to translate into Likpakpaaln. So, with the Gospel – the Konkomba Bible now – we feel God understands our language. And when you read in church you don't need somebody to interpret it for you. No, unless

---

[2] See "OLAC resources in and about the Konkomba language," at http://www.language-archives.org/language/xon.

[3] See *Ethnologue* 2018: "Konkomba," at https://www.ethnologue.com/language/xon.

[4] See *An Introduction to Learning Likpakpaln (Konkomba)* at https://www.sil.org/resources/archives/4818.

you are in a congregation with a mixed group of people who cannot understand Likpakpaaln – then we have to read in English.

The Konkomba have found their soul in the translation of the Likpakpaaln Scriptures. They appear to demonstrate increased confidence in interaction with other people, with a dimishing inferiority complex.

8.6 Other effects of the translated Scriptures

The mother-tongue Scriptures have come to serve a catalytic role in inducing transformation in Konkomba society as in Dagomba society. The degree of effect of the mother tongue Scriptures on them is, however, not the same. One may not see the effect on the urban Dagomba because of the dominant presence of Islam. However, among some rural Dagomba, the effect is tremendous. Clearly among the Konkomba the effect is remarkable. Evidence of this has been obtained through interviews, reports and testimonies.

Both the Dagomba and Konkomba Christians said these Scriptures had improved their marriages and interpersonal relationships. First, the Christian ideal of monogamous marriages is now being embraced. Arranged marriages or exchange marriages where the women had little say are now being resisted. Christian families now respect the marriage choices of their children. The Konkomba Christians who are influential leaders have fought hard to make the Christian form of marriage the preferred choice. The mother-tongue Scriptures are seen to have facilitated this transformational process.

At first, when the Christian community was small, it was difficult for Dagomba Christian men to find Christian women to marry. This situation has changed because there are now many Dagomba Christians and their Scriptures have helped to bring Christians from different denominations together. Dagomba Christians support each other in marriage celebrations and this attracts many Dagombas to the Christian faith. These occasions also offer additional partnership choices for single men and women. Thus, for the Christian Dagomba and Konkomba, their mother-tongue Scriptures have facilitated the marriage process as well as stabilising it.

The mother-tongue Scriptures have served as an instrument of peace not only in marriages but within the community and between different ethnic groups. The message of the Bible on love, forgiveness and respect is promoting peace. The mother-tongue Scriptures also assisted tremendously in finding a solution to the 1994 Northern Conflict involving the Dagomba and Konkomba. The Christian message was available to both parties in their own language during the conflict so that a calming influence by voices of reason, whether by outsiders or members of the contesting parties, could appeal to them from the Bible to restrain from violence and encourage them to choose peace instead of conflict. In this regard, Christian workers played crucial roles in ensuring peace and trust between the warring factions.

Not only does the mother-tongue Bible promote and sustain peace, it further promotes self-esteem. The biblical message that talks of God's love for persons stresses the fact that all human beings are made in the image of God and therefore deserve respect. There seems to be a correlation between receiving mother-tongue Scriptures and fighting against oppression. A case in point is the Gonja and Dagomba who have this perception and so have accused GILLBT of being the cause of the rebellions because by giving the Vagla and Konkomba their mother-tongue Bible, they "had opened their eyes" to resist domination from their traditional overlords. Thus, ethnic groups that hitherto were traditionally subservient to others upon receiving the Bible in their mother tongue began to raise questions as to why they should continue to be dominated by others. For instance, when the Vagla, who were under the Gonja of northern Ghana, had their mother-tongue Bible, they rebelled against their traditional rulers. Though they were punished militarily, the Vagla won morally. Similarly, the Konkomba rebelled against Dagomba rule and wanted to run their own affairs because of the awareness the Likpakpaaln Scriptures brought them. The Dagomba could not crush them and the Konkomba have now been given some autonomy. Professor Gilbert Ansre, in a 2006 interview, demonstrated the power that is released to a people when they receive their mother-tongue Scriptures, as follows:

> God speaks that language, but man also speaks it to God, and it is expanded. Translation into mother tongue implies that their language is also one of God's languages. Speakers of this language can also expand to become people of God – sociologically, psychologically, intellectually, spiritually and come to the realisation that they are also God's children in the fuller sense. One's personality suddenly expands because he becomes God's full man. With the mother tongue Bible comes to the realisation of recipients that other people are the same as they are, why should they bow to them?

Mother-tongue Scriptures not only promote a better understanding of God's message for people, they also fulfil the psychological needs of its speakers or readers, boosting the self-esteem of its users. A non-Christian Dagomba tends to look down on Christian Dagomba and this social stigma has only now lessened because of the Dagomba Scriptures. There is now a Dagomba Christian song that says: *Isa Masiah tibgiti ka ti chandi bonlan nimaa chandi* 'Christ has exalted us, and we now walk like wealthy important persons'. Christian Dagomba are no longer ready to take an inferior status because the Scriptures have affirmed their dignity and identity as people of God.

8.6 Other effects of the translated Scriptures

The mother-tongue translation of the Bible has enhanced the development of Dagbani and Likpakpaaln languages and standardised them. Both the Konkomba and Dagomba affirm that their languages have been enriched and stabilised by the development. Both Konkomba and Dagomba Christians agree that their own grasp of their mother tongue has been enriched by the use of their Bibles. Ansre described in the interview how translation standardises a language and how this promotes a union of the dialects:

> When the language has become standardised, people of that language see themselves as one and union is achieved. Perpetuation of dialects separates a people, for they promote differences. But when it is standardised through graphology or writing, it brings the people together. An example is the Akan of Ghana. When the linguist and Bible translator, Johannes Christaller, sought to standardise the language he used Akuapem because it is intelligible to the Fanti and Asante speakers. However, speakers of these various dialects did not support this and so that union could not be achieved. The truth is that every big language in the world has to be standardised in order to develop. This is the case with English, French, Japanese and others.

With Bible translation promoting formal education and literacy among the Dagomba and Konkomba, enrolment of children among the Dagomba rural folk which was very low or non-existent has experienced remarkable growth. A similar situation has occurred with the Konkomba.

Konkomba and Dagomba Christians were unanimous that their mother-tongue Scriptures have helped in the preservation of their culture. The translation process itself endorses local cultural values and encourages the preservation of the languages. In addition, the literacy programme provides permanent documentation of local history, stories and customs which had been passed orally from generation to generation.

The Dagomba and Konkomba regard the mother-tongue Scriptures as a promoter of good inter-religious relations since the Scriptures enjoin them to live in peace with people of other faiths and to share their Christian faith with them. They are equally enjoined to gently and intelligently answer those who ask questions about the Christian faith by referring to the mother-tongue Scriptures.

One empirical effect of the vernacular Scriptures is in the area of evangelism promotion. Several churches have been planted among the Dagomba and Konkomba. Among the Dagomba, are the PCG, the Baptists, the AG, the Catholics, the Bible Church of Africa (affiliated with SIM) and others. Similarly, the AG, the EPC, the Catholic church, the Evangelical Church of Ghana, an affiliate of Worldwide Evangelisation Crusade, Harvest Covenant Church and others are vigorously engaged in the evangelisation of the Konkomba.

In chapter seven, it was noted that with the coming of the mother-tongue Scriptures, the horizon of the Konkomba and Dagomba has been broadened. Their worldview has been enlarged and they have also opened up to the intellectual world. They therefore give to the intellectual world and at the same time receive from it. Again, the translation of the Scriptures into Likpakpaaln and Dagbani, theologically speaking, implies that these languages have been exalted and attain a transcendent range. They are now God's languages and languages of the people of God.

The Likpakpaaln and Dagbani Scriptures have brought unity to the Konkomba and Dagomba Christians with denominational barriers broken down. Dagomba and Konkomba Christians now see themselves as Christians first before their denominational labels. Dagomba Christians are reported to have hidden Konkomba Christians at the peril of their own lives during the Northern Conflict in 1994. Similarly, the Konkomba hid Dagomba Christians and then sent them to safety during the same conflict. The mother-tongue Scriptures have created a new sense of the people of God among the Dagomba and Konkomba that transcends human barriers.

It can be noted that one other crucial role the mother-tongue Scriptures have played is the indigenisation of Christianity. The use of mother tongue has removed any alien-ness of the Christian faith. Indigenous cultural idioms and symbols are making Christianity take on a more Dagomba and Konkomba character. Each group of Christians can now confidently call Christianity their religion within their worldview.

The Scriptures serve as pastors or evangelists where there are none. The word of God is now accessible to all categories of the Konkomba and Dagomba. Since people can now read God's word in their own mother tongue, they are no longer totally dependent on pastors and evangelists to preach to them on Sundays. This is particularly true with the FCBH programme, in which mother-tongue Scriptures are recorded onto audio programme devices to be distributed among the local people.

These mother-tongue Scriptures further facilitate the development of indigenous leadership. Before the coming of the Bible translation in their own languages, Dagomba and Konkomba churches did not have local pastors. However, the coming of the literacy programmes has paved the way for formal education and training of indigenous pastors. With the PCG, which cherishes formal education and requires at least second-cycle formal education, no Dagomba has become a pastor yet. However, there are many evangelists who have emerged as a result of the Bible translation. Their facilitating role and accompanying literacy have contributed to the spread of the church among the Dagomba and Konkomba.

The translation model has both theological and anthropological import. Theologically speaking, translation in Christian mission proceeds on the understanding that God wants to make Himself known to all peoples in the clearest way possible. Thus, every language has been endowed to become

8.6 Other effects of the translated Scriptures

a vehicle of His mighty gifts of love and grace. From the anthropological dimension, Christian mission embarks on translation to meet psychological and socio-linguistic needs. Unlike Islamic theology, which holds the view that God's will can only be fully known in the Arabic Qur'an, Christian theology sees the mother-tongue Scriptures as the repository of God's revelation to the recipients of that translation.

The Dagomba had been handicapped with respect to access to the stories in the Old Testament prophets and events because they did not have its translation in their mother tongue until 2007, which was after the bulk of study for this book was done. Their knowledge of some of these stories and events was based on what their Muslim neighbours told them from their Qur'an. However, most Dagomba have no direct access to the Qur'an because Islam only facilitates the learning of Arabic in order to be able to read it; they did not have this handicap with the New Testament because it had been translated into Dagbani much earlier. At least with the New Testament, the Dagomba have a legitimate source of studying theology and analysing historical material. It is for this reason that all Dagomba Christians yearned for the Old Testament. Apart from having to learn Arabic to be able to read the Qur'an, some of the Qur'anic narratives and the Biblical ones differ significantly. For example, the story of Daniel in the Bible is different from that of Daniel in the Qur'an, as is the story of Moses. Isaac's role is also totally different in the two; in the Qur'an, it is Ismael whom Abraham offered to God as a sacrifice and not Isaac. The translation of the Bible into Dagbani and Likpakpaaln gives God's message directly in the mother tongue. Theology, history and ethics have been made accessible; readers do not have to learn Arabic first.

Konkomba and Dagomba Christians could not agree more with Sanneh when he spoke with this author of the profound implication of Bible translation into the mother tongue:

> If God speaks our language, then it follows automatically that He affirms us. Thus, He affirms who we are and therefore we are acceptable to Him. Scripture in the language of a people is an implicit endorsement of them. In the context of colonial rule when, for example, Africans were regarded as backward, Bible translation with its specific endorsement of languages, represents a challenge to colonial attitudes, and strengthens the local demand for equality. The basic argument here is that, if God affirms the African, that is, who they are, who is there to say otherwise?[5]

Christian mission to the Dagomba and Konkomba was possible through the translation of the Christian message into Dagbani and Likpakpaaln. This had a rippling effect on all aspects of their lives. The mother-tongue

---
[5] Interview with Professor Lamin Sanneh, 16 July 2003, New Haven, CT, USA.

Scriptures have contributed to the holistic transformation of the Dagomba and Konkomba. The rural Dagomba and Konkomba have experienced empowerment and this has, consequently, overcome the hegemony that was exercised over them. Though Christian mission in certain contexts and eras did not follow the strategy of translation, those in the contexts of the Dagomba and Konkomba did. Christian mission to them could be described using Sanneh's characterisation of a dynamic translation movement (1989:175).

In conclusion, Christian mission is incomplete without translation, which involves the active participation of divinity and humanity. A Dagomba pastor succinctly expressed the importance of Bible translation:

> The work of [Dagbani] Bible translation brings about transformation in communities. May the Lord help and strengthen them so that they can persevere and complete the translation of the Bible.... If you have not touched something you do not yet know its beauty or value. If someone is in a well and tells you to come inside and have a drink, because there is water in it and you give him a calabash and ask him to fetch the water for you, there is some difficulty. However, when you get inside it yourself you will also get all you want. Unless you also enter into the Bible, others may mislead you, but when you experience it yourself you will know the truth for yourself. Personal experience will eliminate any exaggerations or distortions.

Appendix: Dagomba and Konkomba Anthems Sung in Churches

The following popular anthems are sung in multiple churches of various denominations. These songs of anonymous origin illustrate the depth of Christian experience among both groups.

1. Two Dagomba anthems sung in churches

Yisa Kul' Mi Sokam Zaa Yɛla	**Jesus Knows All People**
Yi na ʒi wum ni n zɔ nyɛ Yisa	Have you not heard about Jesus?
N zɔ m-bala, n zɔ m-bala	He is my friend, He is my friend.
Ŋun kɔ ni tooi fa sokam zaa bahi	He alone can deliver all;
N zɔ m-bala, n zɔ m-bala	He is my friend, He is my friend.
Yisa kul' mi sokam zaa yɛla,	Jesus knows about everyone.
O ni sɔŋ ma o yi ko ni,	He will help me by His power.
So ka ŋun nyɛ n zɔ suŋ ka Yisa	No one is a good friend like Jesus;
N zɔ m-bala, n zɔ m-bala	He is my friend, He is my friend.
Yisa daa ka na nti kpi ti zuɣu	Jesus came to die because of us;
N zɔ m-bala, n zɔ m-bala	He is my friend, He is my friend
Yisa daa ka na nti nyaŋ sintani	Jesus came and defeated Satan;
N zɔ m-bala, n zɔ m-bala	He is my friend, He is my friend.

Naawuni Ti Lahabali	God Has Given Us Good News to Share
Naawuni ti lahabali	God has given us a message
Ni ti tɔysi nirba zaa	That we should tell all people,
Ni bɛ deei ti Duuma Yisa	That they should receive Jesus
Ka chɛ n-gul o labbu na	And wait for His return.
Chɛm' ti yɛli ba, Chɛm' ti yɛli ba	Go and tell them, go and tell them,
Ni bɛ dol' la Yisa kɔ	That they should follow only Jesus.
Chɛm' ti yɛli ba, Chɛm' ti yɛli ba	Go and tell them, go and tell them,
Ni bɛ dol' la Yisa kɔ	That they should follow only Jesus.
Yisa yuri zuliya kam zaa	Jesus loves all ethnic groups
Ka daa kpi n-ti ti zaa	And died for us all
Ka lan neei, ka labi zuɣusaa	And rose again and returned to heaven
N' o ti mali ti bebu shee	To prepare our resting place.
Chɛliya ka tiŋ' kam zaa wum li	Let every town hear it
Ka chɛ n-niŋ tuba yom	And repent immediately;
Bɛ yi deei li bɛ ni tiligi	If they receive it they will be saved
Ka kpe Yisa mahim ni.	And enter in His shade.

2. A Konkomba anthem sung in churches

Ilaun Tiga Uwumbor Adichaln Ni Na
Songs We Sing in Churches (Konkomba)

(1) Ndi mba tii Yesu, Yesus lijoo mi
    (I have given myself to Jesus to take care of me.)

(2) Taa nan bi: paacham
    Halleluya taa nan bi taa nanbi paacham
    Hosiyana taa nan bi taa nan bi paacham
    (Our kingdom is in heaven.)

(3) Maa didiliib le ye dulnya ayaan
    Yesu adidiliib le ye dulnya ayaan
    N-yan ya bii ki yaa ka mo ; mua bi ki toor-ee
    (Christians are the salt of the world; when salt loses its taste,
    it becomes useless.)

(4) Gaa chon ado ga chon ado
    Uwumbor aalin roan kiyonbik
    Ga chon ado
    (Plant God's word in your home
    For it gives shade and fruit;
    Plant God's word in your home.)

Archival Source References

(FCBH) Faith Comes by Hearing
(PCG) Presbyterian Church of Ghana
(PRAAD) Public Records Administration and Archives Department

FCBH Report, September 2002. FCBH Archives. Albuquerque, New Mexico. Ms.
FCBH Report, 2003. FCBH Archives. Albuquerque, New Mexico. Ms.
FCBH Report, March 2004. FCBH Archives. Albuquerque, New Mexico. Ms.
PCG Annual Report, 1966. PCG Archives. Tamale. Ms.
PCG Annual Report, 1968. PCG Archives. Tamale. Ms.
PCG Annual Report, 1973. PCG Archives. Tamale. Ms.
PCG Annual Report, 1974. PCG Archives. Tamale. Ms.
PCG Annual Report, 1975. PCG Archives. Tamale. Ms.
PRAAD Accra. ADM 56/1/91 A Report on the Dagomba by the Acting Chief Commissioner, 28 December 1908. Ms.
PRAAD Accra. ADM 56/1/91 Cardinall, A. W., Some Random Notes on the Customs of the Konkombas. Ms.
PRAAD Accra. ADM 56/1/91 Colonial records on the Dagomba. Ms.
PRAAD Accra. ADM 56/1/160 The letter by the Provincial Commissioner's office, 15 February 1915. Ms.
PRAAD Accra. ADM 56/1/160 Wesleyan Mission, establishment of, in the Northern Territories (Case No. 7/1913). Ms.
PRAAD Accra. ADM 56/1/204 (Case No. 78/15, Acc. No. 1390) The Handing Over Notes by the District Commissioner, 1916. Ms.

PRAAD Accra. ADM 56/1/204 Handing Over Report of Yendi District, 1916. Ms.
PRAAD Accra. ADM 56/1/204 (Case No. 78/15, Acc. No.1390) Handing Over Report of Yendi District 5, September 1919. Ms.
PRAAD Tamale. Colonial Report for Yendi District, 1932. Ms.
PRAAD Tamale. Colonial Annual Report, 1932. Ms.
PRAAD Accra. NAG Yendi Diary for January 1918. Ms.
PRAAD Tamale. NRG 8/2/1 A. W. Davies, The History and Organisation of the Kambonse in Dagomba, 1948. Ms.
PRAAD Tamale. NRG 8/2/25 Minutes of the third Dagomba Conference Held at Yendi, on 3 January 1934. Ms.
PRAAD Tamale. NRG 8/2/70 Correspondence between the French and British colonial officers, 3 March 1935 and 24 September 1935. Ms.
PRAAD Tamale. NRG 8/2/70 Konkomba Tribes. Ms.
PRAAD Tamale. NRG 8/2/88 Another testimony of a Veterinary Officer, in support of the Director of Veterinary Services. Ms.
PRAAD Tamale. NRG 8/2/88 Colonial perception of the Konkomba in their accounts in the archives. Ms.
PRAAD Tamale. NRG 8/2/88 Mr. MacDonald's attachment to the Director of Veterinary Service's confidential letter. Ms.
PRAAD Tamale. NRG 8/2/88 The testimony of A. Fulton, Director of Veterinary Service's confidential letter on "Konkomba disturbances–Segbiri" to Ag: Chief Commissioner of the then Northern Territories, 18 March 1941. Ms.
PRAAD Tamale. NRG 8/3/22 Annual Report of the Mandated Area South Mamprusi District, January–December 1930. Ms.
PRAAD Tamale. NRG 8/3/34 Annual Report of the Mandated Area South Mamprusi District, January–December 1930. Ms.
PRAAD Tamale. NRG 8/3/46 An Ethnological Investigation covering the year 1932 and presented by the Acting Chief Commissioner of the Northern Territories, 20 June 1933. Ms.
PRAAD Tamale. NRG 8/3/46 Ethnographical investigation in the Annual Report of 1932. Ms.
PRAAD Tamale. NRG 8/19/3 English Church Mission. Ms.
PRAAD Tamale. NRG 8/19/7 The Chief Commissioner writing to the Colonial Secretary on a Bishop Morin's Memorandum on the subject of conflict between native law and custom and Christian practice which made reference to the disturbance in the Dagaaba traditional area, 1937. Ms.
PRAAD Tamale. NRG 8/19/7 The District Commissioner to the Chief Commissioner, Northern Territories, on the subject, "Christianity and Native Custom," No. 115/28.S. F.1, 5 February 1937. Ms.
PRAAD, Tamale. NRG 8/19/7 The District Commissioner's response to the Chief Commissioner of the Northern Territories letter on the subject, "Christianity and Native Custom," 5 February 1937. Ms.

PRAAD Tamale. NRG 8/34/1 Report on the Mandated area of Togoland under the Kusasi District for the year ending 30 November 1927. Ms.

PRAAD Tamale. Report on the Mandated area of the district area of the District of South Mamprusi for 1925 and 1928. Ms.

Textual References

Aidoo-Dadzie, Galord. 2001. The widowhood rite of the Fante. *Journal of African Christian Thought* 4(1):56–64.

Akrong, Abraham. 1998. The historic mission of the African Independent Churches (AIC). *Research Review New Series* 14(2):56–68.

Amo, Reverend. n.d. The Baptist history, polity and practice. Ms.

Ansre, Gilbert. 1997. *The Evangelical Presbyterian Church: 150 years of evangelization and development 1847–1997.* Ho, Ghana: The Evangelical Presbyterian Church.

Arhin, Kwame, ed. 1974. *The papers of George Ekem Ferguson, a Fanti official of the government of the Gold Coast, 1890–1897.* Leiden: Afrika-Studiecentrum; Cambridge, UK: African Studies Centre.

Azumah, John A. 2001. *The legacy of Arab-Islam in Africa: A quest for inter-religious dialogue.* Oxford, UK: One Word.

Bakar, Moses Mulingna. 1988. The effect of Muslim and Christian missions on the Konkomba of northern Ghana (1700–1987) and its relevance for future Christian mission strategy. Essay for Certificate in Mission Studies, Selly Oak Colleges, University of Birmingham, UK.

Balcomb, Anthony. 1998. Of radical refusers and very willing victims – Interpolations of the missionary message in the stories of Nongqawuse, Nxele, Ntsikana and Soga. *Bulletin for Contextual Theology in Southern Africa & Africa* 5(1 & 2).

Barker, Peter. 1986. *Peoples, languages, and religion in northern Ghana: A preliminary report.* Accra: Ghana Evangelism Committee.

Barker, Peter, and Samuel Boadi-Siaw. 2003. *Changed by the Word: The story of Scripture Union Ghana*. Accra: Scripture Union, African Christian Press, and Asempa Publishers.

Beaumont, Mark. 2005. *Christology in dialogue with Muslims: A critical analysis of Christian presentations of Christ for Muslims from the ninth and twentieth centuries*. Bletchley, UK: The Paternoster Press; Waynesboro, GA: Regnum.

Bediako, Gillian M. 1997. *Primal religion and the Bible: William Robertson Smith and his heritage*. Sheffield, UK: Sheffield Academic Press.

Bediako, Kwame. 1994. Epilogue. In Ype Schaaf, *On their way rejoicing: The history and role of the Bible in Africa*, 241–252. Carlisle, Cumbria, UK: The Paternoster Press; Waynesboro, GA: Regnum Books International.

Bediako, Kwame. 1995. *Christianity in Africa: The renewal of a non-western religion*. Maryknoll, NY: Orbis Books; Edinburgh: Edinburgh University Press.

Bediako, Kwame. 1999. Translatability and the cultural incarnations of the faith. In James A. Scherer and Stephen B. Bevans (eds.), *New directions in mission and evangelization 3: Faith and culture*. Maryknoll, NY: Orbis Books.

Bediako, Kwame. 2001. The role and significance of the translation of the Bible into African languages in the consolidation of the church and its expansion into unreached areas. Paper presented to Wycliffe Bible Translators International Africa Area Forum, Narobi, 2001. In Franklin 2008, p. 10.

Bening, R. B. 1973. Indigenous concepts of boundaries and significance of administrative stations and boundaries in northern Ghana. *Bulletin of the Ghana Geographical Association* 15:7–20.

Bening, R. B. 1975a. Colonial development policy in northern Ghana, 1898–1950. *Bulletin of the Ghana Geographical Association* 17:65–79.

Bening, R. B. 1975b. Location of district administrative capitals in the Northern Territories of the Gold Coast (1897–1951). *Bulletin de l'IFAN, Series B* 37(3):646–666.

Bening, R. B. 1990. *A history of education in northern Ghana 1907–1976*. Accra: Ghana Universities Press.

Berinyuu, Abraham. 1997. *History of the Presbyterian Church in northern Ghana*. Accra: Asempa Publishers.

Berry, LaVerle Bennette and Library of Congress. Federal Research Division. 1995. *Ghana: A Country Study*. Federal Research Division, Library of Congress. PDF: https://www.loc.gov/item/95018891/.

Bible Society of Ghana. 1965. Brochure. Ms.

Blakely, Thomas D., W. E. A. van Beek, and Dennis L. Thomson. 1994. *Religion in Africa: Experience & expression*. London: James Currey.

Boi-Nai, Vincent. 1997. Withcraft mentality as a barrier to women's emancipation: A pastoral reflection. In Jon P. Kirby (ed.), A compilation of papers presented at the Tamale Institute of Cross-Cultural Studies

(TICCS) Witchcraft Mentality Seminars May 26–29 and December 8–11, 1997.

Boi-Nai, Vincent, and Jon P. Kirby. 1998. Catholicism and problem-solving in Dagbon. *Social Compass* 45(4):533–553.

Boi-Nai, Vincent, and Jon P. Kirby. 1999. Popular Catholicism in Dagbon. In Tomas Bamat and Jean-Paul Weist (eds.), *Popular Catholicism in a world church: Seven case studies in inculturation*, 119–156. Maryknoll, NY: Orbis Books.

Bosch, David J. 1991. *Transforming mission*, Maryknoll, NY: Orbis Books.

Bowdich, Thomas Edward. 1819. *A mission from Cape Coast Castle to Ashantee*. London: John Murray.

Bradshaw, Bruce. 2000. Transformational development. In A. Scott Moreau (ed.), *Evangelical dictionary of world missions*, 966. Grand Rapids, MI: Baker Books.

Brukum, N. J. K. 2001. *The guinea fowl, mango and pito wars: Episodes in the history of northern Ghana, 1980–1999*. Accra: Ghana Universities Press.

Buah, F. K. 1980. *A history of Ghana*. London: Macmillan.

Buah, F. K. 1998. *A history of Ghana*. Revised and updated edition. London: Macmillan.

Busia, K. A. 1955. The African worldview. In *Proceedings of the Conference on Christianity and African Culture*, Accra, Gold Coast, May 2–6, 1955. Accra: Christian Council of the Gold Coast.

Catholic Bishops' Conference of Ghana, Justice and Peace Commission. 1984. *Intertribal conflicts in Ghana*. Kumasi, Ghana: Cita Press, Ltd.

Coldham, Geraldine E. 1966. *A bibliography of Scriptures in African languages*, vol. 1. London: The British and Foreign Bible Society.

Comaroff, Jean, and John L. Comaroff. 1989. The colonization of consciousness in South Africa. *Economy and Society* 18(3):267–296.

Comaroff, Jean, and John L. Comaroff. 1997. *Of revelation and revolution, volume 2: The dialectics of modernity on a South African frontier*. Chicago: University of Chicago Press.

Cuthbertson, Greg. 1989. Van Der Kemp and Philip: The missionary debate revisited. *Missionalia* 17(2):77–94.

Dagbani Almanac. 2003. ms.

Debrunner, Hans W. 1967. *A history of Christianity in Ghana*. Accra: Waterville Publishing House.

Der, Benedict G. 1974. Church-state relations in northern Ghana, 1906–1940. *Transactions of the Historical Society of Ghana* 15(1):41–61.

Der, Benedict G. 1983. Missionary enterprise in northern Ghana, 1906–1975: A study in effect. PhD thesis. University of Ghana, Legon.

Der, Benedict G. 1998. *The slave trade in northern Ghana*. Accra: Woeli Publishing Services.

Dickerson, L. 2000. Linguistic theory and linguistics. In A. Scott Moreau (ed.), *Evangelical dictionary of world missions*, 579–580. Grand Rapids, MI: Baker Books.

Donovan, Vincent. 2001 *Christianity rediscovered.* Third edition. Maryknoll, NY: Orbis Books.

Dovlo, Elom. 2001. African culture and emergent church forms in Ghana. *Exchange* 33(1):28–53.

Dovlo, Elom, and Solomon Sule-Saa. 1999. The northern outreach program of the Presbyterian Church of Ghana. *International Bulletin of Missionary Research* 23(3):112–116.

Duthie, Alan S. 1985. *Bible translations and how to choose between them.* Exeter, UK: The Paternoster Press.

Dye, T. Wayne. 1985. *Bible translation strategy: An analysis of its spiritual effect.* Dallas, TX: Wycliffe Bible Translators.

Eberhard, David M., Gary F. Simons, and Charles D. Fennig, eds. 2019. *Ethnologue: Languages of the World.* Twenty-second edition. Dallas, TX: SIL International. http://www.ethnologue.com.

Fage, J. D. 1969. Slavery and the slave trade in the context of West African history. *The Journal of African History* 10(3):393–404.

Franklin, Kirk. 2008. Bible translation as holistic mission. Accessed 6 October 2016. http://www.wycliffe.net/missiology?id=832.

Fredriks, Martha T. 2003. *We have toiled all night: Christianity in The Gambia 1456–2000.* Zoetermeer, Netherlands: Boekencentrum.

Freire, Paolo, 1970. *Pedagogy of the oppressed.* New York: Continuum Press.

Froelich, Jean-Claude. 1954. *La tribu Konkomba du nord Togo.* Dakar: IFAN. Translated by Margrit Bolli as *The Konkomba tribe of northern Togo,* and re-typed by Ingeborg Petermann. Ms.

Fulford, Ben. 2002. An Igbo Esperanto: A history of the Union Ibo Bible 1900–1950. *Journal of Religion in Africa* 32(4):457–501.

Gaiya, Musa A. B. 1993. A history of the Hausa Bible: 1980 edition. *The African Journal of Evangelical Theology* 12(1):54–63.

Gaskin, Ross. 1986. Contextualisation of the gospel among the Konkomba. Minor thesis. Pacific College of Graduate Studies.

Gittins, Anthony J. 2002. *Ministry at the margins: Strategy and spirituality for mission.* Maryknoll, NY: Orbis Books.

Goody, Jack. 1954. *The ethnography of the Northern Territories of the Gold Coast, west of the White Volta.* London: Oxford University Press.

Grubb, Norman P. 1940. Letter, July 26, 1940, from Reverend Grubb to the colonial authorities. Ms.

Hall, Edward. 1983. *Ghanaian languages.* Accra: Asempa Publishers.

Horton, Robin. 1985. Stateless societies in the history of West Africa. In J. F. Ade Ajayi and Michael Crowder (eds.), *History of West Africa.* Harlow, Essex, UK: Longman.

Hostetter, Richard L. 1975. *Distinctive characteristics of Islam in West Africa*. Legon: Institute of African Studies, University of Ghana.
Howell, Allison M. 1997. *The religious itinerary of a Ghanaian people: The Kasena and the Christian gospel*. Frankfurt am Main, Berlin, Bern, New York, and Paris: Peter Lang.
Idowu, E. Bolaji. 1965. *Towards an indigenous church*. London: Oxford University Press.
Iliasu, A. A. 1968. The 'Cambonse' of Mamprusi and Dagomba. Paper presented at the Seminar at the Department of History, University of Ghana, Legon, October 29, 1968.
Jones, Marjorie. 1967. *Black eagle*. Nashville: Convention Press.
Katanga, Justice. 1994a. A new look at the Konkombas – Stereotypes and the road to reconciliation in northern Ghana. *Uhuru* 6(9):19–22.
Katanga, Justice. 1994b. The northern conflict: A historical and ethnographic commentary. Ms.
Kimble, David. 1963. *A political history of Ghana: The rise of Gold Coast nationalism, 1950–1928*. London: Oxford University Press.
Kirby, Jon P. 1988. Inculturation of the Christian message: Claim, reality, consequences. In Joachim G. Piepke (ed.), *Anthropology and mission: SVD international consultation on anthropology for mission*, 68–81, Pune, India, December 29, 1986 to January 04, 1987. Nettetal, Germany: Steyler Verlag - Wort und Werk.
Kirby, Jon P. 1994. Cultural change and religious conversion in West Africa. In Thomas D. Blakely, Walter E. A. van Beek, and Dennis L. Thomson (eds.), *Religion in Africa: Experience and expansion*, 56–71. London: James Currey; Portsmouth, NH: Heinemann.
Kirby, Jon P. 1996. Thoughts about culture: "The politics of religion in northern Ghana." http://www.sedos.org/english/kirby.htm. Accessed 3 October 2004.
Kirby, Jon P. 2006. Ghana's witches: Scratching where it itches. In Stephen B. Bevans (ed.), *Mission and culture: The Louis J. Luzbetak lectures*, 189–224. Maryknoll, NY: Orbis Books.
Kottak, Conrad Phillip. 1999. *Mirror for humanity: A concise introduction to cultural anthropology*. Boston: McGraw-Hill College.
Kottak, Conrad Philip. 2002. *Anthropology: The exploration of human diversity*. Boston: McGraw Hill.
Kraft, Charles H. 2001. *Culture, communication, and Christianity: A selection of writings*. Pasadena, CA: William Carey Library.
Lecestre, Olivier, 1996. The beginnings of Catholic evangelisation in Tamale Archdiocese. Ms.
Legrand, Lucien. 2000. *The Bible on culture: Belonging or dissenting?* Maryknoll, NY: Orbis Books.
Lensch, Christopher K. 2003. Bible translations: Impact on modern languages. *WRS Journal* 10(2):27–30.

Levtzion, Nehemia. 1977. The western Maghrib and Sudan: The hegemony of Songhay. In J. D. Fage and Roland Oliver (eds.), *The Cambridge history of Africa volume 3: From c. 1050 to c. 1600*, 331–462. London: Cambridge University Press.

Lewis, Paul, and Gary Simons. 2017. *Ethnologue: Languages of the world*, edition twenty. https://www.ethnologue.com/country/GH/. Accessed October 19, 2017.

Lidorio, Ronaldo A. 1999. Cultural identity and religious phenomenology: The effect of the gospel in a Konkomba worldview. PhD thesis in Cultural Anthropology – Ethnology. Knightsbridge University, Denmark.

Mahama, Ibrahim. 2004. *History and traditions of Dagbon*. Tamale: GILLBT Press.

Manoukian, Madeline. 1951. Tribes of the Northern Territories of the Gold Coast. In Daryll Forde (ed.), *Ethnographic survey of Africa*. London: International African Institute.

Martinson, H. B. 1994. *The hidden history of the Konkomba wars in northern Ghana*. Accra: Masta Press.

Mazrui, Ali A. 1985. Religion and political culture in Africa. *Journal of the American Academy of Religion* 53(4):817–839.

Mbiti, John S. 1969. *African religions and philosophy*. Nairobi: Heinemann.

Mbiti, John S. 1986. *Bible and theology in African Christianity*. Nairobi: Oxford University Press.

Mbiti, John S. 1994. The Bible in African culture. In Rosino Gibellini (ed.), *Paths of African theology*. Maryknoll, NY: Orbis Books.

McCoy, Remigius F. 1988. *Great things happen: A personal memoir of the first Christian missionary among the Dagaabas and Sissalas of northwest Ghana*. Montreal: The Society of Missionaries of Africa.

Meyer, Birgit. 1999. *Translating the devil: Religion and modernity among the Ewe in Ghana*. Edinburgh: Edinburgh University Press.

Moorhouse, Geoffrey. 1973. *The missionaries*. London: Eyre Methuen.

Mudimbe, V. Y. 1988. *The invention of Africa: Gnosis, philosophy, and the order of knowledge*. Oxford: James Currey.

Naameh, Philip. 2001. The beginning of evangelisation of the north. Paper presented at the Tamale Archdiocesan Pastoral Congress, January 2–5, 2001.

Naden, Tony. 1996. *Time and the calendar in some Ghanaian languages*. Tamale: GILLBT Press.

Nketia, J. H. 1958. The church and culture – The contribution of African culture to Christian worship. In *The church in changing Africa: Report of the All-Africa church conference held at Ibadan, Nigeria, January 10–19, 1958*. New York: International Missionary Council.

Noss, Philip A. 1999. Foreword. In Aloo Osotsi Majola, *God speaks our own languages: Bible translation in East Africa, 1844–1998: A general survey*, vi.

Nairobi, Dodoma, and Kampala: The Bible Societies of Kenya, Tanzania and Uganda.

Oliver, Roland A., ed. 1977. *The Cambridge history of Africa, volume 3: From c. 1050 to c. 1600*. Cambridge: Cambridge University Press.

Opoku, A. A. 1978. *Riis, the builder*. Legon: Institute for African Studies, University of Ghana.

Opoku, Kofi Asare. 1978. *West African traditional religion*. Accra: FEP International Private Limited.

Oppong, Christine. 1973. *Growing up in Dagbon*. Accra: Ghana Publishing Corporation.

Pettifer, Julian, and Richard Bradley. 1990. *Missionaries*. London: BBC Books.

Pilaszewicz, Stanislaw. 2001. History of the Dagomba kingdom in some Hausa Ajami manuscripts. https://archive.is/UenGp. Accessed January 11, 2018. Also found in Smithsonian Libraries African Art Index Project DSI.

Prah, Kwesi Kwaa. 1975. The northern minorities in the Gold Coast and Ghana. *Race and Class* 16(3):305–312.

Prempeh, Samuel. 1977. The Basel and Bremen Missions and their successors in the Gold Coast and Togoland, 1914–1926. PhD thesis. University of Aberdeen.

Pul, Hippolyt A. S. 2003. Exclusion, association and violence: Trends and triggers in northern Ghana's Konkomba-Dagomba wars. *The African Anthropologist* 10(1):39–82.

Quaye, Paa Ekow. 1991. *The Story of the GILLBT*. Tamale: GILLBT Press.

Rattray, Robert S. 1932. *The tribes of the Ashanti hinterland*. Oxford: Clarendon Press.

Saayman, Willem A. 1990. Intercultural evangelisation. *Missionalia* 18(2):308–319.

Sanneh, Lamin. 1974. Amulets and Muslim orthodoxy. *International Review of Mission* 63:95.

Sanneh, Lamin. 1976. Faith and amulets: A spiritual conflict in worship. In John B. Taylor (ed.), *Primal world views: Christian dialogue with traditional thought forms*, 86. Ibadan, Nigeria: Daystar Press.

Sanneh, Lamin. 1983. *West African Christianity: The religious effect*. Maryknoll, NY: Orbis Books.

Sanneh, Lamin. 1985. Christian mission in the pluralist milieu: The African experience. *International Review of Mission* 74(294):199–211.

Sanneh, Lamin. 1987. Christian missions and the Western guilt complex. *The Christian Century*, April 8, 1987:331–334.

Sanneh, Lamin. 1989. *Translating the message: The missionary effect on culture*. Maryknoll, NY: Orbis Books.

Sanneh, Lamin. 1990. Mission and the modern imperative – Retrospect and prospect: Charting a course. In Joel A. Carpenter and Wilbert R. Shenk (eds), *Earthen vessels: American evangelicals and foreign missions, 1880–1980*, 301–316. Grand Rapids, MI: William B. Eerdmans Publishing Company.

Sanneh, Lamin. 1991. The yogi and the commissar: Christian missions and the African response. *International Bulletin of Mission Research* 15(1):2–12.

Sanneh, Lamin. 1993a. *Encountering the West: Christianity and the global cultural process: The African dimension.* Maryknoll, NY: Orbis Books.

Sanneh, Lamin. 1993b. Africa. In James M. Phillips and Robert T. Coote (eds), *Towards the twenty first century in Christian mission,* 89–91. Grand Rapids: William B. Eerdmans Publishing Company.

Sanneh Lamin. 1994. Translatability in Islam & in Christianity in Africa. In Thomas D. Blakely, W. E. A. van Beek, and Dennis L Thomson (eds.), *Religion in Africa.* p. 2. London: James Currey.

Sanneh, Lamin. 1995. Christian missions and the western guilt complex. *Evangelical Review Of Theology* 19(4):393–400.

Sanneh, Lamin. 1996. *Piety and power: Muslims and Christians in West Africa.* Maryknoll, NY Orbis Books.

Sanneh, Lamin. 1997a. Missionary enterprise. In John Middleton, *Encyclopedia of Africa south of the Sahara,* vol. 1. London: Simon & Schuster.

Sanneh, Lamin. 1997b. Theology of mission. In David Ford (ed.), *The modern theologians: An introduction to Christian theology in the twentieth century.* Second edition, 555–574. Cambridge, MA: Blackwell Publishers.

Sanneh, Lamin. 1999. *Abolitionists abroad: American blacks and the making of modern West Africa.* Cambridge, MA: Harvard University Press.

Sanneh Lamin. 2000. Vincent Donovan's discovery of post-western Christianity. In Vincent J. Donovan, *Christianity rediscovered, twenty-fifth anniversary edition,* 151–159. Maryknoll, NY: Orbis Books.

Sanneh, Lamin. 2001. They "stooped to conquer": Cultural vitality and the narrative impulse. In Keith E. Yandell (ed.), *Faith and narrative.* Oxford: Oxford University Press.

Sanneh, Lamin. 2003. *Whose religion Is Christianity?: The gospel beyond the West.* Grand Rapids, MI: William B. Eerdmans Publishing Company.

Schaaf, Ype. 1994. *On their way rejoicing: The history and role of the Bible in Africa.* Akropong-Akuapem, Ghana: Regnum Africa.

Senavoe, Juliana. 2001. Akan widowhood rites: A pastoral response. *Journal of African Christian Thought* 4(1):39–46.

Shaw, R. D. 2000. Bible translation. In A. Scott Moreau (ed.), *Evangelical dictionary of world missions,* 193–196, Grand Rapids, MI: Baker Books.

Sheldon, Steven N. 1999. People groups without adequate access to Scriptures. Ms.

Shinnie, P. L. and Paul Ozanne. 1962. Excavations at Yendi Dabari. *Transactions of the Historical Society of Ghana* 6:87–118.

Sim, Ronald J. 2004. Changing paradigms in Bible translation. http://www.tyndale.org/tsj03/sim.html. Accessed 11 January 2018.

Smalley, William A. 1991. *Translation as mission: Bible translation in the modern missionary movement.* Macon, GA: Mercer University Press.

Smalley, William A. 1995. Language and culture in the development of Bible Society translation theory and practice. *International Bulletin of Missionary Research* 19(2):61–70.

Smith, Noel. 1966. *The Presbyterian Church of Ghana, 1835–1960: A younger church in a changing society.* Accra: Ghana Universities Press.

Sorkpor, Gershon A. 1967. The Mande traders and their role in the political and commercial history of the Gold Coast. Institute of African Studies, University of Ghana, Legon.

Southwell, Neville. n.d. The effect of Bible translation. SIL International Pacific Area, Brisbane. Ms.

Staniland, Martin. 1975. *The lions of Dagbon: Political change in northern Ghana.* Cambridge: Cambridge University Press.

Stott, John. 1975. *Christian mission in the modern world.* Reviewed by James Clark in What is the meaning of mission in today's world?, *Institute for Faith, Work & Economics,* January 6, 2016. https://tifwe.org/mission-in-the-modern-world. Accessed 11 January 2018.

Sule-Saa, Solomon S. 2000. Ethnicity and the church: The case of the Presbyterian Church of Ghana. MTh thesis. University of Natal, South Africa.

Tait, David. 1961. *The Konkomba of northern Ghana.* London: Oxford University Press, for the International African Institute and the University of Ghana.

Talton, Benjamin. 2010. *Politics of social change in Ghana: the Konkomba struggle for political equality.* New York: Palgrave Macmillan.

Tamakloe, Emmanuel F. 1931. *A brief history of the Dagomba people.* Accra: Ghana Government Printing Office.

Thomas, Roger G. 1974. Education in Northern Ghana, 1906–1940: A study in colonial paradox. The International Journal of African Historical Studies, vol. 7, no. 3:427–467. DOI: 10.2307/217253.

Timiadis, Emilianos. 1985. Unity of faith and pluralism in culture: A lesson from the Byzantine missionaries. *International Review of Mission* 74:237–244.

Trimingham, J. Spencer. 1962. *A history of Islam In West Africa.* Oxford and New York: Oxford Universtiy Press.

Turaki, Yusufu. 1993. *The British colonial legacy In northern Nigeria: A social ethical analysis of the colonial and post-colonial society and politics in Nigeria.* Jos: Challenge Press.

Tuurey, Gabriel. 1982. *An introduction to the Mole-speaking community.* Wa, Ghana: Catholic Press.

United Nations Educational, Scientific and Cultural Organization (UNESCO), *Sixth Conference of Ministers of Education and Those Responsible for Economic Planning in African Member States,* Dakar, 8–11 July 1991.

Vanhoozer, Kevin J. 2005. The drama of doctrine: A canonical-linguistic approach to Christian theology. Louisville, KY: Westminster John Knox Press. https://books.google.com/books?isbn=0664223273. Accessed 18 January 2018.

Vansina, Jan. 1985. *Oral tradition as history.* Nairobi: East African Educational Publishers Ltd.

Vansina, Jan. 1989. Oral tradition and its methodology. In Joseph Ki-Zerbo (ed.), *General history of Africa, vol. IV, abridged edition,* 54–61. London: James Currey.

Voorhies. Samuel. 1999. Transformational development: God at work changing people and their communities. In Ralph D. Winter and Steven C. Hawthorne (eds.), *Perspective on the world Christian movement,* 590–591. Pasadena, CA:William Carey Library.

Walls, Andrew F. 2002. *The cross-cultural process in Christian history: Studies in the transmission and appropriation of faith.* Maryknoll, NY: Orbis Books.

Watters, John. 2003. SIL's service in the world. *Intercom* January–March, 2003.

Weiss, Holger. 2005. Islam, missionaries and residents: The attempt of the Basel Missionary Society to establish a mission in Yendi (German Togo) before World War I. In Ulrich van der Heyden and Holger Stoecker (eds.), *Mission und macht im wandel politischer orientierungen* 173–186. Stuttgart: Franz Steiner Verlag.

Whiteman, Darrell. 1990. Bible translation and integral development. In Philip C. Stine (ed.), *Bible translation and the spread of the church: The last 200 years,* 120–141. Leiden: E. J. Brill.

Wilks, Ivor. 1975. *Asante in the nineteenth century: The structure and evolution of a political order.* London: Cambridge University Press.

Wilson, Elizabeth A. Galley. 1955. *Making many rich.* Springfield, MO: Gospel Publishing House.

Wilson, William A. A. 1972. *Dagbani: An introductory course.* Tamale: Self published.

World Missionary Conference. 1910. Report of Commission 2: The church in the mission field. Edinburgh: Oliphant, Anderson & Ferrier.

Yakuba, Abudulai. 2006. *The Abudulai-Andani crisis of Dagomba: A historical and legal perspective of the Yendi skin affairs.* Accra: MCP Ltd.

Index

Abakah, Kwasi 98–99
Aboriginal Rights Protection
  Society 85
Accelerated Development Plan for
  Education 156
acephalous people/groups 2, 57
  see non-centralised societies
Adventist Relief Association 114
African traditional (primal) religion
  110n, 134–135
  among Dagomba 33, 47–51
  fulfilled by Christianity 129,
    135, 173, 179–180
  among Konkomba 73–77
  and translation process 133–140
agricultural efforts 17, 95, 107,
  114, 182.
  Agricultural School and Training
    College (Bimbilla) 102
  Agricultural Settlement "Mile
    7" Programme (Tamale)
    105–111
  Saboba Agricultural Project 124

Yendi Agricultural Station 102
  see also van den Broek
Ajami manuscripts (Hausa/Arabic)
  27–28
Ajuoga, Matthew 19
Akan culture 44, 48, 50, 135, 164
Akonsi, Mr. (first Konkomba
  Christian) 122
Akrong, Abraham 127
Alando, Stephen 111
Amo, Reverend 103
amulets (*saba*) 49, 51
Ansre, Gilbert 102, 198–199
anti-hegemony see hegemony
Anufo (*also* Chokosi) (people) 31, 114n
Anufo churches 109
Asante (*Kambonga* people)
  hegemony/impact on Dagomba
    34–35, 66–67
Assemblies of God (AG)
  Assemblies of God Relief
    Services 114
  and Dagbani translation 115–116

219

mission to Dagomba 94–97, 120
mission to Konkomba 72,
    122–123, 159
Atakora, Simon 99

baga see diviners/soothsayers
Bagmae, Solomon 148
Bakar, Moses Mulingna 77
Balcomb, Anthony 7
Baptist missions 102–104
    Baptist Training Centre 103
Barker, Peter
    on Dagomba 52
    on Konkomba 78–80
    on Mamprusi 33
    survey of northern Ghana 6
Basare/Basari (people) 31, 35, 68
    language 91
    and WEC 126
Basel Mission 88–92, 115–116,
    120, 121, 123, 157
Bediako, Gillian 134–135
Bediako, Kwame 9, 79, 179n
Bekpokpam, sing. *Okpokpandja*;
    Okpokpampi (Konkomba
    autonym) 59, 61
Bendor-Samuel, John 131–132
Bening, R. B. 32–33, 86
Bible Church of Africa 47
Bible Society of Ghana 115,
    117–118, 120, 142, 149
    Translators' Course 105
Bimoba/Bimwaba (people) 68–69,
    170–173
    Bimoba (vernacular) Bible
        170–173, 189
Binabiba, Winston 148, 163, 165,
    166, 176
bininkpieb ('ancestors') 75
birth rituals
    Dagomba 43
    Konkomba 168
Boi-Nai, Vincent 53–54, 100–101

Bradley, Richard 7
Braintrust (at Tamale) 107
Bremen Mission 88, 102, 123,
    123–124, 157
Buchwalter, Beulah 94
buga/wuna ('lesser divinities'/
    nature spirits) 48–49
burial/funeral rituals 183
    Dagomba 44, 80
    Konkomba 80, 163–164, 168
Busagri, Dekpiema 99
Buxton, T. F. 90

Cardinall, A. W. 53, 73, 87
Carter, Douglas and Sarah 103
Cather, D. C. 103
Catholic missions
    among Dagomba 98–101, 107,
        120, 146
    among Konkomba 54, 72, 123,
        146n, 159
    Catholic Relief Service 114
    Society of Missionaries of Africa
        98–99
    Society for the Propagation of
        the Divine Word 146
    White Fathers 87–88, 98–100,
        127, 157
centralised (chiefly) societies/
    political system 2
    e.g. Dagomba, Gonja, Mamprusi
        2, 26
    dominate non-centralised groups
        32, 34, 60
    hierarchical/structured 40
    see also hegemony; Indirect Rule
Chamba (Konkomba subgroup) 35
chief (*na/naa*) 30, 40
    eminent (*na yiri*) 33
    king/paramount/'Lion of
        Dagbon' (*ya na*) 35, 36, 40,
        46, 52, 70, 96, 184
chieftaincy (*naam*) 26, 36, 38, 52–54

Index: C

Christian Council of Ghana 114
Christian mission
  and colonial rule 83–88, 122, 128, 192
  and colonialism 13–14, 19, 22
  concept of 1n3, 2n7
  contrast with Islam 8, 10, 20, 92, 112–113, 201
  cultural imperialism of 3, 22, 181, 186
  cultural learning important 116
  among Dagomba 83–120
  as a dynamic translation movement 3, 4, 9, 182, 191
  history of 6–7, 13, 15, 192
  indigenous consciousness increased by 18, 158, 191–202
  among Konkomba 121–143
  new approach 15–17
  role of translation in 115, 128, 130, 133, 185n22, 191, 202
  Sanneh's hermeneutic of 8, 145–189, 193–202
  and social change 156, 182–183, 186
  study methodology 4, 11–15
  translatable 9, 10, 20, 200
  as translation and anti-hegemony 3, 4, 8, 10, 11–15, 24, 115
  and Western Guilt Complex 12–13
  and Western hegemony 22, 193–194
  see also hegemony; Sanneh
Christian Service Committee 105, 109
Christianity
  as alien/foreign religion
    from colonial era 89, 120, 121
    from cultural differences 113–115, 183
  effect of vernacular translation 124, 136, 160, 171, 175, 178n16, 200
  among Dagomba 25, 54, 83–120, 149–158, 194–195
  indigenous African 9, 21–24, 174, 177–178, 200
  among Konkomba 57–81, 121–143, 158–173, 195–197
  role in society 197–200
  translatability 10, 18, 129, 185
  as vernacular translation 3, 9, 11–24, 173–189
  Western *see* Western Christianity
  World 23–24, 174–175
  see also colonialism; hegemony
Circumcision rituals
  Dagomba 43–44
  Konkomba 80
clans/clanship 57, 66, 68, 71, 72, 78, 137
colonialism (colonial authority/rule)
  British 31, 84, 86, 98
  and Christian missions
    as collaborators 13–14, 17, 22
    control by authorities 87
    among Dagomba 83–88, 93–94
    ethnocentric perspective 7, 22, 125, 127–128
    during World Wars 90, 95, 115, 124, 146, 193
    as obstacle 83, 88, 145–146
  cultural imperialism
    and acceptance of Christianity 127–128, 193
    and vernacular translation 19, 21–24, 181
  among Dagomba
    division of Dagbon 31
    favoured by British 31–32, 66–67

history 83–98, 120
  and Western education 45–46
economic policy 86, 155–156
education 45–46, 155–156, 177, 182
evangelism/missions as
  and economic policy 86
  and ethnocentric perspective 127–128
  media perspective 22, 193
  political causes 16
French 22–23, 61, 84, 98
German 31, 84, 90–91, 98
  and World Wars 115, 193
hegemony
  and vernacular translation 14, 143, 189, 194
  Western perspective 13–14, 20–24, 193
among Konkomba
  authorities resented 59, 61–62
  Dagomba hegemony opposed 58–67
  view of Christianity 121
language policy 98, 157, 186, 194
media 7, 22–23, 58, 70
missionaries during
  and authorities 17, 88, 92, 98
  ethnocentric perspective 7
and Moslems/Islam/Muslims
  colonial policy 83–87, 94, 146
  World Missionary Conference (1910) 87
in Northern Territories 84–88, 192
records 28
  on Dagomba 55
  ethnographic studies 89
  on Konkomba 58
repression/liberation
  and Christian missions 13, 127–128, 181

effect of vernacular translation 19, 23n, 181, 186, 201
in southern Ghana 86
Western Guilt Complex 12–13
  and Enlightenment 13, 128
see also Indirect Rule; Luggard
Comaroff, Jean and John L. 7, 186, 193
conscientised 54
conversion
  of Bimoba 171–172
  of Dagomba
    factors involved 83, 104, 151, 195
    Islam as obstacle 46, 97, 112, 195
  fear of 46, 152
  to indigenous African Christianity 9
  to Islam *see* jihads
  of Konkomba 54
  of Sanneh 4, 12–13
  political implications 16
  and vernacular translation 15, 54, 101, 104–105, 151, 155, 171–173, 195
Cow War (1940) 62–64
Crouch, Marge 134
cultural imperialism
  see imperialism

Dagaaba (area) 85
Dagaaba (people) 158
Dagban daba, Dagban doo
  see traditionalists
Dagbani/Dagbane/Dagbanli (Dagomba language)
  classification and relationships 38–39
  development of 183–184, 195, 199–200

Index: D

early studies of 90–93, 100, 116–120
in education 67, 72, 96, 100
Dagbani scriptures
  early translation 91, 100, 115–117
  effect on Dagbani language 148
  as foundation of belief 101
  influence of Islam 53, 96, 157
  literacy programme 119–120
  native speaker involvement 116–117
  New Testament 96, 116
  Old Testament 117
  and traditional culture 113, 115, 117
  usage/social change 148–158
  see also organisations involved in translation
Dagbon Kingdom
  Asante hegemony 35–36
  colonial era 31–32
  history 30
  and Konkomba 60, 81
  ritual areas 40
Dagomba
  Christian mission among 83–120
  history and culture 25–55
  Dagomba-Konkomba War (1994) (*also called* Guinea Fowl War; Northern Conflict)
    Christian ministry during 195, 200
    and Dagomba hegemony 64, 182
    and Konkomba ethnic pride 71
    and Nanumba hegemony 69
    religious factors 113–114
    and vernacular translation 197–198
  and Sanneh's hermeneutic of mission 145–158, 173–189
  and vernacular translation 194–195
  see also Dagbani
dance/dancing 45, 78, 126, 172, 177
Davies, A. W. 27, 30
death rituals/beliefs
  among Dagomba 44
  among Konkomba 80, 163–164, 168
Debrunner, Hans 123
Denominations
  church structure 114
  countries of origin 98
  involved with Dagomba and Konkomba 5, 47
  multi-ethnic/multi-lingual 19
  multi-/inter-denominational 107, 111, 118, 124
  non-denominational organisations 117, 130
  rivalry 83, 192
  seen as foreign 93
  and southern Christians 93, 95
  support for translation 143
  unity 120, 175, 180, 197, 200
  see specific denominations
Der, Benedict
  colonial rule 86, 98
  education/literacy 182
  missionary attitudes 126
  social change 100, 156, 182, 183
Diari Dapare 66
diviners/soothsayers
  among Dagomba 41–43, 49, 110
  effect of vernacular translation 172, 180
  among Konkomba 68, 75, 76, 80, 163
Donovan, Vincent 23n
drummers (*lunsi*) 25–27, 55, 59, 110, 116
Duthie, Alan S. 134

education
    anti-hegemony 37
    by Baptists 103
    and Christian missions 17, 180
    and colonial authorities 85–88
    Dagomba attitudes 45–46, 97, 119
    for girls 46
    Konkomba attitudes 57, 72
    among Konkomba 131, 133, 160–162, 166
    by Presbyterians 104–107
    Qur'anic 46
    by Catholics 100
    social change 40, 121, 155–157, 182, 186
    and vernacular translation 189, 195, 199–200
    by WEC 125–126
    see also Shirer
Edwards, Riley 117
enskin(ment)/enstool(ment)
    Dagomba 36
    Konkomba 60
    of Shirer 96
    of van den Broek 108
ethnic conflicts
    causes 62, 64, 71, 81, 113–114
    Christian response 195, 197–198, 200
    see also Dagomba-Konkomba War
ethnic consciousness/identity/pride
    of Dagomba 36, 37, 43
    of Konkomba 68, 70–72
    enhanced by vernacular translation 18, 157, 176
    threatened by Dagomba hegemony 54
ethnic groups
    Asante hegemony 35
    British policy 84–86
    Christian influences
        on churches 19
        on identity 157, 176, 196
        on inter-group relations 195–199
    cultural similarities 26, 32, 37, 54, 66
    Dagomba hegemony 27, 32, 37, 54, 66
    identity/pride
        Dagomba 36, 37
        Konkomba 60, 68, 71–72
    Mamprusi *na yiri* seniority 33, 45
    origins 34
    relations with Dagomba 33–36, 52
    relations with Konkomba 62, 68–70
    see also specific groups; map 2; Dagomba-Konkomba War; centralised societies; non-centralised societies
Evangelical Church of Ghana 5, 125, 199
Evangelical Presbyterian Church (EPC)
    among Dagomba 94, 101–102
    educational/developmental projects 72, 102, 123
    among Konkomba 72, 121, 123–124, 199
Ewe (people)
    Christians 81, 101
    church 101–102, 120
    language 102, 124

Faile, George 103
FCBH (Faith Comes By Hearing; formerly Hosanna)
    among Dagomba 118–119, 150–155, 200
    among Konkomba 161, 200
Ferguson, George Ekem 84, 90
fertilisers 109
festivals/celebrations
    Bible Week Celebration 142

among Dagomba 26, 42, 44–45, 111, 113, 157, 197
and Islam 42, 45, 51–52, 111, 113
among Konkomba 78–79, 180
National Farmer Celebration 102
and vernacular Scriptures 179–180
fiddlers (*gunji*) 25–27, 54–55, 59, 110
First World War *see* World Wars
Fisch, R. 90–91
Fish War (1946) 64
Fisher, Robert 93
'Fortress Christianity' 15
Foster, James E. 103
Frafra (people) 160
Frempong, Justin 134, 142, 149, 158–160, 169
French colonial authority
 and British 98
 colonial rule 61
 and Dagomba 84
 and Konkomba 61
Froelich, Jean-Claude 59, 73

Gambaga (town) 32–33, 35, 69
 witch camp 49
Garlock, H. B. 95
Gaskin, Ross 78, 80, 180
gates/houses (royal families) 38, 152, 184
genealogy 26, 72, 116n
German colonial authority
 and British 84
 colonial rule 90
 cooperation of Basel and Bremen Missions 123
 and Dagbani 91
 and Dagomba 84
 division of Dagbon kingdom 31
 effect of World Wars 90, 98, 115, 193

GILLBT (Ghana Institute of Linguistics, Literacy, and Bible Translation)
 and Bible translation 132–135, 146, 178–179
 and Dagbani Literacy Project 115, 119–120
 and Dagomba-Konkomba conflict 182, 198
 and FCBH 149
 and Konkomba literacy 130, 133, 142–143, 159, 166, 187
 mission statement 132
 Nassim Habif prize 178
 and SIL International 130–131, 146
 and vernacular literacy 131
Gonja (people)
 and Asante 35
 classification 26, 30–32
 and Dagomba 34, 52, 66
 and Konkomba 60, 70, 176, 198
 Gonja Bible/literacy program 125
 and WEC 125
Grubb, Norman P. 124–125
grungna/grundoo (slave) 32, 37
Grushi (people) 35
Guinea Fowl Festival (*Kpini*) 45
Guinea Fowl War (1994)
 see also under Dagomba-Konkomba War
gulkpena (Tamale chief) 95
gunji see fiddlers
Gushiego chiefdom 64

Handing Over Report 66–67
Haruna, Adam 111
Harvest Covenant 159, 199
Hausa (people) 29, 52, 53, 83, 91, 141
 see also Ajami chronicles

hegemony
  challenged by Christianity 20,
    181–189
  Christian mission as
    anti-hegemony
    indigenous African
      perspective 10, 14
    Sanneh's perspective 3,
      22–24, 145–189
  by Asante 35–36
  by Dagomba 2, 54, 81
  Konkomba response 65, 81
  by Nanumba 69
  by southern Christians 106
  vernacular translation as
    anti-hegemony
    human dignity affirmed 181,
      186
    redemptive effect 148, 189,
      193–194, 202
    Sanneh's perspective 8,
      22–23
  Western 20–23, 189, 193
  see also Christian mission
    as translation and
    anti-hegemony
Hickcok, Guy 94
Horton, Robin 28, 57
Howell, Allison 180
human rights see under rights
Huppenbauer, Hans 90–91

Idowu, Bolaji 114
Idowu, Mr. and Mrs. 102
Igbo (people) 141
  Igbo Union Bible 141
Iliasu, A. A. 27
illiteracy 27n7, 88, 90, 105, 111, 119
imam(s) 45, 53
Imoro, Ibrahim 120
imperialism, cultural 3, 20–24,
  127–128, 181
  imperialist ideology 10

Indirect Rule (by British colonial
    authorities)
  and administrative capitals 33
  brainchild of Lord Luggard 31n16
  and Christian missions 31nn16,
    83–85
  effect on Konkomba 60, 63, 70
  favoured centralised societies
    27, 28, 31–32
Irvine, R. A. 30
Islam/Muslim
  Ajami literature 27–28
  and audio programmes (of
    vernacular translation of New
    Testament) 150–155
  contrasts with Christianity
    centres 9
    indigenous cultural practices
      8, 10, 111, 157
    forgiveness/reconciliation
      153, 184
    language use 4, 7–8, 10, 20,
      146
  colonial policy 83–88, 92, 146
  among the Dagomba 42–45,
    49, 51–55, 80–81, 96–97,
    152–157
  challenge to Christian missions
    93, 97, 102, 112–113, 153
  conversion to 28–29
    see also jihads
  among the Konkomba 77–78,
    122, 127
  Dyula Muslims 29, 49
  kaffir ('pagan'/non-Muslim) 55
  language use 28, 117
  militant see jihads
  Sanneh background 3–4, 11–12,
    193
  sects 47
  and vernacular translation 149,
    194–195, 201
  see also *mallams*, Qur'an
  see also jihad(s)

Jesus Film 120, 145, 161–163, 174
jihad(s)/jihadists 8, 28–29, 46, 51–52
Jones, Marjorie 102–103
Jones, W. J. A. 86
juju(s) (spiritual power) 51, 150–151, 163, 172

kaffir ('pagan'/non-Muslim) 55
Kambonga (southerners/Asante) 93, 106, 120
  Kambonsi Jangli (Ashanti mosque) 99
kambonse/kambonsi (traditional military formation/infantry) 27, 34, 65
kambong naaneme (warriors) 35
Kasena (people) 180
Katanga, Justice 32, 53
kayaye ('porter') 86
Kekpokpam (Konkomba homeland) 59, 61
Ken Radach Memorial Centre 97
kenjaa ('lesser gods') 74–75
kente (multicoloured fabric) 178
kesuo ('general evil') *see* witchcraft, sorcery
Kies, Immanuel 90
Kimble, David 6
King, Solomon 123
Kirby, Jon 53–54, 70, 100–101, 109, 114
kola (cola) nut 43n30, 76, 97
Konkomba
  Christian missions among 121–143
  history and culture 57–81
  Sanneh's hermeneutic of mission 145–202
  and vernacular translation 158–170, 195–197
  see also Likpakpaaln
  see also under Dagomba

Kottak, Conrad Phillip 22, 109n
KOYA (Konkomba Youth Association) 71, 79, 161, 174, 180
Kpandai (town) 125–126
Kutin, David 123
Kwansa, A. L. 85, 107

Laubach, Frank C.
  The Story of Jesus 105
Lecestre, Olivier 98–99
Leigh, Walker 88
Likpakpaaln (Konkomba language)
  audio/video recording in 133, 186–187
  classification and relationships 60, 67–68
  development of 143, 162, 175–176, 182, 187–188, 196
  in education 72
  linguistic studies of 130, 141
  literacy programmes 130, 143, 162, 166, 178, 148
  vernacular translation 81, 130, 133, 143
    delay in 121–122, 124
    effect of 158–169, 175, 178–179, 197–201
    indigenous resources 133, 137, 147
literacy 23n, 182–189
  Bimoba 120–123
  Dagomba 39, 96–97, 102–103, 105, 119
  Dagomba Literacy Programme 115, 119–120
  Konkomba 130–133, 142, 154–169, 199–200
  Northern Outreach Literacy Programme 47
Littleton, Mr. (missionary) 102–103
louar'k/loual, sg. ('spirits') 74
Luggard, Lord 31n16

lunsi (counsellor to royalty, geneologist, cultural expert) see drummers
luul (vanishing medicine) 76

Mabihi language family 38–39
Mahama, Ibrahim 29
Majola, Aloo 129
malgu na ('development chief') see Shirer
mallam ('Muslim cleric') 110
 and festivals 45
 and marriage 41–43
 rebukes 184–185
 and rituals 53
 and traditional divination/guidance 49, 76
 and witchcraft 50
Mamprugu territory (Mamprusi kingdom) 32, 33, 35, 68, 103, 154
Mamprusi (people) 26–30, 33–34, 68–69
 and Christianity 184–185
 classification 26, 38
 cultural similarities 26, 41, 44–45, 68–69
 origin 26–27, 30
 relationships 33–34, 44, 68–69, 154, 170
Mankron, David 123
Manoukian, Madeline 41–42, 59
marginalisation
 of Konkomba and other non-centralised societies 28, 30, 31, 60, 65, 196
 of minority group languages 141n
 overcoming/empowerment 78, 156, 188
 of rural Dagomba 38
 of women 18, 95
marriage
 arranged 41, 197
 betrothal 41, 68, 79, 164
 Christian 150, 163–164, 183, 197
 courtship 42
 among Dagomba 39–42, 113, 175
 elopement 41
 exchange marriages 68–69, 79, 164, 197
 forced 79, 161, 164, 170
 intermarriage 70–71
 among Konkomba 41, 68–69, 161, 164
 premarital sex 69, 79
Mazrui, Ali A. 7–8
Mbiti, John 1, 129, 138–139, 173
Methodists (Wesleyan) 88, 93
"Mile 7" Programme (Tamale) 105–111
missionary enterprise
 challenges 93
 among Dagomba 91, 93
 early efforts 15
 education and development 156, 182
 indigenous involvement 191–194
 Islamic 20
 among Konkomba 126–127, 134, 143
 modern missions 17
 and translation 115, 146–147
Missionary Society of Africa (S. M. A.) 99
Mole-Dagbani (*also* Mole-Dagomba; More-Dagbani; Mooré-Dagbani) groups
 customs 39, 40–41, 43, 49
 language 38
 origins 26–27, 29–30
 see also specific groups
Moorhouse, Geoffrey 7
Morin, Oscar 88
Mossi (*also* Moshi) (people)
 language 38

Index: M–N

origins 26, 30, 34
relationships 33, 34, 77
mother tongue
  see vernacular language
Mudimbe, V. Y. 7

na/naa ('chief') 30, 40
  Bilpila-*Naa* Abukani Tiah 97
  Na Andani (c. 1892) 31
  Na Andani Ziblim 52
  Na Gariba (c. 1830) 34
  Na Gbewaa (Gbewa)
    (c. 1320–1365) 26, 30, 34
  Na Luro (c. 1554–1570) 60
  Na Zangina (c. 1750) 51–52,
    53, 112
  the Nalerigu *na* 69
  (Soo) Naa Mogri 184, 185
  see also ya na
na yiri ('overlord, king') 33
naam ('chieftaincy') 26, 36, 38
Naameh, Philip 83
naanima ('traditional rulers') 31,
  36, 48, 53
Naawuni ('King God') 47–48, 51,
  117, 147, 195
  Naawuni Kundi Palli (New
    Testament in Dagbani) 116
  Naawuni yili ('God's home')
    48
Nafeba (language) 133
Nafeba (people) 60
Nalerigu (town) 33
  Medical Centre 103
names (vernacular terms) 116
  Asante terms 35
  names for God
    see Naawuni (Dagomba)
    importance of use 137–140,
      147, 175, 195
    see Uwumbor (Konkomba)
names/naming (personal names)
  (*suuna*) 43, 157, 168

Nanumba (people)
  customs 41, 45
  hegemony 69
  language 38, 154
  loyalty to Islam 102
  origins 26–27, 30
  relationships 33–34, 69–70
National Farmer celebration 102
Natomah, C. J. 104
Nawuri (people)
  and Konkomba 70
  and WEC 125–126
Ndan be Wuni ('eternal, sufficient
  God') 117
New Life for All Programmes 109
NGO (non-governmental
  organisation)
  among Dagomba 46
  Christian 114, 142, 149
  and social change 156
njog ('sorcerer's medicine') 76
Nkrumah, Kwame 156
non-centralised (acephalous)
  societies 2, 58
  e.g. Bimoba, Konkomba 58, 170
  clan-based 57, 68, 72, 78
  conversions among 54, 105
  dominated, despised 31, 71
  features of 57–58
  historical sources, lack of 28, 59
  land claims 54, 60, 65
  marginalised, vulnerable 28,
    30–32, 58, 196
  rights 54, 81, 164, 176
  stateless 28, 54
  subjugated by Indirect Rule
    31–32
  see also clans/clanship; ethnic
    loyalty/pride; hegemony;
    marginalisation; stateless
    societies
Northern Conflict (1994)
  see also Dagomba-Konkomba War
Northern Outreach Programme 47

Northern Territories/Region
  Christian missions 1–2, 84–100, 111, 121–125
  Dagomba 30, 52, 55
  education 46, 87
  ethnographies 6, 88, 89
  FCBH radio programmes 153–154
  Indirect Rule 31
  trade 3–35, 84
  see also Nalerigu Medical Centre
Noss, Philip 129
Nyaba, Solomon 95–96
Nyagse/Nyaghse (1476–1492) 30

organisations involved in translation
  see Assemblies of God Mission; Basel Mission; Bible Society of Ghana; FCBH; GILLBT; PCG; RILADEP; SIL; UBS; WEC; White Fathers
oubwa see diviners/soothsayers

patrilineal society 36, 43, 72
Pettifer, Julian 7
Photius (Patriarch of Constantinople AD 810–895) 8
pregnancy 43, 157
Presbyterian Church of Ghana (PCG) 104–111
  Christian Service Committee 105, 109
  see also van den Broek
Pul, Hippolyt A. S. 37, 65, 71

Quaye, Paa Ekow 119–120
Qur'an/Qur'anic
  access requires Arabic 201
  and Arabic/Qur'anic education 39, 46, 183
  and Christianity 112, 131n, 154, 201
  customs and rituals 42, 53, 77–78
  names in 117
  not translatable 10

Radio Savannah/Ghana Broadcasting Corporation
  effect of Scripture broadcast 118–119, 149–155
  languages broadcast 39, 154, 183
Rattray, Robert S. 2n, 6
Red Hunter *see* Tohajie
rights
  effects of vernacular translation and literacy 164, 167, 176, 189, 196
  human rights 81, 85, 164, 176
  land ownership 65
  self-rule 54, 176
  women's rights 164
Riis, Andreas 139
RILADEP (Rural Integrated Literacy and Development Programme) 160, 162, 166
rituals
  see specific rituals
Rosingh, Frits 104–106, 111

Saayman, Willem 7
Saboba
  Christian missions 122–126, 159, 161, 178n16
  clinic 72
  Dicheem community 159
  education 72
  festivals 78

Konkomba capital 65, 141, 148
language 126, 133, 141
Saboba Agricultural Project 124
Saboba Secondary Technical 159
Saboba Town Development Committee 65
Toma Assemblies of God Church 159
Trinity Foundation Church 159
Sanneh, Lamin
biography 3–4, 11–13
Christian mission as translation 3, 8–10, 11–24, 115, 191–202
hermeneutic of mission 3, 5, 145–148, 185–189
Schimming, Otto and Julia 90–91
Scripture Union (SU) 111–112
Seaman, Mr. and Mrs. John 124–125
Second World War *see* World Wars
Shirer, Lloyd and Margaret 94–96, 116
shrines
Dagomba 48, 50, 77
Konkomba 30, 60, 68, 75
SIL (Summer Institute of Linguistics/SIL International)
among Dagomba 184
and GILLBT 131–133
among Konkomba 130, 133, 142, 146, 159
Sissala (people) 160
skin, stool *see* enskin
slave/slavery/slave raiding
by Asante and Dagomba 35, 64, 70
attitudes toward 7, 32, 35, 37, 77, 169
ending 23
Konkomba resistance 54, 59
and missionary movement 15, 17, 89
societal change 54, 156

Society of Missionaries of Africa (White Fathers) *see* Catholic missions
Society for the Propagation of the Divine Word *see* Catholic missions
son-nya see witchcraft/sorcery
son-nya sung ('good witchcraft') 50
Soo Naa Mogri 184, 185n21
Spratt, David and Nancy 105
stateless society *see* non-centralised society
Steele, Mary 133, 146
suliminga adiini ('white man's religion') 120
sulinboma na ('goodwill chief')
sulinminsi ('white people') 89
Sumaila Ndewura Jakpa Lanta 34

Tait, David 61, 64–69, 75
talisman 52, 157
Tallensi (people) 38, 41
Tamakloe, Emmanuel 29, 30n10
Tamale
Assemblies of God missions in 95–97
administrative capital 32–33, 55
Baptist missions in 103–104
Baptist Training Centre 103
Basel Mission in 90
Catholic missions in 98–100, 150, 155
FCBH broadcasts in vicinity 150–155
population and religions in 47, 52–53, 97
Presbyterian Church of Ghana missions in 104–112
see also Mile 7 Programme
Tamale Christian Church 95
Wesleyan Mission in 92–93

ten'dana/ten'danba ('priests of the earth') 30, 40, 78
Tia, Peter 119
Togo/Togoland
  British and German rule 31, 99, 123
  and Konkomba 59, 65, 68, 123
Tohajie (*also* 'Red Hunter') 27, 29–30, 34, 38
totem 40, 47, 72
traditionalists
  among Dagomba 44, 47, 52, 101, 184
  among Konkomba 75, 139, 148, 161–165
translation
  and anti-hegemony 20–23, 181, 193–194, 198
  and Christian mission 185–189
  destigmatisation of indigenous cultures 15, 18
  early attempts 115–116
  effects of 14–15, 189, 197–202
    on Bimoba 170–173
    on Dagomba 149–158, 183
    on Konkomba 127–128, 129–130, 141, 148, 158–170
    testimony of Yussif (Dagomba evangelist) 151
    testimony of "doctor" (Dagomba evangelist/ FCBH supervisor/ pharmaceutical seller) 151
  and empowerment 18–23, 158, 166, 202
  indigenous resources 133–140, 147, 161, 200
  Islamic perspective on 10, 20
  need for 89, 105, 114–115, 124, 127–128
  process of translation 140–143
  reception of translated Scripture
    by Dagomba 91, 146, 148–149, 194–195
    by Konkomba 146, 195–197
  Sanneh's perspective 3, 8–10, 14–15, 18–24, 189
  see also organisations involved in translation; vernacular language
Trimingham, J. Spencer 51, 85
Turaki, Yusufu 85
Tuurey, Gabriel 29, 58

UNESCO (United Nations Education, Scientific and Cultural Organization) 178
United Bible Societies 117–118
United church 93
Uwumbor/Woumbor ('supreme God'/ Creator) 59, 73–75, 137, 147

Vagla (people) 198
van den Broek, A. P. 105–111, 117
  enskinned *sulinboma na* ('goodwill chief') 108
  'Pastor for the Dagomba' 109
van Nierop, Arrie 117
Vansina, Jan 26n1
vernacular language (*also* mother tongue)
  authentic missions 17
  effective communication 6, 9, 19, 54, 115, 179
  and conversion 98, 173–174
  and Dagomba 194–195
  growth of Christianity 20, 169
  and Islam 20
  and Konkomba 180–188, 195–197
  literacy 142, 162

preservation of language and culture 19, 168, 178–179, 195
See also translation
Volta Region
  churches in 159
  Evangelical Presbyterian Church seminary 123–124
  groups/languages in 58n, 60, 126, 191
  minimal historical records 58

Wa (town) 83, 98
warizam (traditional barber) 44
Watherson (Governor) 90
Wedam, Manfred 111
Weed, Gretchen 133
Weiss, Holger 90–91, 116
Wesleyan Mission 88, 92–93, 120
Westermann, Dietrich 191
Western Christianity 3, 15, 31, 54, 83, 100–101, 174
  among Dagomba 113–115
  among Konkomba 126–127
Western Christian mission/ missionary enterprise 2n7, 7, 9, 10, 12–16, 90
Western colonialism *see* colonialism
Western education *see* education
Western Guilt Complex 12–13
Western hegemony *see* hegemony
Western missionary perspective 7, 12, 22, 90, 125, 128
Western scholars/media
  on Christian mission as cultural imperialism 3, 7, 20–23, 193–194
  research benefitted by Christian mission 140, 174
  and Western Guilt Complex 13–14
Weston, Arnold 95

White Fathers *see* Catholic missions
Whiteman, Darrell 182
Wilks, Ivor 35
Wilson, Elizabeth A. Galley 94–95
Wilson, William A. A. 38n25
Winter, Klaus 124
witchcraft/sorcery
  Christian response 50, 93n11, 100, 155, 163
  among Dagomba (*son-nya*) 49–50
  among Konkomba (*kesuo*) 76
  witch camps 49–50, 76–77
woman/women
  education 103–104, 111, 166, 170
  empowerment 18, 164, 166, 179
  exchange marriages 69, 197
  and Konkomba architecture 68
  (first) pregnancy (*presigu/prisigu*) 43, 157
  rights *see under* rights
  roles 39–42, 100, 164, 183
  women's groups 102, 160, 162
  see also burial rituals; Indirect Rule, effect on Konkomba; marriage; witchcraft
World Christianity 23–24, 174–175
World Vision International (WVI) 114, 142
World Wars
  First 90, 93, 115, 123–124, 146
  Second 95
Worldwide Evangelisation Crusade (WEC) 124–126
  see also Evangelical Church of Ghana
Woumbor see Uwumbor
Wujangi, Kenneth 187, 196
wulana ('linguist') 35
Wumbee, Daniel 40, 116
  and Dagbani OT 117, 130

Wuni, Isaac Issah 111
Wycliffe, John 148

ya na ('king', 'Lion of Dagbon';
    supreme authority in Dagbon) 35,
    36, 40, 46, 52, 95, 96, 152, 184
  Ya Na Andani Sigili (reign
    1700s) 35
  Ya Na Yakubu II (reign 1974–
    2002) 38, 70, 152, 184
  Ya Na Salifu (Billa Billa) III
    (reign 1950's) 102
Yahaya, Moses 27, 39
Yakubu, Abudulai (lawyer) 6
Yankazia (town/people) 133
Yendi (town/district)
  Assemblies of God Mission in
    94–96, 116
  Basel Mission in 90, 116, 146
  Catholic missions in 99
  Dagomba traditional capital 33,
    34, 60, 66n18, 77
  Dagomba in 38, 53, 66, 84, 184
  Evangelical Presbyterian Church
    in 101–102, 124
  Konkomba in 61–62, 64, 66,
    70–71
  Konkomba claim to 60
  lion as totem of 40
  skin gates of 38
  Yendi Agricultural Station 102
yidanaa ('family head') 43
Yoruba (traders/church) 81,
  102–103

SIL International® Publications
Publications in Ethnography Series
ISSN 0-0895-9897

48. **Environmental invasion and social response: Of a forest and those who dwell therein,** by Douglas M. Fraiser, 2019, 155 pp., ISBN 978-1-55671-395-8.

47. **Bajju Christian conversion in the Middle Belt of Nigeria,** by Carol V. McKinney, 2019, 202 pp., ISBN 978-1-55671-398-9.

46. **Baranzan's people: An ethnohistory of the Bajju of the Middle Belt of Nigeria,** by Carol V. McKinney, 2019, 238 pp., ISBN 978-1-55671-399-6.

45. **Acclimated to Africa: Cultural competence for Westerners,** by Debbi DiGennaro, 2017, 163 pp., ISBN 978-1-55671-386-6.

44. **The heart of the matter: Seeking the center in Maya-Mam language and culture,** by Wesley M. Collins, 2015, 205 pp., ISBN 978-1-55671-375-0.

43. **African friends and money matters.** Second edition, by David E. Maranz, 2015, 293 pp., ISBN 978-1-55671-277-7.

42. **Ensnared by AIDS: Cultural contexts of HIV and AIDS in Nepal,** by David K. Beine, 2014, 357 pp., ISBN 978-1-55671-350-7.

41. **The Norsk Høstfest: A celebration of ethnic food and ethnic identity,** by Paul Thomas Emch, 2011, 121 pp., ISBN 978-1-55671-265-4.

40. **Our company increases apace: History, language, and social identity in early colonial Andover, Massachusetts,** by Elinor Abbot, 2007, 279 pp., ISBN 978-1-55671-169-5.

39. **What place for hunters-gatherers in millennium three?** by Thomas N. Headland and Doris E. Blood, eds. 2002, 130 pp., ISBN 978-1-55671-132-9.

38. **A tale of Pudicho's people,** by Richard Montag. 2002, 181 pp., ISBN 978-1-55671-131-2.

SIL International® Publications
7500 W. Camp Wisdom Road
Dallas, Texas 75236-5629 USA

General inquiry: publications_intl@sil.org
Pending order inquiry: sales@sil.org
publications.sil.org

Rev. Dr. Solomon Sumani Sule-Saa holds a BA (Hons) from the University of Ghana (1996). He also completed an MTh (2000; University of Natal, South Africa) on the topic, "Ethnicity and the Church: The Case of the Presbyterian Church of Ghana," followed by a PhD (2007; Akrofi-Christaller Institute of Theology, Mission and Culture, Akropong-Akuapem, Ghana) on which this book is based.

Dr. Sule-Saa has held several positions in the Presbyterian Church of Ghana, including Director of Ecumenical and Social Relations, Director of the Presbyterian Interfaith Research and Resource Centre, Accra, and Director of the Presbyterian Lay Training Centre, Tamale. He also served on the Northern Regional Peace Council from 2015–2018. He is currently Director of Centre for Interfaith Studies and Engagement in Africa (CISEA) (under the Akrofi-Christaller Institute), a full-time lecturer at the Akrofi-Christaller Institute, and a member of the board of the Ghana Institute of Linguistics, Literacy and Bible Translation (GILLBT). He has a passion for ecumenical issues and a special interest in language and mission in northern Ghana.

www.ingramcontent.com/pod-product-compliance
Lightning Source LLC
Chambersburg PA
CBHW050137240426
43673CB00043B/1703